For the garden is the only place there is, but you will not
   find it
Until you have looked for it everywhere and found
   nowhere that is not a desert.
The miracle is the only thing that happens, but to you it
   will not be apparent
Until all events have been studied and nothing happens to
   you that you cannot explain.
And life is the destiny you are bound to refuse until you
   have consented to die.

For the Time Being
W. H. AUDEN

A SOCIOPOLITICAL READING
OF MARK'S GOSPEL ————————————————————

A Reordering of Power

HERMAN C. WAETJEN

Fortress Press   Minneapolis ————————————————

Library of Congress Cataloging-in-Publication Data

Waetjen, Herman C.
  A reordering of power.

  "A translation of the Gospel according to Mark": p.
  Bibliography: p.
  1. Bible. N.T. Mark—Criticism, interpretation, etc.
  2. Sociology, Biblical. I. Bible. N.T. Mark. English.
  1989. II. Title.
  BS2585.2.W32 1989   226'.0367   88–45251
  ISBN 0–8006–2319–3

Printed in the United States of America   1-2319
97   96   95   94   93   2   3   4   5   6   7   8   9   10

To MARY

There are two births; the one when light
   First strikes the new awaken'd sense;
The other when two souls unite,
   And we must count our life from thence:
When you loved me and I loved you
Then both of us were born anew.

               —William Cartwright

Contents

Prologue

"Stat rosa pristina nomine, nomina nuda tenemus." With this Latin declaration Umberto Eco ends his novel *The Name of the Rose.* The aphorism could be appended to the Gospel According to Mark as well and, for that matter, to the other Gospels of the New Testament: "The original rose stands by name." That is, what the author saw or perceived is conveyed to us, the readers, by name or in the form of signs. But "we apprehend the name empty." The words of a printed page are only the textual signals that bear the semantic potential of the book. Like the notes of a musical composition, which must be sung or played to make music, the words of a text must be read in order to produce meaning.

But intelligent reading is required, especially if the book, like the Gospel According to Mark, originated in another society in the distant past. For the repertoire that has been used to constitute this literary composition and the strategies that have been embedded in its text to facilitate the actualization of meaning are not as immediately transparent as those of a twentieth-century narrative would be. Interpretation is, of course, unavoidable as the act of reading takes place; but it should be an experience, indeed, the creative experience of bringing the signified to life and not an exercise in explanation.

Like the musical notes of a composition, therefore, the words must be authentic to the text. They must be genuine parts of the whole conceived and constructed by the author in order to constitute the aesthetic unity of the literary work. Every part and particle is critical—definite articles, prepositions, verb tenses, number (singular and plural), and the sentence construction—for all combine to form the unity of the text and the potentiality of meaning that it conveys. From the signified of the individual parts and particles an understanding of the whole arises, while at the same time the structure of the whole governs the determination of the individual parts. Meaning is generated by the reader's reciprocal interaction between the parts and the whole.

Obviously, then, the signs or words of a text are decisive for the production of meaning. But ironically, while text criticism serves as an indispensable method for as precise an establishment of the original Greek of Mark's Gospel as possible, English translations generally do not appear to be particularly concerned about its careful and faithful reproduction in the vernacular. Of course, their primary and certainly justifiable objective is maximal lucidity and transparence. But all too often vital signs and textual signals are lost in the process because they eluded the translators or because they were misjudged or rationalized by them. An absence of class consciousness and attendantly an ignorance of the realities of class, sex, and race which determine a text's meaning foreordain a limited or even a distorted comprehension, because certain textual signs remain invisible or are explained away. A hermeneutical perspective that is brought to bear on texts originating in another sociocultural "world" without being informed by the disciplines of sociology, cultural anthropology, and an appropriate literary criticism is doomed to misconstruction and misinterpretation. An attempt has been made in this book to enable readers of Mark's Gospel, a text that originated in the agrarian society of the Roman Empire of the last quarter of the first century (A.D. 73–75), to explore its narrative world and to actualize its semantic potential more effectively by employing a method of reading that correlates these three disciplines.

Part One intends to prepare the reader for an experiential interaction with a new translation of the Gospel that is offered in Part Two. The former presents an introduction to the realities of class encountered in the narrative, analyzed with the aid of historical sociology and its reconstruction of the social stratification of agrarian society. Attendantly the socioeconomic context of the Gospel is elucidated in relation to the same realities of class that its narrative mirrors and in which it originated. Finally, literary critical guidance derived from

Wolfgang Iser's "theory of aesthetic response" is delineated in order to promote the creative experience of actualizing the text's meaning.

Part Two offers a translation of the Gospel that has undergone continuous revision since 1978. Words and phrases especially significant for the production of meaning are in boldface. An effort has been made to reproduce as much of the rustic character of Mark's Greek as possible within the bounds of intelligibility. This includes following the author's syntax in the sentence construction of the translation. The style of narration seems to approximate oral storytelling and is reflected in the use of conjunctions at the beginning of almost every sentence and the apparently awkward change of verb tenses within a sentence or from sentence to sentence. The latter deserves particular attention in order to appreciate the sophisticated sensibility of the narrator to the realities of time that are developed in the story world. Additional punctuation has been used to foster clarity. More important, however, any word that appears more than once in the original Greek text is translated with the same English equivalent whenever possible for the sake of consistency building. As a result, the translation may seem to be eccentric, strange, even inept; but it is hoped that these very qualities will contribute to a new experience of meaning. Since key words are woven through the text in order to produce an intricate pattern of themes, a literal rather than a literary translation will, it is hoped, enable the reader to perceive wordplays and thematic developments and consequently foster a more meaningful interaction with the story world of the Gospel.

Because individual words often bear the weight of consequential meaning, precision in transposing the text into English has been a major preoccupation. A controversial example is the preposition "into" *(eis)* in Mark 1:9. What is the significance of Jesus' baptism **"into the Jordan"**? Does it correspond to or contrast with the earlier reference (1:5) to the Jews from Judea and Jerusalem letting themselves be baptized **"in the Jordan River"**? The latter confessed their sins; nothing of the kind is attributed to Jesus. Why? Was he sinless? If so, in what respect? And what measuring stick should be used to determine the nature of sinlessness? If, according to 1:4, John is preaching a baptism of **repentance** unto the forgiveness of sins, can the conclusion be validly drawn that Jesus' baptism "into the Jordan" stands in contrast to the baptism of the Jews from Judea and Jerusalem "in the Jordan River confessing their sins"? His baptism appears to correspond to John's proclamation and can therefore be regarded as an act of repentance. Consequently he is the only Jew who experiences the fulfillment of John's promise in 1:8; he alone receives the baptism of the holy Spirit. His baptism, however, is not a ritual of purification, a washing away of accumulated uncleanness, such as was practiced by the Qumran Essenes. Mark 10:38–39 links it to Jesus' forthcoming death. Accordingly, his repentance, expressed by his baptism "into the Jordan," must be an eschatological experience of death and his subsequent baptism by the holy Spirit an eschatological experience of re-creation or resurrection.

Although it is often claimed that the prepositions *en* ("in") and *eis* ("into") are used interchangeably in Hellenistic Greek, this generalization cannot be assumed to hold true for a specific literary composition until all the occurrences of these prepositions have been examined and compared. The subsequent use of *eis* in 1:10, 12, 14, 21, 28, 29, 35, 38 et al., and of *en* in 1:4, 13, 16, 19, 20, 23, et al., indicates that this principle cannot be imposed on Mark's Gospel.

Part Three, the longest section of the book, is divided according to my perception of the Gospel's intrinsic structure and conveys my performance of meaning. It intends to be more than an exercise in explanation. Indeed, it is hoped that this interpretation will serve as a second text of Mark's Gospel with which the reader can interact, especially in the light of her or his production of meaning arising out of the earlier reading of the Gospel, and, as a result, be enabled to realize more of its semantic potential.

As Part One emphasizes, Part Three presupposes that Mark's Gospel is a narrative world reflecting the career of Jesus in its original sociohistorical context but nevertheless a literary construct created by an anonymous author to whom tradition has assigned the name of Mark. As suggested in the book title, *A Reordering of Power,* the text of the Gospel of Mark has been read in the light of historical sociology in order to locate individuals, groups, and institutions within the socioeconomic pyramid of Roman Palestine, to determine the extent of their socioeconomic well-being, and to ascertain their relationship to the means of production. Hence the subtitle of the book: *A Sociopolitical Reading of Mark's Gospel.* The sociology of millennialism has also been appropriated for a more adequate understanding of the phrases "the kingdom of God" and "the Son of Man," as well as the millennarianism of Jewish apocalypticism from which they were derived. Kenelm Burridge's investigation of millennialism in *New Heaven, New Earth: A Study of Millenarian Activities* has proven to be exceptionally helpful, particularly his analysis of the second phase of millennial movements in which a prophet emerges and becomes the representative of the new human being for the new moral order that is anticipated. A pertinent example is the *bar nasha* ("son of a human being") of Jewish apocalypticism in Dan. 7:13–14, who is subsequently interpreted to be the eschatological community of "the saints of the Most High" in Dan. 7:27 but who as *ben adam* ("son of a human being") is identified with the prophet Daniel in Dan. 8:17. In the same way Jesus, after his experience of eschatological death and re-creation (Mark 1:9–11), arises from the Jordan River as the embodiment of a new humanity generated by God and proceeds to give expression to this self-understanding by his appropriation of the epithet "the Son of the Human Being" or, to convey this eschatological reality in a more contemporary and less androcentric way, "the New Human Being." An attendant consequence of his divine re-creation is his entry into "a reordering of power."

The identification of unclean spirits and demons with specific social, religious, and military institutions in Part Three presupposes an interpretation of *1 Enoch* 6:1—16:3 that is also determined by the sociology of millennialism. Unfortunately it cannot be reproduced here, but it is supported independently by Paul Hollenbach's essay "Jesus, Demoniacs, and Public Authorities: A Socio-Historical Study," *JAAR* 44/4 (1981) (see Part Three, n. 20), an analysis that utilizes "recent social-scientific literature on possession and exorcism" in an attempt to explain and understand these phenomena more fully.

Finally, aspects of cultural anthropology are also drawn into the service of the production of meaning. One particularly important example is the recognition of "the mountain" in Mark 3:13; 5:11; 6:46; and 11:23 as a cosmic navel or architectonic center—to use the terminology of Mircea Eliade in *Cosmos and History: The Myth of the Eternal Return.* "The mountain" in Mark's story world generally remains unidentified, but its most satisfactory interpretation is that of a cosmic center where a community that enters into covenant with God is born or reborn. Although the idea of a "new Israel" may not be explicitly conveyed in Mark's Gospel or, as some would also argue, in the New Testament, it is implied by Jesus' selection of twelve men on "the mountain" in 3:13, after his earlier rejection by the synagogue (3:6).

These dynamics of my reading the text of Mark's Gospel in order to generate meaning have been evolving ever since I wrote a doctoral dissertation on the Gospel According to Matthew and subsequently revised it for publication under the title *The Origin and Destiny of Humanness: An Interpretation of the Gospel According to Matthew.* The earlier gropings, at times misled by an authorially oriented intuitionist hermeneutics, were corrected and synthesized with the indispensable help of Wolfgang Iser's writings, especially *The Act of Reading.* The model of the interplay between the text and the reader, developed independently in part but clarified and amplified by Iser's "theory of aesthetic response" for the interpretation of Mark's Gospel (see Part Three), is set forth in the third chapter of *The Act of Reading* under the heading "Grasping the Text."

Speaking comprehensively, the horizon of understanding that has affected the employment of sociological theory, cultural anthropological insights, and reader response criticism in this work and determined my interaction with the text of Mark's Gospel has been formed, partially at least, by the experiences of three sabbatical leaves in the so-called Third World. Research and study in three African nation-states—Kenya, South Africa, and Zimbabwe—as well as teaching university and seminary students in these countries, have contributed significantly to the expansion and enrichment of the hermeneutical circle in and through which the interpretation of Part Three has been generated.

Other obligations must also be recorded: to those students, both in the United States and in Africa, who joined me in this enterprise and provided challenging questions and stimulating discussions; to Harold W. Rast and John A. Hollar of Fortress Press for their indispensable role in editing and publishing this manuscript; to Greg Lambert for enabling me to perceive more clearly certain ambiguities in my hermeneutical synthesis; to Paul Gifford for proposing the idea of boldfacing what I consider to be the key words and phrases in Mark's Gospel; to the Board of Trustees of San Francisco Theological Seminary for a sabbatical leave to complete this work which had been initiated on a previous sabbatical at the Federal Theological Seminary in Pietermaritzburg, South Africa; to the University of Zimbabwe for the privilege of teaching in the Department of Religious Studies in exchange for free housing while producing the final draft of this book; to my father-in-law, Harry C. Struyk, for his untiring efforts to put the first half of the manuscript on a computer disk and for assistance in reading the galleys; to my daughters, Thembisa and Lois, who could not accompany us on this sabbatical but nevertheless inspired me to complete this work and offered invaluable suggestions to improve the clarity of my writing, and to Lois, who eventually assumed the task of putting the second half of the manuscript on a computer disk; to my son, Dave, for the enrichment of many shared experiences during this year and the encouragement communicated in and through them; and finally most of all to my wife, Mary, without whose enthusiastic support this book could never have been written.

University of Zimbabwe   HERMAN C. WAETJEN
Harare, Zimbabwe
April 1987

Abbreviations

ASTI	*Annual of the Swedish Theological Institute*
CBQ	*Catholic Biblical Quarterly*
ER	*Ecumenical Review*
FRLANT	Forschungen zur Religion und Literatur des Alten und Neuen Testaments
HTR	*Harvard Theological Review*
JAAR	*Journal of the American Academy of Religion*
JBL	*Journal of Biblical Literature*
JSNT	*Journal for the Study of the New Testament*
NTS	*New Testament Studies*
PEFQ	*Palestine Exploration Fund Quarterly*
TDNT	*Theological Dictionary of the New Testament*
THKNT	Theologischer Handkommentar zum Neuen Testament
USQR	*Union Seminary Quarterly Review*
ZNW	*Zeitschrift für die neutestamentliche Wissenschaft*

Glossary

AGRARIAN SOCIETY. A generic type of society based on agriculture that is made possible by the invention of the plow and the harnessing of animal energy and that therefore generates a greater economic surplus which in turn leads to population growth and labor specialization.

ANACOLUTHON. A broken or incomplete sentence construction or one kind of construction abandoned in the middle of a sentence in favor of another. For example, Mark 3:16–17; 4:31–32; and 5:23.

ASYNDETON. A lack of connecting links supplied by particles and conjunctions or the omission of conjunctions which ordinarily join coordinate words or clauses. For example, Mark 3:35; 4:28; 5:39b; and 6:26.

ESCHATOLOGY. An orientation toward the reality of a new moral order in the future which determines conduct and activity in the present.

IMPLIED AUTHOR. The sum total of choices that a real author makes in telling a story: the repertoire selected to constitute the narrative, the strategies embedded in the text to foster the interaction between the reader and the text, the kind of narrator chosen to tell the story, the plot line to structure the narrative, and the characters to carry out the action.

IMPLIED READER. The role to be played by the actual reader laid down in the text by the implied author. "A network of response-inviting structures which impel the reader to grasp the text"; "all those dispositions necessary for a literary work to exercise its effects" (Iser).

JEWISH APOCALYPTICISM. Manifestations of millennialism which originated in different periods of postexilic Jewish history and expressed themselves in anonymous and pseudonymous literature.

MILLENNIALISM. Movements of oppressed and dispossessed people who reject the present moral order and look forward to the terrestrial reality of a new heaven and a new earth.

POLLUTION SYSTEM. Or a system of binary oppositions. A social construct that divides the world into the two realms of the sacred and the secular, the clean and the unclean, good and evil.

SIGNIFIED. The referent of a linguistic sign or word, the concept or object to which it refers.

SIGNIFIER. The sound image component of a linguistic sign or word.

THE RULE (OR KINGDOM) OF GOD. The eschatological or millennial reality of a new moral order that is terrestrial, corporate, and total.

THE SON OF MAN OR THE NEW HUMAN BEING. The eschatological or millennial reality of a new humanity, embodied in the individual person of Jesus, in which the dualistic pollution system of clean and unclean has been replaced by the corporate reality of the one and the many.

THEORY OF AESTHETIC RESPONSE. A literary critical theory represented by Wolfgang Iser that focuses on the process of reading and the interaction between the reader and the text.

TRIBUTARY MODE OF PRODUCTION OR REDISTRIBUTION SYSTEM OF EXCHANGE. A form of economic exchange in which the deployment of labor as a function of political power is exercised by the ruling elite who extract the agricultural surplus from its peasant producers, redistribute it among themselves, and use it to maintain their power and privilege.

Introduction:
Reading Mark's Gospel
Today

The Gospel According to Mark is a story world artistically constructed by an immensely creative and powerful storyteller.[1] It is an integrated narrative in which all of its content is coherently related to itself and constitutes an independent, self-contained, and systemic universe with its own inherent structures of time and space. In no way is it a copy of the world in which it originated, in spite of its reflection of the social, economic, political, cultural, and religious realities of its agrarian context in the first-century Roman-occupied Palestine and Syria. Its arrangement of narrative units does not arbitrarily correspond to the historical progression of events in the public career of Jesus of Nazareth. It is not a documentary record of the past but an aesthetic literary creation—like a novel—and as such it forms its own world. Consequently it can be comprehended only in terms of itself and not by any historical investigation of its content in relation to the quest of the historical Jesus. While it mirrors aspects of Jesus' life from his baptism under John to the witness of his resurrection, it is not a transparent window through which the historical progression of his career can be viewed. It is not to be identified with the literary genre of biography.[2] Its subject matter is neither mimetic nor historical but

1. See Norman R. Petersen, "'Point of View' in Mark's Narrative," *Semeia* 12 (1978): 97–121, esp. 115, which convincingly argues that Mark's Gospel is a genuine literary composition, indeed a "narrative world." See also David Rhoads and Donald Michie, *Mark as Story: An Introduction to the Narrative of a Gospel* (Philadelphia: Fortress Press, 1982), 1–5. On textual structure as story world, see Wolfgang Iser, *The Act of Reading: A Theory of Aesthetic Response* (Baltimore and London: Johns Hopkins University Press, 1980), 35.

2. See Charles H. Talbert, *What Is a Gospel? The Genre of the Canonical Gospels* (Philadelphia: Fortress Press, 1977). Talbert attempts to categorize the Gospels as "ancient biographies."

ideological. Yet it also cannot be interpreted within the referential framework of early Christian thought or its evolutionary development. Mark's Gospel is not simply a witness to a prevailing view of the Christian faith or a confessional system of truth whose meaning can be determined by pinpointing its life situation. It is not a reproduction of any given reality. It is a reformulation of the already formulated good news of Jesus Christ. Composed in the form of a story, it is a world creatively constructed out of materials of tradition and social conventions available to the author. As such it cannot be validated by historical inquiry or literary criticism. It authenticates itself in the process of reading and its attendant production of meaning.

How can contemporary readers enter into this story world intelligently and effectively without being predetermined in their comprehension of the text by a preunderstanding that has been formed by socialization in a particular religious environment and class context that may not correspond to that which the text presupposes? How can contemporary readers become "informed readers" who possess the literary competence and semantic acumen to perform the role of actualizing the meaning encoded in the Gospel? For meaning, if it is understood as an effect to be experienced rather than as a set of ideas to be grasped, is only potentially present in Mark's text and is constituted by a role that must be played if it is to be realized.[3]

Because that role has been structured into the text with prodigious care by the author, its realization of course cannot occur without some form of contact with the text. What kind of contact the original addressees had with it is difficult to determine. Given their socioeconomic identity as rural peasants and artisans who very likely were illiterate, the text may have been read publicly; and entry into its story world was made by hearing rather than seeing.[4] Yet on the basis of 13:14, the narrative itself appears to presuppose readers rather than hearers. Perhaps both had access to the text. Although the autograph itself has not survived—and of course also the hermeneutical act of

3. Iser, *The Act of Reading*, 10.

4. So also Rhoads and Michie, *Mark as Story*, 143 n. 1. On the illiteracy of the peasantry, see Gerhard E. Lenski and Jean Lenski, *Human Societies: An Introduction to Macrosociology*, 4th ed. (New York: McGraw-Hill, 1982), 177. Yet on the basis of Mark 13:14, it must be acknowledged that some of the original addressees must have been literate.

reading it publicly and privately in its entirety—the original text can be reconstructed with a fair degree of accuracy using both the external and the internal modes of text criticism.[5] In all probability, therefore, the Gospel with all of its original encoded signals and strategies for the actualization of its meaning is recoverable. Yet even a plausibly reconstructed autograph cannot assure an adequate production of its semantic potential by contemporary readers, for the instructions of the text are completely foreign to most of them. The words or signifiers that convey the instructions for the production of meaning are encoded in Hellenistic Greek and, more specifically, the Hellenistic Greek of the uneducated lower-class residents of the rural countryside. Of course, many translations of Mark's Gospel have been published, but most of them are inadequate because they generally are not alert to the signs and signals of meaning embedded in the text and therefore do not render them with corresponding English equivalents in order to enable contemporary readers to enter into the role designed by the author. What translation, for example, renders the noun *phōs* in 14:54 correctly as "light" instead of rationalizing the author's intention and substituting that which seems more logical? Did Peter warm himself "at the fire" or "toward the light" while out in the courtyard of the high priest's palace awaiting the outcome of the trial? If the text is to realize its intended effects, the translation must approximate the Greek original as closely as possible.[6] For individual words are often freighted with far-reaching implications and tantalizing ambiguities, guiding the potential effects of the literary work. Moreover, the repetition of words and phrases for amplification and continuation of themes should be respected and rendered with the same modern equivalents. Such a more or less literal translation into the vernacular of contemporary readers will at least initiate the process of interaction and consistency building.

Nevertheless, philology alone cannot guarantee the fulfillment of the underlying intention of the text or the resolution of its indeterminacies. As Wolgang Iser says, "The written utterance continually transcends the margin of the printed page in order to bring the

5. Bruce M. Metzger, *The Text of the New Testament: Its Transmission, Corruption and Restoration*, 2d ed. (Oxford: Clarendon Press, 1968), 209–11.

6. The only translation I know of that appears to do this is in Rhoads and Michie, *Mark as Story*, 7–34; but even they render the Greek word *phōs* as "fire."

addressee into contact with nontextual realities."[7] How, then, will contemporary readers make contact with the Gospel's "nontextual realities" and actualize the potential effects of the literary work?

The production of meaning by the original recipients of Mark's text was illuminated and stabilized by the author's utilization of a stock of material familiar to them, material that included the realities of context, oral tradition, and literary quotations and allusions. If there is no acquaintance with any of this material, the result can only be disorientation and misconstruction. Traveling through an ancient text without any guidelines derivable from its content must be as bewildering as the contemporary world of relativity and quantum mechanics would be for anyone whose universe was structured according to Newtonian physics. Since the picture of Jesus that is offered by the Gospel is conditioned by the realities of context that permeate the author's stock of material, its comprehension requires some knowledge of Mark's "extratextual" world. As Iser asserts, "Speech acts are not just sentences. They are linguistic utterances in a given situation or context, and it is through this context that they take on meaning."[8]

Two contexts, however, merge in the story world of the Gospel: that of Roman-occupied Palestine in which Jesus conducted his ministry and that of Roman-occupied Syria in which the text originated. Because of their coalescence it is difficult to determine whether the details of a particular episode reflect the past realities of Jesus' context, which have been retained in the transmission of the tradition, or the present realities of Mark's "extratextual" world, which have been incorporated into tradition in order to contemporize the story for the addressees. The houses in which Jesus meets with his followers (3:20, 31–35; 9:33; 10:10) probably reflect the institution of the house church in Mark's time rather than in Jesus' time.[9] The house whose roof is dug through in order to present a paralytic to Jesus may resemble the rural houses of the Gospel's addressees instead of an actual house in the "city" of Capernaum (2:4). The division of the crowd into groups of fifty and one hundred at the feeding of the five

7. Iser, *The Act of Reading*, 55.

8. Ibid.

9. The house of 3:20 appears to be a place of hospitality and is similar to houses in the early Christian movement where hospitality was offered and where eventually Christian communities formed. See Abraham J. Malherbe, *Social Aspects of Early Christianity*, 2d ed. enl. (Philadelphia: Fortress Press, 1983 [1977]), 60–91.

thousand (6:40) probably intimates, as has often been observed, the size of Christian congregations in the "extratextual" world of the author.

In spite of this fusion of context, both belong to the same sociocultural system; indeed, the one is continuous with the other. All of their individual aspects—the geophysical, the socioeconomic, the political, the religious, and the cultural—are systemically interrelated and constitute a generic type of society which historical sociologists have identified as advanced agrarian.[10] The structures of social class and economic distribution that dominated and determined agrarian life are mirrored or at least presupposed in the story world of the Gospel. The elucidation of Mark's fused contexts requires a skeletal reconstruction of the society in which Jesus and his contemporaries and the author and addressees of the Gospel lived. A graphic representation of its class-segmented pyramid discloses its hierarchical structure and facilitates class identification of its individual characters and groups and simultaneously reveals the class orientation of Jesus' ministry. It will serve as a useful frame of reference for an analysis of various aspects of the narrative.

Agrarian societies were based on agriculture, and land was the primary source of wealth and power. Whoever controlled the state determined the ownership of the land and the distribution of the agricultural surplus produced by the peasants. Three individuals appear in the story world of Mark's Gospel who are located at the pinnacle of this pyramidally constituted world and who therefore are oriented toward and engaged in the maintenance of this systemic order and its fundamental realities of the unequal distribution of power and wealth.

Herod Antipas, the son of Herod the Great, was typical of agrarian rulers. A client king of Rome and regent of Galilee and Perea,[11] he continued his father's policy of legitimating his claim to the ownership of virtually all the land over which he ruled, including at least a part of

---

10. Lenski and Lenski, *Human Societies*, 82–98, 180–217.
11. See the summary of Antipas's rule in Mary Smallwood, *The Jews Under Roman Rule* (Leiden: E. J. Brill, 1976), 183–87.

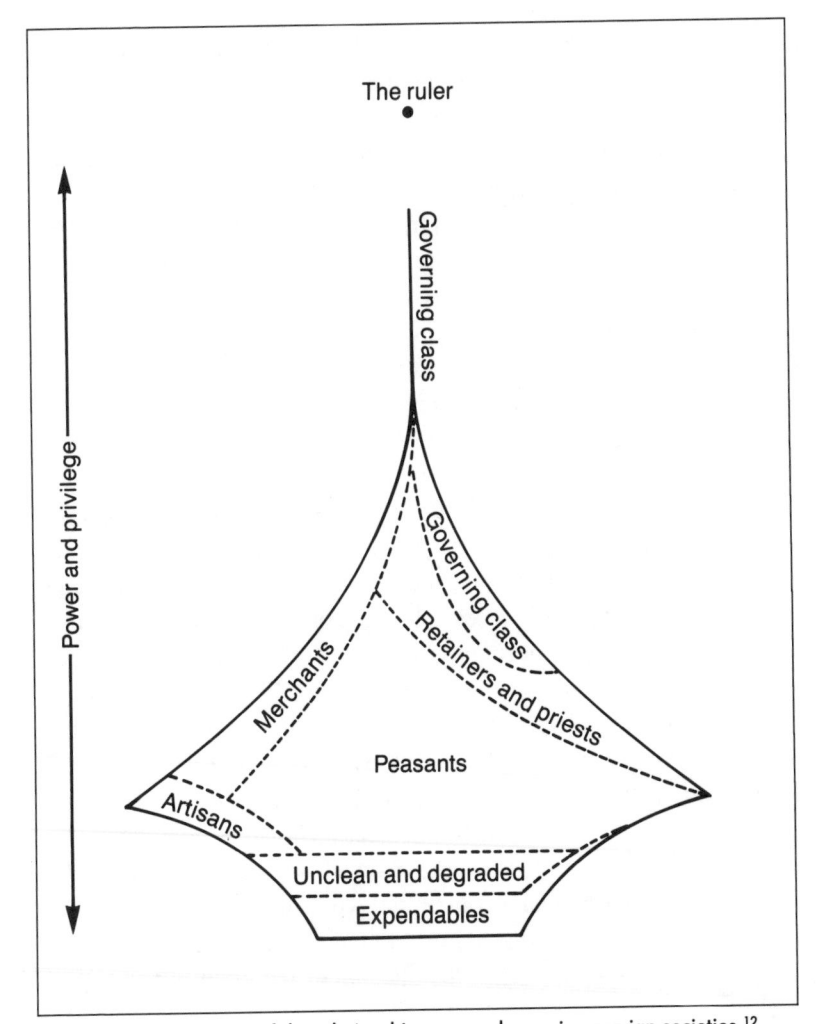

A graphic representation of the relationship among classes in agrarian societies.[12]

12. Gerhard E. Lenski, *Power and Privilege: A Theory of Social Stratification* (New York: McGraw-Hill, 1966), 284. In the 4th ed. of *Human Societies* (p. 211) the Lenskis present a revised figure of the stratification of agrarian society, eliminating "the degraded," which they appear to absorb into the peasantry and the artisans. The expendables remain at the very bottom of the socioeconomic pyramid.

the Sea of Galilee, on the basis of the proprietary rights of kingship.[13] Those who worked his land or lake, peasant farmers and fishers, were required to pay high rents and taxes, perhaps as much as one-fourth or even one-third of their annual production.[14] The dispossession and the marginalization of the lower classes, in particular the peasants and the rural artisans who depended on them, resulting from a concentration of unjust rents and taxes, crop failures, loss of land, and unemployment, constitute the socioeconomic context of Jesus' ministry in the narrative world of the Gospel.

Second, Pontius Pilate, one of Herod's contemporaries, represented the supreme rule of the Roman emperor in administering the imperial province of Judea (15:1–15). According to Josephus, he was notorious in his flagrant abuses of power involving violations of both Roman and Jewish law as well as deliberate provocation of Jewish piety.[15] As with other procurators of Rome, his chief preoccupation during his administration was self-aggrandizement for his eventual retirement from office and return to Rome. His relationship to the Jewish aristocracy, particularly the high priest and the Sanhedrin, is not explicated in Mark's Gospel, but it appears to have been determined by a policy of expediency, and that may account for his willingness to hand Jesus over to crucifixion (15:15).

After the procurator the high priest was the most powerful individual in Roman-occupied Palestine. In the story of Jesus' trial (14:53–64) he is not named, but in the other Gospels he is identified as Caiaphas. A willing collaborator with Rome, he was, however, subject to the patriarchal authority exercised by his father-in-law and predecessor in office, Annas or Ananus I, who dominated domestic

13. Compare G. Lenski's characterization of agrarian rulers in *Power and Privilege* (pp. 214–16) with Harold W. Hoehner's critical life of *Herod Antipas* (Cambridge: Cambridge University Press, 1972), esp. 75–79; on Herod and John the Baptizer, 110–71; on Herod and Jesus, 184–250; and on the problem of tribute during his rule, 298–302.

14. Douglas E. Oakman, "Palestinian Land Tenure and Tenancy Under the Early Roman Empire," a special comprehensive paper presented to the Faculty of the Graduate Theological Union in partial fulfillment of the requirements for the degree of Doctor of Philosophy, Berkeley, Calif., 15 April 1984, pp. 27–28. For a general survey of taxes, rents, and tithes that peasants were forced to pay at different periods of history in different agrarian societies, see G. E. Lenski, *Power and Privilege*, 266–70. See also Wilhelm Wuellner, *The Meaning of "Fishers of Men"* (Philadelphia: Westminster Press, 1967), 43–44, 63.

15. Smallwood, *The Jews Under Roman Rule*, 160–74.

politics by controlling the governing consistory of the temple, the "chief priests," and the high council of the Sanhedrin which he had reorganized during his term of office.[16] The first of these two bodies, the "chief priests," formed the board of directors of the temple which supervised the sacred complex and its sacrificial system. That included the concession of selling the animals used for the daily sacrifices. They were also responsible for the administration of the treasury and its collection of the various taxes and tithes that were imposed on the people.[17] The temple, therefore, was the central institution in Judaism that controlled the Jewish "tributary mode of production," the system that extracted the economic surplus from its primary producers, the peasant cultivators and shepherds, and redistributed it among the upper class, specifically to the members of the ruling aristocracy, the priesthood and the administrative apparatus of the government.[18]

The seventy members of the Sanhedrin, or High Council, of Jerusalem, who concurred with the high priest's condemnation of Jesus (14:64), were drawn from the Jewish sacred and secular aristocracies and consisted of chief priests, elders, and scribes (14:53; 15:1). Acting as a kind of parliament under the Roman procurators, this assembly shared the responsibilities of governing the Jewish polity with the high priest. Many of them were absentee landlords of large estates in various regions of Palestine; and, as is estimated by the parable of the wicked tenants in 12:1–12, they were also the enemies of the peasants who worked their land, because they dispossessed them of their agricultural surplus through inordinately high rents.[19]

The scribes, who are encountered in Mark's narrative, were a professional guild of jurists who served the Jewish polity as the official

16. This is reflected in John 18:12–28. See Bo Reicke, *The New Testament Era: The World of the Bible from 500 B.C. to A.D. 100*, trans. David E. Green (Philadelphia: Fortress Press, 1968), 142–45.

17. Reicke, *The New Testament Era*, 146–47.

18. For the model of this exchange system, see T. F. Carney, *The Shape of the Past: Models and Antiquity* (Lawrence, Kans.: Coronado Press, 1975), 172–86. See also Fernando Belo, *A Materialist Reading of the Gospel of Mark*, trans. Matthew J. O'Connell (Maryknoll, N.Y.: Orbis Books, 1981), 60–81.

19. M. Rostovtzeff, *The Social and Economic History of the Hellenistic World*, 3 vols. (Oxford: Clarendon Press, 1941), 1:270. See also Simon Applebaum, "Economic Life in Palestine," in *The Jewish People in the First Century*, ed. S. Safrai and M. Stern, Compendia, 2 vols. (Assen and Amsterdam: Van Gorcum, 1960; vol. 2 published in association with Fortress Press), 2:656–64.

interpreters of the law. Those "coming down from Jerusalem" on various occasions (3:22; 7:1) may have been members of the Sanhedrin (11:27; 14:1, 53; 15:1), while the scribes of Galilee (2:6, 16; 9:14) probably were attached to local synagogues. According to 12:38–40, they exploited their prestige and power for self-aggrandizement at the expense of a true administration of justice. Jesus' cancellation of the temple institution and with it the systems of pollution and redistribution that it maintained turned their growing animosity into an active pursuit of his destruction (11:18).

Closely allied with the scribes were the Pharisees, the popular champions of "separation" from all forms of pollution and defilement. They had adopted the rigorous purity code of the priesthood, along with its ritual observances, in order to impose it on Jewish society at large for the realization of an ideal covenant community. But by compromising with the ruling class so that the norms of Levitical purity might govern the life of the Jewish people, they stabilized and perpetuated the political status quo with all of its injustices and inequalities. In Mark's story world they are quickly alienated by Jesus' rejection of their traditions of the elders, many of which, in his judgment, promoted injustice (7:1–13). In their opposition to him they did not hesitate to enter into a plot with the Herodians to kill him (3:6; 12:13). The latter were political supporters of the Herodian family and, while therefore also pro-Roman, they may have advocated the reestablishment of the earlier undivided kingdom of Herod the great.[20]

Many of these Herodians, Pharisees, and local scribes may be classified as retainers in the employ of the governing class who enjoyed a standard of living above that of the lower levels of society and therefore also tended to identify with it and its interests.[21] Others among them included household servants, tax collectors, professional soldiers, and many other kinds of officials. In Mark's Gospel they are represented by Levi the tax collector, who performed the work of transferring the economic surplus of the peasant producers to the ruling elite but who followed Jesus into discipleship. Also belonging to

20. Smallwood, *The Jews Under Roman Rule*, 163.
21. On retainers, see G. Lenski, *Power and Privilege*, 243–56.

this segment of society are the guards or petty officials of the Sanhedrin who received Jesus "with blows" (14:65).

The peasantry constituted the largest class of agrarian society.[22] Living in the rural countryside, they worked the land under a tributary or redistribution system of exchange,[23] and because they were dispossessed by exorbitant rent funds, different kinds of taxes, and compulsory labor, amounting to up to four-fifths of their total agricultural produce, they were usually subjected to a life of abject poverty.[24] In Mark's Gospel, Simon Peter and his brother Andrew, who are introduced as net-casting fishers, are to be counted among them (1:16). They own no boat, and their fishing therefore may be limited to standing waist deep in the water throwing out their hand nets "at the bay of the seven warm springs south of Capernaum where 'the fishes come up in shoals on account of the water from the springs.' "[25] Zebedee and his two sons, James and John, who are also engaged in the fishing business, own a boat, and therefore can fish throughout the lake dragging long seine nets behind them and eventually pulling them up onto the land (1:18–20). Because they are able to catch large quantities of fish, they also enjoy a greater measure of affluence from their sale and can afford to hire day laborers for the maintenance of their equipment and consequently the continued success of their enterprise. But like Peter and Andrew, they too must pay a large percentage of their catch as a rent fund to the tax collectors of Herod Antipas. The

22. Lenski and Lenski, *Human Societies*, 266–78. See also Eric R. Wolf, *Peasants*, Foundations of Modern Anthropology Series (Englewood Cliffs, N.J.: Prentice-Hall, 1966).

23. Again, see Carney, *The Shape of the Past*, 172–75. See also Eric R. Wolf, *Europe and the People Without History* (Berkeley and Los Angeles: University of California Press, 1982), 79–88.

24. Oakman, "Palestinian Land Tenure," 28. For a vivid description of peasant life in the rural countryside, see G. E. M. de Ste. Croix, *The Class Struggle in the Ancient Greek World* (London: Gerald Duckworth & Co., 1981), 9–19, 205–75. See also Wolf, *Peasants*, 1–17.

25. Wuellner, *The Meaning of "Fishers of Men*," 39. See also J. G. Duncan, "The Sea of Tiberias and Its Environs," *PEFQ* (1926): 20. But see esp. E. W. G. Masterman, *Studies in Galilee* (Chicago: University of Chicago Press, 1909), 39–40, on fishing with casting nets. Wuellner examines the fishing traditions of other cultures but does not view his data in the light of sociological theory or give careful consideration to the signifiers by which the evangelist Mark differentiates between the economic status of the two pairs of brothers in 1:16–20. Note his distinction between two classes of fishers on p. 63. In his judgment the two pairs of brothers "were anything but the idyllic and naive fishermen of Galilee's lower proletariat."

last peasant to appear in Mark's story world is Simon the Cyrenian, who carried the transverse beam of Jesus' cross to Golgotha. According to 15:21, he came into Jerusalem "from [the] field."

Artisans and craftspeople were usually drawn from the peasantry as labor specialization increased.[26] Many of them, in fact, were peasants disinherited by the institution of primogeniture and compelled to enter a craft in order to make a living. Generally their income was not as high as that of the peasants, upon whom many of them depended for work; and some of them were so poor that they were unable to marry and raise a family. In the narrative world of Mark's Gospel, Jesus had been a carpenter before he submitted to John's baptism of repentance and was called into a new vocation (6:3).

Two large groups formed the lowest ranks of agrarian society: the degraded and the expendables.[27] The former consisted of "defiled" and unskilled laborers—tanners, shepherds, prostitutes, porters, burden bearers, miners, and others—who were engaged in offensive and ritually unclean work or sold their body or animal energy. The latter segment occupied the very bottom of the societal ladder and formed a large mass of unemployed or nonproductive people: beggars, vagrants, thieves, outlaws, lepers, and others. Of these two groups the expendables were the more deprived and dehumanized, subject to continuous malnutrition and disease. The leper of 1:40–45, whom Jesus cleansed and returned to a fuller life in society, is one of them. Blind Bartimaeus, who is seated at the edge of the way outside Jericho, is another (10:46). The rural crowds of Galilee who follow Jesus, whose diseased, demented, blind, deaf, and mute he heals (3:7–12), whom he feeds in the wilderness (6:34–44; 8:1–9), who hear and understand his parables (4:1, 33), and who become his new family (3:20, 31–35) are to be located at these lowest levels of agrarian society. The crowds of Mark 11—12, who are eventually stirred up by the chief priests to choose Barabbas and cry out for Jesus' execution (15:11, 15), are the urban dispossessed who, although they are profoundly alienated from their political and religious leaders, are economically dependent on the charity of the temple institution which the latter administer.

26. G. E. Lenski, *Power and Privilege*, 278–81. See also Ste. Croix, *Class Struggle in the Ancient Greek World*, 269–75.

27. G. E. Lenski, *Power and Privilege*, 280–84.

These class identifications and associations, presupposed by the evangelist, would be made quite naturally by the recipients of the Gospel because they themselves participated in the same realities of agrarian society that the story world reflects.[28] The two worlds, that of Roman-occupied Palestine during Jesus' ministry and the "extratextual" world of Mark's Gospel, are essentially equivalent. Predominant in both of them are the actualities of class structure and class struggle manifested in the exploitation and dispossession of the lower classes by the governing aristocracy and its retainers. The traditions of Jesus' public career, therefore, which recount his involvement in the class conflict of his society and his actualization of "the kingdom of God" in a context of appalling poverty, hunger, unemployment, disease, and powerlessness, are profoundly relevant to Mark's addressees. Indeed, their own class identity would be a decisive factor in their interaction with the story. For it would determine which characters they will regard sympathetically and which they will view with suspicion and hostility, which episodes will have the greatest impact on them and which feelings, instincts, and intuitions are evoked by the development of the plot line. It would affect their evaluation of the different points of view, attitudes, responses, actions, and reactions encountered in the story.[29]

Such an interchange would be all the more effective if the story world actually confronted them with their counterparts, individuals and groups involved in conditions and circumstances that correspond to their own. A textual excavation of the author's vocabulary, explanations, plot development, and narrative detail reveals that the original addressees are in fact represented in the story in terms of their geophysical location, ethnic identity, and class membership. Mark's intended audience proves to be "a sort of fictional inhabitant of the text" and embodies "not only the concepts and conventions of the contemporary public but also the author's desire to link up with these

28. That the realities of class, class structure, and class conflict are not nineteenth- or twentieth-century constructions but actually existed and were acknowledged in antiquity is shown by Ste. Croix, *Class Struggle in the Ancient Greek World*, 69–80.

29. Of course, in their hearing or reading of the Gospel they will be guided by the narrator, but they will quickly discover a correspondence between their lower-class perspective and the point of view of the narrator. So also Petersen, " 'Point of View' in Mark's Narrative," 109.

concepts and work on them—sometimes just portraying them, sometimes acting upon them."[30]

Accordingly, the Latinisms found in the Gospel hint at the geophysical location of its intended recipients: *modios* (peck measure) in 4:21; *legiōn* in 5:9, 15; *spekoulatōr* ("executioner") in 6:27; *dēnarion* (a Roman silver coin) in 6:37; 12:15; and 14:5; *xestēs* (a liquid measure about equal to a pint) in 7:4; *kēnsos* ("tax") in 12:14; *kodrantēs* ("a penny") in 12:42; *phragelloun* ("to flog") in 15:15; *praitōrion* ("governor's residence") in 15:16; and *kenturiōn* ("centurion") in 15:39, 44, 45. Although they have been regarded as evidence for a life situation in the city of Rome,[31] a sociological analysis, as Werner Kelber has made, indicates that these words are military and economic terms that reflect a context of Roman-occupied territory and not the sociocultural milieu of Rome. If this text had originated and been addressed to an audience in the capital city, a sociologically different set of Latinisms—domestic, social, and even religious in character— would have been assimilated.[32]

Other features of the Gospel's vocabulary enable a more precise identification of its geophysical location. While the word *polis* ("city") occurs eight times in the text—twice referring to Capernaum and three times to Jerusalem—the word *kōmē* ("village") appears seven, possibly eight, times. The unusual term *kōmopoleis* (probably referring to market towns) is used once in 1:38, and the word *agros* ("field") in either the singular or the plural eight times. Although Jesus works in Capernaum and other cities of Galilee (1:45; 6:56), his ministry, in the story world of Mark, is concentrated in the villages and fields of the rural countryside (1:38; 6:56; 8:27; 11:1, 2, 11, 12; 14:3). Correspondingly it seems probable that the original addressees of the Gospel were village folk residing in a rural territory that, as the Latinisms suggest, was occupied by Roman legions and exploited by Roman business entrepreneurs and traders. The Semitic influence that

---

30. Iser, *The Act of Reading*, 33.

31. So, e.g., Belo, *A Materialist Reading*, 97, 122, 167. Belo brings a Marxist analysis to bear on Mark's Gospel and its content, and disappointingly still locates its origin in Rome.

32. Werner H. Kelber, *The Kingdom in Mark: A New Place and a New Time* (Philadelphia: Fortress Press, 1974), 129.

is also evident both in the Semiticisms of the text and in the transliterations of Aramaic words into Greek implies an area in which Greeks and Jews lived side by side.[33]

On the basis of the strategy of the author's plot line, it may even be possible to name the exact province. The exorcism of the Gerasene demoniac concludes with an anomaly: instead of charging the restored individual to remain silent, as he does throughout his ministry, Jesus sends him back to his home and his society to "report to them how much the Lord has done for you and (how) he showed you mercy." This reversal may be a feature of "the implied reader" signaling the addressees of the Gospel that the beginnings of the Christian mission in their own region originated when Jesus established God's rule in the countryside of Gerasa—by defeating a legion of demons—which, in spite of the rejection of the ruling elite, was continued by the proclamation of the demoniac whom he had liberated. An equally dramatic turning point is reached in the exorcism of a gentile girl (7:24–30). When Jesus withdraws into the regions of Tyre in order to seek seclusion, a Greek mother succeeds in locating him and by her wisdom constrains him to exorcise the demon that has taken possession of her daughter. She is the only person in the story world of the Gospel who addresses Jesus with the divine appellation "Lord." His subsequent itinerary of going out of the regions of Tyre, through Sidon to the Sea of Galilee, up into the middle of the Decapolis (7:31), is not an indication of the author's inadequate knowledge of Palestinian-Syrian geography but of the opening of the gentile mission (7:34) and its deeper penetration into gentile territory.[34] Once again the origin of the Christian mission to the gentiles is linked to Jesus' career, and, like the earlier episode in the countryside of Gerasa, it occurred in southern

33. On Semiticisms in Mark, see Vincent Taylor, *The Gospel According to St. Mark: The Greek Text with Introduction, Notes and Indexes* (London: Macmillan & Co., 1952), 59–66; and Howard Clark Kee, *Community of the New Age: Studies in Mark's Gospel* (Philadelphia: Westminster Press, 1977), 101–2, 190–201 n. 6.

34. Kee believes this itinerary is "scarcely credible." Historically yes, but not if the Gospel is presumed to be a story world with its own structures of time and space (*Community of the New Age*, 103). See T. A. Burkill, *New Light on the Earliest Gospel* (Ithaca, N.Y., and London: Cornell University Press, 1972). Burkill asserts that both 5:1–20 and 7:24–30 owe their "place in the gospel to a desire on the evangelist's part to show that the apostolic mission to the Gentiles found prefigurement in the Messiah's earthly career."

Syria.[35] Certainly the ethnic identity of these Greek-speaking people as gentiles is upheld by the narrator's explanation of such Jewish customs as the Pharisaic ritual of ceremonial washing in 7:3–4 and the translation of various Aramaic words and phrases into Greek: *Boanērges* (3:17); *talitha koum* (5:41); *korban* (7:11); *ephphatha* (7:34); *abba* (14:36); *Golgatha* (15:22); and *Eloi, Eloi, lama sabachthani* (15:34).

Other features of the Gospel indicate that these rural gentile Christians belonged to the lower-class strata of Roman-occupied Syria. They appear to have been primarily peasants and artisans. All of the parables and metaphors that Jesus utilizes in his teaching relate to agriculture: the sower (4:3–9), the seed growing secretly (4:26–29), the mustard seed (4:30–32), the wicked tenant farmers (12:1–11), and the fig tree (13:28), or to various aspects of the lower-class culture: marriage (2:19–20), mending garments (2:21), and wine making (2:22). The link between "fields" and "family," that is, the family of "brothers, sisters, mother, father, children," which Jesus draws in response to Simon Peter's claimed renunciation and sacrifice, discloses the bond between the land and the institution of the extended family among the peasantry (10:29–30). Simon the Cyrenian, who was pressed into service by the Romans to carry the transverse beam of Jesus' cross, as has already been observed, is described in 15:21 as "coming from [the] field." He is a peasant. The comparison that is made to describe the intensity of Jesus' transfiguration is derived from the craft of bleaching: His garments "became very shining white such as a bleacher on earth is unable to make so white" (9:3).[36] Finally, only Mark's Gospel identifies Jesus vocationally as a carpenter (6:3).[37]

35. So also Kee, *Community of the New Age*, 102. Obviously this episode in Matt. 15:21–28 holds a different significance for the evangelist Matthew. See Herman C. Waetjen, *The Origin and Destiny of Humanness: An Interpretation of the Gospel According to Matthew*, 2d ed. (San Rafael, Calif.: Crystal Press, 1978), 167–68.

36. The analogy is not employed in the parallel episodes of Matthew's or Luke's story world. The former utilizes apocalyptic imagery (17:2), while the latter attempts no comparisons at all (9:29). Mark's analogy must have been meaningful to his addressees, some of whom may have been involved in the craft of bleaching.

37. In the parallel passage of Matt. 13:55 Jesus is designated "the son of the carpenter." He cannot be a carpenter in Matthew's story world, for from the very beginning he is the Messiah, "king of the Jews." Matthew's Gospel is addressed to upper-class Christian Jews.

Accordingly, his power and privilege in the socioeconomic pyramid of Roman Palestine would correspond to that of the poorer peasants. For the Gospel's addressees of peasants and craftspeople, therefore, Jesus, in view of his own class membership, would serve as a model of how the dispossessed and the oppressed can enter into a reordering of power in order to recover what God willed to all human beings at creation (Ps. 8:4–6).

Mark's folk tale of John the Baptizer's martyrdom reflects the animosity of these lower classes toward their lawless and self-serving rulers. John's death is attributed to the injustice of the debauched political elite. Herod Antipas fears John and, in contrast to Josephus's account in *Antiquities* 18.116–19, hears him gladly and even defends him. But he, Herod, is basically a weak-willed profligate. It is his wife, Herodias, who, because she holds a grudge against John, wants to put him out of the way. But she has no opportunity until Herod's scruples are overwhelmed by his carousing and the sensuous dance performed by her own daughter. John's head is brought into the banquet, like a piece of meat served up on a platter.[38] The same evaluation of their leaders is manifested at the end of the Gospel in the account of the Sanhedrin's abusive, even sadistic humiliation of Jesus after his condemnation to death: "And some began to spit at him and to cover his face and to beat him and to say to him, 'Prophesy!' And the retainers received him with blows" (14:65).

These factors of geographical location, ethnic identity, and class orientation alone would not constitute the disposition of the text's addressees, but they would be merged into their ideology and its set of values. Their point of view as a whole would be engaged in a reciprocal relationship with the text. It is, in fact, an essential component of the system of perspectives represented in the story world, expressed by one or more of its characters but appropriately those who occupy the same levels of the stratified agrarian society reflected in the Gospel.[39] These are the disciples of Jesus who have been drawn in the image of the text's addressees. They are not depicted historically but

---

38. Note the differences in Matthew's version of the story, which corresponds more closely to Josephus's account. Herod, not Herodias, wanted to put John to death, yet he carried out his design only when his inhibitions were overcome by self-indulgence.

39. According to Iser, *The Act of Reading*, 35: "As a rule there are four main perspectives: those of the narrator, the characters, the plot and the fictitious reader."

ideologically in order to mirror the disciples outside the story. The latter, by observing their counterparts in the story as they interact with Jesus and others, are confronted more directly with the disposition of their own discipleship and consequently brought face-to-face with both its resources and its deficiencies. Obviously that disposition is not identical to the effect or outcome that the story is intended to have but that which is to be challenged and even changed as a result of their interaction with it. To draw upon Wolfgang Iser's analysis of the act of reading:

> The intended reader [addressee] ... marks certain positions and attitudes in the text, but these are not identical to the reader's role, for many of these positions are conceived ironically ... so that the reader is not expected to accept the attitude offered to him [her] but rather to react to it.[40]

In addition to the disposition of these characters which reflect the point of view of the addressees, there are other perspectives conveyed by the authorial constructs of the narrator, the plot line, and the attitudes and positions of the other characters.[41] Together they constitute the hypothetical figure of what is called "the implied reader" which is embedded in the text and "embodies all those predispositions necessary for a literary work to have its effect."[42] Since the message that is to be communicated is not a set of concepts but an experience arising out of a participation in the story, the role of the addressees consists essentially of interacting with the "response-inviting structures" of the implied reader or the author's schematized set of perspectives in order to produce the subject matter of the text.

The evangelist has chosen the rhetorical instrument of an omniscient narrator to tell the story of "the beginning of the good news of Jesus Christ,"[43] but in the vernacular of the uneducated lower classes, characterized by crudity of snytax and grammar, anacoluthons and asyndetons, mixed verb tenses, and a variety of conjunctions introduc-

40. Ibid., 33.
41. Ibid., 35.
42. Ibid., 34; also 34–38. See also Wolfgang Iser, *The Implied Reader: Patterns of Communication in Prose Fiction from Bunyan to Beckett* (Baltimore: Johns Hopkins University Press, 1975), perhaps esp. the concluding chapter (pp. 274–94).
43. Petersen, " 'Point of View' in Mark's Narrative," 105–6. For a detailed discussion of the omniscient narrator of Mark's Gospel, see Rhoads and Michie, *Mark as Story*, 35–43.

ing virtually every sentence. According to Etienne Trocmé, "the main feature of Mark's style is its rusticity."[44] Of course, the Hellenistic Greek of the narrator may, in fact, be identical to the language of the author, but in any case its employment conveys the story with rapid movement, fresh vitality, and dramatic impact. Standing outside the story and speaking in the third person, yet being an invisible presence inside the story by directing the plot line of the narrative and shaping the character and speech of the actors, the omniscient narrator functions somewhat like a contemporary producer of a sports event. Television cameras have been placed at various strategic angles overlooking the playing field. As the action unfolds, the producer will utilize different cameras and lenses to channel different perspectives to the viewer. It may be a close-up of an individual player throwing, carrying, or kicking the ball, or a more comprehensive view of the defensive unit attempting to stop a particular play, or even a conjunction of two pictures showing a touchdown or a goal being scored on one side of the screen and simultaneously the crowd in the stands rising to its feet screaming in wild ecstasy on the other side of the screen. In the same way the omniscient narrator channels to the addressees a close-up of Jesus performing the actions of his ministry: teaching in parables, exorcising demons, and healing the sick, followed by a composite of responses from different individuals and groups, and sometimes even holding a scene in temporary suspension while another is followed to its conclusion. In Mark 4 the great crowd of people wait on the beach (4:1–9) while Jesus addresses his disciples with exhortations intended only for them (4:10–25) and then returns to tell two more parables (4:26–32) to the crowd. In 14:53–72 the episodes of Jesus' trial and Peter's denial are dramatically intertwined. From time to time the narrator overtly enters the story in order to inject a clarifying remark (e.g., 6:52 or 9:6), explain certain customs foreign to the addressees (7:3–4), and translate the Aramaic words and phrases that have been

44. See the helpful discussion of Mark's language in Etienne Trocmé, *The Formation of the Gospel According to Mark*, trans. Pamela Gaughan (Philadelphia: Westminster Press, 1975), 68–72. "The author of Mark was content to use the vocabulary current in his milieu. His syntax also presents certain peculiarities, all to be explained by the influence of the spoken language, or of Aramaic" (p. 70). See also the analysis of Mark's vocabulary, syntax, and style by Taylor (*The Gospel According to St. Mark*, 45–52).

used, possibly to draw the addressees into the historical authenticity of the story world that is being constructed.[45]

Perhaps the foremost value of the use of an omniscient narrator lies in its capacity to convey scenes and episodes that are not available to any of the characters in the story but are intended specifically for the benefit of the addressees. Crucial instances of this strategy are the descent of the holy Spirit into Jesus and the words that the Heavenly Voice addresses to him (1:10–11), the temptation in the wilderness (1:12–13), and Jesus' agonizing prayer in the field of Gethsemane (14:35–41). As a result, the disciples outside the story, the addressees of the Gospel, acquire a comprehension of Jesus' person and work that the disciples inside the story do not have. The advantage that they gain, however, is hazardous, for it can be turned against them in their interaction with the story. What will be the outcome of their confrontation with their own quality of discipleship, mirrored as it is in the Gospel by Jesus' followers, which they will be forced to evaluate from a new transcending point of view that begins to crystallize out of the fresh insights they receive from an omniscient storyteller?

The different perspectives expressed in and by the narrative, as well as the traditions that have been appropriated to convey them, must have been both familiar and unfamiliar to the recipients of the Gospel. Yet how much of the author's stock of material they were acquainted with beforehand seems impossible to determine. At least some of it must have been familiar to them, and its utilization by the author would ensure the illumination and stabilization of meaning that is to be actualized. At the same time, there would also have been new, unfamiliar material—the distinctive repertoire of the author—which would arouse the curiosity and maintain the interest of the audience.[46] The combination and conjunction of both, the familiar perspectives and traditions carefully selected and removed from their original

---

45. According to Petersen (" 'Point of View' in Mark's Narrative," 110), "The frequent explanatory commentary on Jewish words or customs establishes this difference between the competence of actors and readers in their respective worlds, but it also implies the narrator's competence in the codes of both worlds. . . . Literarily, the effect of such commentary is of a double nature. On the one hand it posits a distance between the reader in his world and the actors in theirs, while on the other hand it serves to bridge the two worlds and bring the reader close to the world of the actors."

46. Iser, *The Act of Reading*, 69–70.

context and function, and the fresh, unfamiliar material strategically introduced into a new plot, would produce a new configuration of semantic potential. The eventual outcome, as has already been suggested, resulting from an adherence to the instructions of the text, would be an original standpoint enabling the addressees to transcend the limitations of their own discipleship by viewing a reality "that would never have come into focus as long as . . . habitual dispositions were determining [their] orientation."[47]

The opening verse of the Gospel intimates that they were unfamiliar with "the beginning of the good news of Jesus Christ." That beginning may, in fact, include the entire story, as the narrator tells it, for even though the addressees may be familiar with individual episodes and events, they have never before been confronted with a coherent, consistent account of how the Christian movement began. For what is disclosed in the Gospel's opening Old Testament quotations is the divine prospect of a new **way**. In view of the repeated use of *hodos* ("way") in the text, indeed sixteen times, the tantalizing possibility emerges that what may have been the Christian movement's earliest self-designation has been adapted for a novel undertaking. It is to serve as a key signifier in this story of the construction of the way.

Of course, both Old Testament quotations reproduce more or less accurately what is familiar to the addressees from their own hearing of the reading of the Septuagintal text in their liturgy of worship. But not only have these quotations been detached from their original scriptural context and placed at the beginning of a story, they have also been revised to convey as clearly as possible a fundamental paradox that will permeate the entire narrative. For their juxtaposition raises the critical question of who, in fact, is supposed to be coming. The problem is already implicit in the first quotation, which appears to be a conflation of Mal. 3:1 and Exod. 23:20. According to the original version of Mal. 3:1, it is Yahweh! Yet according to Exod. 23:20, it is a third party, Israel! Moreover, it is curious that neither of the main verbs of these two quotations has been retained; an altogether new one

---

47. Ibid., 35. Contemporary readers cannot enter into such an original experience of interaction with the familiar (placed into a new context) and the unfamiliar in order to construct a new experience of meaning. Perhaps with a more precise translation of the Gospel, some historical-sociological understanding, and some literary-critical guidelines to serve them in their act of meaning, they may begin to fulfill the underlying intention of the text.

has been substituted, the verb *kataskeuazein* ("to construct"). The second citation—the one, in fact, that has been derived from Isaiah—clearly anticipates, at least in its original context, the coming of Yahweh, whose way will be prepared by the repentance of the people. What is the correlation between these two verses? What relevance do they have for the story that is to be told?

The narrative that follows will convey answers to these questions, but the text must be translated accurately in order to enable contemporary readers to receive the proper instructions from the narrator for the production of the signified.[48] If contemporary readers are indeed alert, they cannot but respond with astonishment to the climax that is reached at the end of this initial episode of the Gospel and the subtle manner in which it resolves the contradiction posed by the juxtaposition of the opening Old Testament quotations. Of course, the answer is not immediately obvious. It arises out of the experience of taking the text seriously as it stands, without any rationalizations drawn from historical conjecture and, at the same time, limiting any questions to the narrative world that has been entered.

Therefore, when the storyteller maintains that "the entire Judean countryside and all the Jerusalemites" came to John for baptism, that is not to be treated as a historical fact that requires historical corroboration. It is reality for the world of Mark's Gospel and must be taken seriously, if the contrast of Jesus as the only Jew from Galilee who presents himself to John for baptism and experiences the fulfillment of John's promise (1:8) is to have its impact. Moreover, what is not said in the text must not be read into it. If Jesus did not confess his sins at his baptism, as the Jews from Judea and Jerusalem did, it must not be assumed, on the basis of ecclesiastical dogma, that he had no sins to confess. Something else may be implied by the narrator's choice of the signifiers, "he was baptized into the Jordan."

Although different points of view are communicated throughout the subsequent narrative, the storyteller's own perspective is primary and is conveyed both in and through the development of the plot and in and through the portrayal of Jesus. He is, of course, the central character, and his person and work dominate the story. But while his

---

48. See the translation that follows (Part Two) and compare it to any other English version.

activities are recounted broadly and explicitly, his identity emerges more subtly, even though at the outset he is acknowledged as God's beloved son. The narrator develops a "stereoscopic" view of Jesus that combines two discrete typologies that are held in dialectical tension as they emerge in the course of the plot.[49] On the basis of his re-creation or resurrection by the holy Spirit as he arises out of the water of the Jordan River, he is "the Son of Man" or, preferably, "the New Human Being" whom the Heavenly Voice identifies as "my beloved son." But at the same time he is also an Elijah figure, who, like John the Baptizer with whom he shares this typology, serves as God's forerunner in order to construct the way through death and into resurrection for his followers.

The plot line unfolds this dialectical identity of Jesus within an essentially circular construction of the narrative. The opening scene introduces the Elijah-like activity of John the Baptizer as God's forerunner but quickly focuses on the one who fulfills his call to repentance. Jesus launches his new career as God's surrogate in his home province of Galilee. By his preaching, teaching, and healing he makes the long-anticipated millennial reality of God's rule present to his contemporaries, particularly the oppressed and dispossessed masses of Galilee. He expands his activity into territory of Gerasa, east of Lake Galilee, and eventually into the regions of Tyre, even penetrating northward as far as Sidon in order to inaugurate the gentile mission.

Among all of the people he encounters in his itineracy, some are called to be "fishers of human beings." Unlike the crowds who enjoy the benefits of his eschatological mission, they are not to be simply beneficiaries of his ministry. While the former participate in the reality of God's rule and are identified by him as his new family (3:31–35), they are summoned into a discipleship that will eventually involve them in a collaborative role of fulfilling God's will. Instruction and training, of course, are indispensable, and both are given throughout the time of Jesus' work in Galilee. Above all, he is the model they are to emulate in their discipleship. Indeed, they are called to be his accom-

---

49. R. Alan Culpepper (*Anatomy of the Fourth Gospel: A Study in Literary Design* [Philadelphia: Fortress Press, 1983], 33) uses this term to characterize the narrator's point of view in the story world of the Gospel According to John. I have appropriated it because of its aptness in describing the dialectical Christology of Mark's Gospel.

plices in incarnating the millennial reality of the New Human Being which he embodies.

But as the narrative continues, the addressees of the Gospel, the disciples outside the story, become more aware of the difficulties that the disciples inside the story have in comprehending Jesus' mission and his efforts to fulfill it, both in their lives and in their Galilean world. Among them he continually encounters ignorance, misunderstanding, and stubborn resistance. The discovery that it is necessary for Jesus to explain his parables to his disciples while the crowd has no difficulty in grasping them must be disturbing to the addressees. This surprising disclosure can only challenge them to scrutinize their own capacity to hear and see, especially in the light of the warning that Jesus issues to his disciples inside the story in response to their lack of understanding: "Take heed how you hear!"

Any new uneasiness arising within the addressees about the quality of their own discipleship might be intensified by the episode of the stilling of the storm. What is faith after all, if Jesus rebukes his community of followers even when they have turned to him for help in a moment of crisis?

Through the perspective of the plot line the narrator extends the measure of Jesus' stature of the New Human Being by recounting the impressive feats of conquering a legion of demons, delivering a woman from the oppression of the pollution system, and raising a girl from the dead. In view of these experiences the addressees can only assume that the disciples inside the story are gaining a more comprehensive sense of Jesus' person and work. Indeed, they may even be able to answer for themselves the christological question they raised at the conclusion of the stilling of the storm (4:41). For the disciples outside the story, the addressees, who already know the secret of Jesus' identity, these mighty works should come as no surprise.

After Jesus' rejection in his hometown of Nazareth, the disciples are sent forth on an internship to preach repentance and exorcise unclean spirits. By this time they should be ready to undertake such a commission, and indeed they prove they are. In addition to the activities that Jesus prescribed, they even heal the sick by anointing them with oil. Their success must be reassuring to the addressees. When Jesus therefore subsequently invites them to undertake the feeding of the multi-

tudes (6:37)—a natural inclination in the light of his ultimate intention—their startled reaction is to question the reasonableness of his
expectation. How can two hundred days' wages, two hundred denarii,
be enough to satisfy the hunger of so many people? But then what kind
of impact did their own mighty works of casting out demons and
healing the sick have on them?

At this point, what tensions are the disciples outside the story
feeling? With whom do they find themselves identifying? Are they able
to grasp the seemingly unlimited possibility that belongs to Jesus in the
light of his entry into a reordering of power at his baptism by the holy
Spirit, unlimited possibility which he wants his disciples to share in as
well? The story of Jesus walking on the Sea of Galilee underlines this
reality of unlimited possibility by intimating that the destiny of the
New Human Being is nothing less than realizing the potentiality of
God. Yet after describing the overwhelming astonishment of the disciples, the narrator injects the remark, "For they did not understand
about the loaves, but their heart had been hardened." Will the addressees comprehend the relationship between the possibility of walking on water and the possibility of feeding the multitudes?

Curiously Jesus and his disciples do not arrive at the destination he
had prescribed. What kind of judgment does that evoke from the
addressees—especially when Jesus is unable to avoid a confrontation
with the religious elite on his disciples' lack of observance of the
regulations of ritual purity and subsequently feels the necessity of
withdrawing into the gentile territory of Tyre? That, as has already
been noted, leads to the "heavenly opening" of the gentile mission
(7:34) and a concomitant feeding of gentile multitudes, events that
would confirm the sensibilities of Mark's gentile addressees.

But the plot line, with its return to the inadequacies of the disciples,
must evoke further consternation. For their continued hardness of
heart and incapacity to hear and see leads Jesus to denounce them
with the same words of Isaiah 6 that he directed to "those outside" his
new family (8:17–21). They are like the blind human being who
requires a second touch of Jesus' restoring hand in order to see clearly
and be capable of true perceptions (8:22–26). Peter's confession of
8:29 confirms this. Even the dazzling experience of Jesus' metamorphosis does not trigger new comprehension. The general
powerlessness and ineffectiveness of the disciples are openly displayed

by their inability to exorcise the unclean spirit of epilepsy. Instead, they sublimate by engaging the scribes in debate (9:14). Jesus therefore is constrained to end his Galilean ministry by resuming his teaching of his disciples but this time in peripatetic seclusion (9:30–31).

As they enter Judea, after leaving Galilee, Jesus assumes the Elijah role which John the Baptizer had played for him and **goes before** his disciples in order to construct the way for them into vicarious death and resurrection. Even though he continues to elucidate his destiny, they show no signs of grasping what he is telling them. Yet, unlike the rich ruler, they have expressed a radical repentance by leaving family, house, and fields to follow him. They are overwhelmed with both fear and amazement (10:32), but their anticipation is turned toward themselves and their self-aggrandizement (10:35–40). They acknowledge that they can drink the same cup and be baptized with the same baptism as Jesus, but they do not comprehend what that involves. During their celebration of the Passover with Jesus they are incorporated into the body of the New Human Being which he will establish permanently through his death and resurrection. But subsequently at his arrest in Gethsemane they all abandon him and flee into the night. Only the women return and share in the agony of his crucifixion. Yet by not fulfilling their commission and rallying the disciples to follow Jesus into Galilee, they end the story with a default that has been endemic of the discipleship portrayed by the narrator throughout the Gospel.

In the usual ending of the narrative, which, in fact, is not an ending,[50] there is an underlying intention that is not expressed by the text but that must nevertheless be fulfilled. A signified must be constructed by the disciples outside the story that is not denoted by the signifiers.[51] Jesus has been raised from the dead. But this is not the good news that the three women are to bear to the other disciples. Rather, they are charged to remind them of the words Jesus had spoken to them before his arrest. "After I am raised, I shall go before you into Galilee." Although the women flee from the sepulcher and say

---

50. Norman R. Petersen, "When Is the End Not the End? Literary Reflections on the Ending of Mark's Narrative," *Interpretation* 34 (1980): 151–66. See below, pp. 248–50, where Petersen's essay is treated at greater length.

51. See Iser, *The Act of Reading*, 67.

nothing to anyone, the possibility that the addressees must take seriously, in spite of the silence of the women, is that the disciples may have remembered those words of 14:28, followed Jesus back to Galilee, and experienced the reality of his resurrection. The signifier that the youth employs, "He is **going before** you," implies that Jesus is continuing to play the role of the forerunner, which he assumed in 10:32, and if the disciples will follow him into resurrection, as they followed him into death, they will experience their own re-creation as New Human Beings and, like Jesus in 1:11, be acknowledged by God as "my beloved daughters and sons." The realization of that possibility will signify their entry into a reordering of power and, in collaboration with the risen Jesus, the continuation of the construction of The Way.

The story ends as it began. According to the testimony of the youth (16:5–7), Jesus has been resurrected and is going back to Galilee. If the ending is like the beginning, and if the beginning presupposes the ending, Jesus' return to the province in which he inaugurated God's rule connotes the opening of a second career and the resumption of his former activity. Although the addressees have no certainty about the outcome of the possibility that the text presumes, their own pondering of the signified which they have constructed should eventually confront them with the underlying intention of the text which they and only they themselves can fulfill. Sooner or later they must determine whether, in consequence of their following their own forerunner, the evangelist Mark, who through the literary creation of a story world has constructed the way for them, they have followed Jesus to Galilee, experienced the reality of his resurrection, entered into a reordering of power, and are committed to the continuation of the construction of the way.

A Translation of the Gospel According to Mark

1:1-8 The beginning of the good news of Jesus Christ, as it is written in the prophet Isaiah:

"Look, I send my messenger before your face who will construct your **way**. A voice of **shouting in the wilderness,** 'Prepare **the way** of the Lord; make his paths straight.' "

John the Baptizer happened in the wilderness proclaiming a baptism of **repentance** toward forgiveness of sins. And the entire Judean countryside and all the Jerusalemites were going out to him, and they were letting themselves be baptized by him **in** the Jordan River confessing their sins. And John was wearing camel's hair and a leather belt around his waist, and he was eating grasshoppers and wild honey. And he was proclaiming saying, "The one stronger than I comes after me, whose thong of his sandals I stooping down am not worthy to loosen. I baptized you with water, but this one will baptize you with the holy Spirit."

1:9-13 And it happened in those days (that)* Jesus came from Nazareth of Galilee, and he was baptized **into** the Jordan by John. And immediately going up out of the water he saw the heavens being **torn apart** and the Spirit going down like a dove **into** him. And a voice happened out of the heavens, "You are my beloved son, in you I began

N.B. Three verses are not included in this translation of Mark's Gospel: 7:16; 11:26; and 15:28. In all probability they are later scribal interpolations and consequently are deleted from critical editions of the Greek New Testament.

*Words placed in parentheses do not appear in the Greek text but have been added for the sake of intelligibility.

to take pleasure." And immediately the Spirit casts him out into the wilderness; and he was in the wilderness forty days being tested by Satan, and he was with the wild beasts, and the angels were ministering to him.

1:14-20 And after John was delivered up, Jesus came into Galilee proclaiming the good news of God and saying, "The right time has been fulfilled, and **the rule of God** has approached. Repent and believe in the good news." And going along at the edge of the Sea of Galilee he saw Simon and Andrew, the brother of Simon, casting nets **in** the sea; for they were fishers. And Jesus said to them, "Come on after me, and I will make you become fishers of human beings." And immediately leaving the nets, they followed him. And going on a little he saw James the son of Zebedee and John his brother and (he saw) them in the boat restoring the nets. And immediately he called them; and leaving their father Zebedee in the boat with the hired hands, they went off after him.

1:21-28 And they come into Capernaum; and immediately on the sabbath entering into the synagogue he began teaching. And they were overwhelmed at his teaching, for he was teaching them as (one) having authority and not as the scribes. And immediately there was in their synagogue a human being with an unclean spirit, and he cried out saying, "What (is there) between us and you, Jesus Nazarene? Did you come to destroy us? I know who you are, the holy one of God!" And Jesus rebuked him saying, "Be muzzled and come out of him." And convulsing him and making a great outcry the unclean spirit came out of him. And all were astounded so that they continued to dispute saying, "What is this? A new teaching with authority! He even commands the unclean spirits and they obey him." And his fame went out immediately everywhere into the entire region of Galilee.

1:29-31 And immediately coming out of the synagogue, they went into the house of Simon and Andrew with James and John. Now Simon's mother-in-law was bedridden with a fever, and immediately they tell him about her. And approaching **he raised** her taking hold of her hand; and the fever left her, and she was ministering to them.

1:32-34 Now when evening came, when the sun set, they were bearing to him all the sick and the demonized; and the entire city was gathered together at the door. And he healed many sick with different kinds of diseases, and he cast out many demons, and he was not permitting the demons to speak, because they knew him.

1:35–39 And arising very early while it was still dark, he went and departed into a wilderness place; there he was praying. And Simon and those with him pursued him, and they found him and say to him, "All are looking for you!" And he says to them, "Let us go elsewhere into the neighboring market towns in order that I might preach there also; for this I came out." And he went into their synagogues throughout all of Galilee proclaiming and casting out demons.

1:40–45 And there comes to him a leper begging him and falling on his knees, saying to him, "If you want, you are able to cleanse me." And being moved with compassion, stretching out his hand, he touched him and says to him, "I want, be cleansed!" And immediately the leprosy went away from him, and he was cleansed. And being furious with him he immediately cast him out and says to him, "Keep on seeing to it that you say nothing to anyone! But go show yourself to the priest and offer up for your cleansing the things which Moses prescribed for a witness to them." But he going out began to proclaim loudly and to spread widely the word, so that he is no longer able to enter a city openly, but was outside in wilderness places; and they were coming to him from all directions.

2:1–12 And after some time when he came into Capernaum again, it was heard that he is in a house. And many were gathered together so that there was no room, not even around the door, and he was speaking the word to them. And they come bearing to him a paralytic being carried by four. And not being able to bring (this one) to him on account of the crowd, they took away the roof where he was, and digging through they lowered the mat on which the paralytic was lying. And seeing their faith, Jesus says to the paralytic, "Child, your sins are forgiven." Now some of the scribes were seated there and reasoning in their hearts, "Why does he speak so? He is blaspheming. Who is able to forgive sins except God alone?" And Jesus, immediately knowing in his spirit that they are reasoning so within themselves, says to them,

"Why do you reason these things in your hearts? What is easier: to say to the paralytic, 'Your sins are forgiven,' or to say, 'Arise and take your mat and walk'? But so that you know that **the Human Being** has authority to forgive sins on earth"—he says to the paralytic—"to you I say, arise, take your mat and go to your house." And he was raised, and immediately taking his mat he went out in view of all, so that all went out of their minds and continued to glorify God saying, "We never saw anything like this!"

2:13–17 And he went out again **at the edge of the sea,** and the entire crowd was coming to him, and he taught them. And going along he saw Levi, the son of Alphaeus, seated at the revenue table, and he says to him, "Follow me." And arising he followed him. And it happens he is reclining (at dinner) in his house, and many revenue collectors and sinners were reclining with Jesus and his disciples, for they were many and they were following him. And the scribes of the Pharisees, seeing that he eats with sinners and revenue collectors were saying to his disciples, "He eats with revenue collectors and sinners!" And hearing Jesus says to them, "The ones who are healthy have no need of a physician but the ones who are sick; I did not come to call the just but sinners."

2:18–22 And the disciples of John and the Pharisees were fasting. And they come and say to him, "Why do the disciples of John and the disciples of the Pharisees fast, but your disciples do not fast?" And Jesus said to them, "Are the groomsmen able to fast while the bridegroom is with them? As long as they have the bridegroom with them, they are not able to fast. But the days will come when the bridegroom will be taken from them, and then they will fast on that day. No one sews a patch of unshrunk cloth on an old garment; otherwise the patch takes away from it, the new part from the old, and the tear becomes worse. And no one casts new wine into old skins; otherwise the wine tears the skins, and the wine and the skins are lost."

2:23–28 And it happened on the sabbath that he is traveling along through the grainfields, and his disciples began to make a **way** plucking the heads of the wheat. And the Pharisees were saying to him, "Look, why are they doing on the sabbath that which is not lawful?"

And he says to them, "Did you never read what David did when he had need, and he was hungry and those with him? He went into the house of God at the high priesthood of Abiathar, and he ate the loaves of the Presence, which is not lawful to eat except for the priests, and he gave to those who were with him." And he was saying to them, "The sabbath happened on account of the human being and not the human being on account of the sabbath; so that **the Human Being** is the Lord also of the sabbath."

3:1–6 And he went into a synagogue again, and there was a human being there having a withered hand; and they were watching closely if he would heal him on the sabbath, so that they might accuse him. And he says to the human being having the withered hand, "Arise into the middle (here)." And he says to them, "Is it lawful to do good on the sabbath or to do evil, to save a life or to kill?" But they were remaining silent. And looking around at them with anger, being grieved at the hardness of their hearts, he says to the human being, "Stretch out your hand!" And he stretched (it) out, and his hand was restored. And going out the Pharisees immediately were holding counsel with the Herodians against him so that they might destroy him.

3:7–12 And Jesus with his disciples withdrew **to the sea,** and a large multitude followed from Galilee, from Judea and from Jerusalem and from Idumea and Transjordan and around Tyre and Sidon, a large multitude hearing the things which he does came to him. And he said to his disciples that a little **boat** should stand ready for him on account of the **crowd** so that they do not press upon him. For he healed many so that such who had scourges fell on him in order that they might touch him. And unclean spirits, when they were observing him, were falling before him, and were crying out saying, "You are the son of God!" And he was rebuking them loudly that they should not make him known.

3:13–19 And he ascends into **the mountain,** and he summons the ones whom he wanted, and they went to him. And he made **twelve** in order that they might be with him and in order that he might send them forth to preach and to have authority to drive out demons. And he made **the twelve,** and he bestowed on Simon the name Peter; and

James the son of Zebedee and John the brother of James, and he bestowed on them the name Boanerges, that is, "sons of thunder." And Andrew and Philip and Bartholomew and Matthew and Thomas the son of Alphaeus and Thaddeus and Simon the Cananaean and Judas Iscariot who also delivered him up.

3:20–27 And he comes into a **house;** and there comes together again a **crowd,** so that they are not even able to eat bread. And his relatives hearing went out to take hold of him, for they were saying, "He's gone out of his mind!" And the scribes, who were coming down from Jerusalem, were saying, "He has Beelzebul," and "By the chief of the demons he casts out demons." Summoning them he was speaking to them in parables, "How is Satan able to cast out Satan? And if a kingdom is divided against itself, that kingdom is not able to stand. And if a house is divided against itself, that house is not able to stand. And if Satan arose against himself and was divided, he is not able to stand but has an end. Accordingly no one entering the house of the strongman is able to plunder his property unless he first binds the strongman, and then he will plunder his house.

3:28–30 "Amen I say to you, all offenses and blasphemies will be forgiven human beings, as much as they blaspheme. But whoever blasphemes against the holy Spirit has no forgiveness at any time, but is guilty of an eternal offense." For they were saying, "He has an unclean spirit."

3:31–35 And his mother and his brothers come, and, standing **outside** they sent to him calling him. And a crowd was seated around him, and they say to him, "Look, your mother and your brothers and your sisters **outside** are seeking you." And answering he says to them, "Who is my mother and brothers?" And looking around at the ones seated around him he says, "See, my mother and my brothers. Whoever does the will of God, this is my brother and sister and mother."

4:1–9 And again he began to teach **at the edge of the sea.** And a very large **crowd** is gathered together to him so that he, boarding the boat, is seated **on the sea,** and the whole **crowd** was on the land (facing) **toward the sea.** And he began teaching them many things in parables;

and he was saying to them in his teaching, "Listen! Look, the sower went out to sow. And it happened in the sowing some fell at the edge of **the way,** and the birds came and gobbled it up. And other fell on rocky ground where it did not have much earth, and immediately it sprang up because it had no depth of earth; and when the sun arose it was scorched, and because it had no root it was withered. And other fell into thorns, and the thorns grew up and choked it, and it did not give fruit. And others fell into good earth, and it was giving fruit, growing up and increasing, and was bearing unto thirty and in sixty and in one hundred." And he was saying, "Who has ears to hear, let him/her hear."

4:10–12 And when he was alone, the ones around him with the twelve were asking him (about) the parables. And he was saying to them, "To you the mystery of **the rule of God** has been given; but to **those outside** all things happen in parables so that

"Looking they look and they do not see, and hearing they hear and they do not understand, lest they turn around and it is forgiven them."

4:13–20 And he says to them, "Don't you know this parable, and how will you understand all the parables? The sower sows the word. And these are the ones at the edge of **the way** where the word is sown; Satan immediately comes and takes the word sown into them. And likewise these are the ones being sown on rocky ground, who, when they hear the word, immediately receive it with joy; and they do not have root in themselves but are temporary. Then when pressure or persecution happens on account of the word, they are immediately scandalized. And others are the ones being sown into the thorns; these are the ones hearing the word, and the cares of the age and the beguilement of wealth and the cravings for all the other things entering in choke the word and it becomes unfruitful. And those are the ones sown on good earth who hear and receive the word and bear fruit in thirty and in sixty and in one hundred."

4:21–23 And he was saying to them, "Does the lamp come in order that it should be placed under a peck measure or under the reclining couch? Not in order that it should be placed on the lampstand? For nothing is secret that will not be disclosed; neither did (anything) happen hidden but that it will come into the open. If anyone has ears to hear, let him/her hear!"

4:24–25 And he was saying to them, "Keep on being aware of how you hear! With the measure you measure it will be measured to you, and it will be added to you. For who has, it will be given to him. And who does not have, even that which he has will be taken from him."

4:26–29 And he was saying, "So is **the rule of God:** as a human being casts seed on the earth, and as he sleeps and rises night and day, and the seed sprouts and grows long, how he does not know. The earth bears fruit by itself: first grass, then ear, then full grain in the ear. And when the fruit allows, he immediately sends for the sickle, for harvest has come."

4:30–32 And he was saying, "How shall we compare **the rule of God** or with what parable shall we put it? Like a grain of mustard which, when it is sown on the earth, smallest of all the seeds on the earth, and when it is sown, it grows up and becomes greater than all the vegetable bushes and makes big branches, so that the birds of the sky are able to nest under its shade."

4:33–34 And with many such parables he was speaking the word to them, **even as they were able to hear.** And without parables he was not speaking to them, but privately he was **explaining all things to his own disciples.**

4:35–41 And on that day when it was evening he says to them, "Let's cross over to the other side." And leaving the **crowd,** they take him as he was in **the boat,** and other boats were with him. And a great storm of wind happens and the waves were casting up into the boat so that **the boat** is already filling up. And he was asleep on **the** pillow in the stern. And they arouse him and say to him, "Teacher, is it no concern to you that we are perishing?" And arising he rebuked the wind and said to the sea, "Silence! Be muzzled!" And the wind ceased and a great calm happened. And he said to them, "Why are you so cowardly?

How (is it) you do not have faith?" And they were terribly frightened, and they were saying to one another, "Who then is this, for even the wind and the sea obey him?"

5:1–20 And they came to **the other side of the sea** into the country of the Gerasenes. And as he was going out of **the boat,** there met him from the tombs a human being with an unclean spirit who had his home in the tombs. And even with a chain no one was able to bind him, because he had been bound often with shackles and chains, and the chains were torn apart by him and the shackles broken in pieces, and no one was strong (enough) to subdue him. And through every night and day in the tombs and in the mountains he was crying out and bruising himself with rocks. And seeing Jesus from a distance he ran and worshiped him, and crying out with a great voice he says, "What (is there) between me and you, Jesus, son of the most high God? I adjure you by God that you do not torment me." For he was saying to him, "Come out, unclean spirit, from the human being!" And he asked him, "What is your name?" And he says to him, "My name is Legion, for we are many." And he was begging him earnestly that he not send them away out of the country. Now there was at the mountain a great herd of swine grazing; and they begged him saying, "Send us into the swine so that we may enter into them." And he allowed them. And going out the unclean spirits entered into the swine, and the herd rushed down the cliff into the sea, about two thousand, and they were drowned in the sea. And the ones grazing them fled and reported (it) to the city and to (the people in) the fields. And they came to see what it is that has happened. And they come to Jesus, and they observe the demoniac seated, clothed and being of sound mind, the one having had the legion, and they were frightened. And the ones seeing recounted to them how it happened to the demoniac and about the swine. And they began to beg him to go away from their regions. And as he embarks into the boat, the one who was demonized was begging him that he might be with him. And he did not permit him but says to him, "Go to your house, to your people and report to them how much **the Lord** has done for you and (how) he showed you mercy." And he went away and began to proclaim in the Decapolis the great things Jesus did for him, and all were marveling.

5:21–34 And when Jesus crossed over again in **the boat** to the other side, a large crowd was gathered together to him, and he was **at the edge of the sea.** And one of the synagogue rulers[1] comes and, seeing him, falls at his feet and begs him earnestly saying, "My daughter is at the point of death, so that coming you put hands on her, so that she is saved and may live." And he went off with him. And a large **crowd** was following him and pressing around him. And a woman being in a flow of blood **twelve years** and suffering many things by many physicians and spending everything she had and receiving no help but rather coming into a worse condition, she hearing the things about Jesus, (and) coming in the crowd behind (him), touched his cloak. For she was saying, "If only I touch his clothes, I'll be saved." And immediately the source of her blood was dried up, and she knew in her body that she was healed of her scourge. And immediately Jesus, knowing exactly in himself (that) power had gone out of him, turning around in the crowd, was saying, "Who touched my clothes?" And his disciples were saying to him, "You see the crowd pressing around you and you say, 'Who touched me?' " And he was looking around to see the one having done this. Now the woman being frightened and trembling, knowing what has happened to her, came and fell before him and told him the truth. But he said to her, "Daughter, your faith has saved you! Go into peace and be restored from your scourge."

5:35–43 While he is still speaking they come from the synagogue ruler's (home) saying, "Your daughter died. Why still trouble the teacher?" But Jesus, hearing the word spoken, says to the synagogue ruler, "Don't be afraid! Only keep on believing!" And he did not permit anyone to accompany him except Peter, James and John, the brother of James. And they came into the house of the synagogue ruler. And he observes commotion and (the ones) weeping and wailing loudly, and entering he says to them, "Why do you make a commotion and weep? The child did not die, but she is sleeping." And they were ridiculing him. But he, casting all (of them) out, takes the father of the child and the mother and the ones with him and goes into where the child was. And taking hold of the child's hand, he says to her, **"Talitha koum!"** which is translated, "Little girl, I say to you, arise!" And

---

1. Most manuscripts include "by name of Jairus," but it may be a scribal interpolation based on Luke 8:41. It does not appear in Matt. 9:18.

immediately the little girl stood up and walks about. For she was **twelve years** old. And immediately they went out of their minds with ecstasy. And he gave strict orders to them that no one should know this; he also said (that something) be given to her to eat.

6:1–6 And he went out from there and comes into his hometown, and his disciples follow him. And when it was sabbath he began to teach in the synagogue. And the many hearing were overwhelmed saying, "From where (do) these things (come) to this one? And what (is) the wisdom given to him? And such mighty works happen through his hands! Is this not the carpenter, son of Mary, the brother of James and Joses and Judah and Simon? And are not his sisters here with us?" And they were scandalized by him. And Jesus was saying to them, "A prophet is not without honor except in his hometown and among his relations and in his house." And he was unable to do any mighty work there, except putting his hands to a few sick people he healed (them). And he marveled at their unbelief.

6:7–13 And he was going round about the villages teaching. And he summons the twelve and began to send them out two by two, and he was giving them authority (over) the unclean spirits. And he charged them that they should take nothing into (the) **way** except a staff alone, not bread, not knapsack, not a copper (coin) for the belt, but shod (with) sandals, and "you shall not wear two undershirts." And he was saying to them, "Wherever you enter into a house, remain there until you go out from there. And whatever place does not receive you nor hear you, departing from there shake off the dust under your feet for a testimony to them." And going out they proclaimed that they should repent, and they were casting out many demons and anointing many sick people with oil and healing.

6:14–29 And King Herod heard, for his name became manifest and they were saying, "John the Baptizer has been raised from the dead and on account of this the mighty deeds of power are at work in him." But others were saying, "It is Elijah." And others were saying, "A prophet like one of the prophets." Now Herod hearing was saying, "The one whom I beheaded, John, he was raised." For Herod himself, sending forth, took hold of John and bound him in prison on account of

Herodias, the wife of Philip, his brother, because he married her. For John was saying to Herod, "It is not right for you to have your brother's wife." Now Herodias had a grudge against him and was wanting to kill him and was not able. For Herod feared John, knowing him (to be) a just and holy man, and he was protecting him, and hearing him was greatly disturbed, and yet he was hearing him gladly. But an opportune day came when Herod gave a banquet on his birthday for his courtiers and for the tribunes and for the leading citizens of Galilee, and when the daughter of Herodias herself entered and danced, it was pleasing to Herod and the ones reclining at the table with (him). So the king said to the little girl, "Request of me whatever you wish, and I will give you." And he swore to her, "Whatever you request, I will give you up to half of my kingdom." And going out she said to her mother, "What shall I request?" And she said, "The head of John the Baptizer." And going in immediately with haste to the king she asked saying, "I request that you give me at once on a platter the head of John the Baptizer." And deeply grieved, the king, because of the oaths and the recliners, did not want to refuse her. And immediately sending the executioner, the king ordered his head to be brought. And going, he beheaded him in prison and brought his head on a platter and gave it to the little girl, and the little girl gave it to her mother. And hearing, his disciples came and took his corpse and put it in a tomb.

6:30–44 And the apostles are gathered together with Jesus and they reported to him all the things which they did and which they taught. And he says to them, "Come by yourselves into a desert place and rest yourselves a little." For many were coming and going, and they did not even have time to eat. And they went away in **the boat** into a desert place alone. And many saw them going and they knew exactly, and by land from all the cities they were running there together and they arrived ahead of them. And going out he saw a large **crowd,** and he was moved with compassion for them, because they were like sheep not having a shepherd, and he began to teach them many things. And when it was already a late hour his disciples approaching him were saying, "The place is desolate and it is already a late hour. Dismiss them so that, going off into the surrounding fields and villages, they may buy for themselves something they may eat." But answering he said to them, "You give them (something) to eat!" And they say to him, "Going off shall we buy bread for two hundred **denarii** and give it to them to eat?" But he says to them, "How many loaves do you have? Go see." And knowing they say, "Five and two fish." And he gave orders to them that all recline in groups on the green grass. And they lay down group by group in hundreds and in fifties. And taking the five loaves and the two fish, he, **looking up to heaven,** blessed and broke the loaves, and he was giving to the disciples so that they might distribute to them, and the two fish he divided to all. And all ate and were satisfied, and they took up (of) the crumbs and of the fish the sum total of **twelve wickerwork baskets.** And those eating the bread were five thousand men.

6:45–52 And immediately he **compelled** his disciples to board **the boat** and to go before (him) to the other side **to Bethsaida** while he dismisses the **crowd.** And taking leave of them, he went off into the mountain to pray. And when evening came the boat was in the middle of the sea, and he alone on the land. And seeing them tortured in rowing, for the wind was against them, he comes to them around the fourth watch of the night walking on the sea; and **he was wanting to pass them by.** But seeing him walking on the sea they thought that he is a ghost, and they cried out; for all saw him and were in an uproar! But he immediately spoke with them and says to them, "Keep on being courageous! **I am.** Stop being afraid!" And he went up to them into **the boat,** and the wind ceased; and in themselves they went absolutely out of their minds. For they did not understand about the loaves, but their hearts had been hardened.

6:53–56 And crossing over to the land they came **to Gennesaret** and they anchored. And as they disembarked from **the boat,** immediately the ones recognizing him ran around that whole region and began to bear the sick on mats (to) where they were hearing that he is. And wherever he was entering into villages or into cities or into fields they placed the sick in the marketplaces, and they were begging him that they might touch even the fringe of his cloak. And as many as touched him were saved.

7:1–13 And the Pharisees and some of the scribes coming from Jerusalem are gathered together with him. And seeing some of his disciples that with impure, that is unwashed, hands, they eat bread; for the Pharisees and all the Jews unless they wash their hands with (the) fist[2] do not eat, holding fast to the tradition of the elders. And (coming) from market, if they do not cleanse themselves, they do not eat; and there are many other things which they received to hold fast: washings of cups, and jugs and kettles. And the Pharisees and the scribes asked him, "Why do your disciples not walk according to the tradition of the elders, but eat bread with impure hands?" So he said to them, "Appropriately did Isaiah prophesy about you hypocrites, as it is written, 'This people honors me with lips, but their heart remains far away from me. And they worship me in vain teaching teachings (which are) commandments of human beings.' Leaving the commandment of God, you hold fast to the tradition of human beings." And he was saying to them, "Appropriately you nullify the commandment of God so that you may observe your traditions. For Moses said, 'Honor your father and mother,' and 'Let the one who speaks evil of father or mother surely die.' But you say, 'If any human being says to father or to mother, **"Korban"**—which is gift, whatever you are owed from me,' you no longer allow him to do anything for his father or mother. You make void the word of God by your tradition which you handed down. And you do many similar things."

7:14–15 And summoning the **crowd** again, he was saying to them, "Hear me all and understand. Nothing is outside a human being which, entering into him, is able to defile him. But the things coming out of a human being are the things defiling the human being."

7:17–23 And when he entered a **house** away from the **crowd,** his disciples were questioning him (about) the parable. And he says to them, "So you also are without understanding? Do you not comprehend that everything outside entering into the human being is unable to defile him because it does not enter into his heart but into the belly and comes out into the latrine purifying all foods?" But he was saying that the thing coming out of the human being, that defiles the human being. For from inside the heart of human beings evil thoughts come forth, fornications, thefts, murders, adulteries, greeds,

---

2. Some manuscripts read "frequently" instead of "with the fist."

wickednesses, deceit, debauchery, an evil eye, blasphemy, arrogance, foolishness. All these things come out from within and defile the human being.

7:24–30 And arising from there he went away into the districts of Tyre. And entering into a house he was wanting no one to know, and he was unable to escape notice. But a woman whose young daughter had an unclean spirit, immediately hearing about him, coming, fell down at his feet. Now the woman was Greek, a Syrophoenician by race. And she asked him that he cast out the demon from her daughter. And he was saying to her, "First let the children be satisfied, for it is not good to take the bread of the children and throw (it) to the house dogs." But she answered and says to him,[3] "**Lord,** even the house dogs under the table eat of the crumbs of the children." And he said to her, "Because of this word go! The demon has gone out of your daughter." And returning to her house she found the child lying on the couch and the demon gone out.

7:31–37 And coming out again from the districts of Tyre he went through Sidon to the Sea of Galilee up into the middle of the districts of the Decapolis. And they bring to him a deaf (human being) with a speech impediment, and they beg him that he put (his) hand to him. And taking him away from the crowd alone he cast his fingers into his ears and spitting he touched his tongue, and **looking up into heaven** he groaned and says to him,[4] "**Ephphatha,**" which is, "**Be opened** once and for all!" And his ears were opened, and immediately the bond of his tongue was loosed, and he was speaking normally. And he gave orders to them that they speak to no one. But the more he ordered them, even more they were proclaiming. And they were overwhelmed beyond measure saying, "He has done all things well, and he makes the deaf hear and the mute speak."

8:1–10 In those days again when there was a large crowd and they had nothing they might eat, he summoning his disciples, says to them, "I

---

3. Many manuscripts include "Yes" before "Lord," but it is a suspect reading.

4. The pronoun *autō* is ambiguous. More immediately it refers back to "heaven." But it may also be the antecedent for deaf person.

am moved with compassion for the **crowd** because they continue with me already **three days** and they have nothing they might eat. And if I dismiss them hungry into their homes, they will give out on **the way;** and some of them are from far away." And his disciples answered him, "Where will anyone be able to satisfy these with bread in[5] the desert?" And he asked them, "How many loaves do you have?" And they said, "Seven." And he instructs the **crowd** to recline on the ground; and taking the seven loaves, giving thanks, he broke and gave to his disciples so that they might serve, and they served the **crowd.** And they had a few small fish, and blessing them he said (that) these also be served. And they ate and were satisfied, and they took up an abundance of crumbs, **seven mat-baskets.** Now they were about four thousand, and he dismissed them. And immediately boarding the boat with his disciples, he came into the regions of Dalmanoutha.

8:11–13 And the Pharisees came out and began to debate with him, seeking from him a sign from heaven, testing him. And groaning deeply in his spirit he says, "Why does this generation seek a sign? I'll say 'Amen' to you if a sign will be given to this generation!" And leaving them he, boarding the boat again, went off to the other side.

8:14–21 And they forgot to take bread, and except for **one loaf** had nothing with them in **the boat.** And he ordered them saying, "Look! Keep on being aware of the leaven of the Pharisees and the leaven of Herod!" And they were reasoning with each other that they have no bread. And knowing he says to them, "Why do you reason that you have no bread? Don't you know yet or understand? Do you have your heart hardened? Having eyes don't you see? And having ears don't you hear? And don't you remember when I broke the five loaves for the five thousand? How many full **wickerwork baskets** of crumbs did you take up?" They say to him, "Twelve." "When the seven for the four thousand, the fullness of how many **mat-baskets** of crumbs did you take up?" And they say, "Seven." And he was saying to them, "Don't you understand yet?"

8:22–26 And they come into Bethsaida. And they bring to him a blind

---

5. Here the Greek preposition means "on."

(human being), and they beg him that he touch him. And taking the hand of the blind (human being) he led him out of the village, and spitting into his eyes, placing his hands on him, he questioned him, "Do you see anything?" And **gaining sight** he was saying, "I see human beings, like trees I see them walking." Then again he placed his hands on his eyes, and he **opened his eyes wide** and was restored, and he was **able to see all things clearly.** And he sent him into his house saying, "By no means enter into the village!"

8:27–33 And Jesus and his disciples came out into the villages of Caesarea of Philip. And on the way he questioned his disciples saying to them, "Who do human beings say I am?" And they said to him saying, " 'John the Baptizer,' and others 'Elijah,' but others 'one of the prophets.' " And he asked them, "But who do you say I am?" Answering Peter says to him, "You are the Messiah." And he rebuked them that they speak to no one about him. And he began to teach them that it is necessary for **the Human Being** to suffer many things, and to be rejected by the elders and the chief priests and the scribes and to be killed and after three days to rise up. And with plainness he was speaking the word. And Peter taking him aside began to rebuke him. But turning about and seeing his disciples he rebuked Peter and says, "Get away from behind me, Satan, for you do not think the things of God but the things of human beings."

8:34–38 And summoning the **crowd** with his disciples he said to them, "If anyone wants to come after me, let him deny himself and take up his cross and follow me. For whoever wants to save his life will lose it; but whoever loses his life on account of me and the gospel will save it. For what does it benefit a human being to gain the whole world and forfeit his life? For what will a human being give (as) an exchange for his life? For whoever is ashamed of me and my words in this adulterous and sinful generation, **the Human Being** will also be ashamed of him when he comes in the glory of his father with the holy angels." And he was saying to them, "Amen I say to you that there are some of these standing here who will by no means taste of death until they see **the rule of God having come in power.**"

9:1–13 And after six days Jesus takes Peter and James and John and leads them up into **a high mountain** privately alone. And he was transformed before them, and his clothes became very shining **white** such as a bleacher on earth is unable to make so white. And there appeared to them Elijah with Moses, and they were conversing with Jesus. And Peter speaking up says to Jesus, "Rabbi, it is good for us to be here, and let us make three tents, one for you and one for Moses and one for Elijah." For he did not know what he was speaking for they had become terrified. And a cloud came overshadowing them, and a voice came out of the cloud, "This is my beloved son, hear him!" And suddenly looking about they no longer saw anyone except Jesus alone with them. And as they descended from the mountain he gave orders to them that they recount to no one the things they saw except when **the Human Being** rises up from the dead. And they took hold of the word debating with each other what it is: "to rise up from the dead." And they were questioning him saying, "The scribes say that it is necessary for Elijah to come first." But he said to them, "Elijah indeed coming first will restore all things! And how has it been written of **the Human Being,** that he suffers many things and is made nothing? But I say to you, Elijah in fact has come, and they did to him such things as they were wanting, even as it has been written of him."

9:14–29 And coming to the disciples they saw a large **crowd** around them and the scribes debating with them. And immediately seeing him the whole **crowd** was stunned and running up they were greeting him. And he questioned them, "What are you disputing with them?" And one of the **crowd** answered him, "Teacher, I brought to you my son having a mute spirit; and whenever it seizes him, it tears him and he foams and grinds his teeth and becomes stiff. And I spoke to your disciples that they might cast it out, and they were not strong enough." And responding to them he says, "O unbelieving generation! How long shall I be with you? How long shall I put up with you? Bring him to me." And they brought him to him. And seeing him the spirit immediately convulsed him, and falling to the ground he was rolling (about) foaming. And he questioned of his father, "How much time is it since this has happened to him? And he said, "From childhood, and frequently, and it casts him into fire and into water so that he might destroy him. But if you can do anything, help us, being moved with compassion toward us!" And Jesus said to him, "If you can! All things (are) possible to the one who believes!" Immediately crying out the father of the child was saying, "I believe! Keep on helping my unbelief!" Now Jesus seeing that a **crowd** is running together rebuked the spirit saying to it, "Mute and deaf spirit, I command you, come out of him and never again enter into him." And crying out and convulsing him terribly he came out. And he became like dead so that the many were saying that he died. But Jesus taking hold of his hand **raised** him, and he arose. And when he came into a **house** his disciples were questioning him privately, "(Why) were we unable to cast it out?" And he said to them, "This kind is able to come out by nothing except prayer."

9:30–32 Coming out from there they were going along through Galilee, and he was not wanting that anyone should know. For he was teaching his disciples and was saying to them "**The Human Being** is going to be delivered up into (the) hands of human beings, and they will kill him and being killed he will arise after three days." But they were not understanding the matter, and they were afraid to question him.

9:33–37 And they came into Capernaum. And being in the house he asked them, "What did you argue (about) on **the way?**" But they were keeping silent; for they had discussed with each other on **the way** who (would be) greatest. And sitting down he called the twelve, and says to them, "If anyone wants to be first, he will be last of all and a minister of all." And taking a child he stood it in their midst, and embracing it he said to them, "Whoever receives one of these children in my name receives me; and whoever receives me, does not receive me but the one who sent me."

9:38–50 John said to him, "Teacher, we saw someone casting out demons in your name who is not following us, and we tried to stop him because he was not following us." But Jesus said, "Don't stop him! for there is no one who will do a mighty work in my name and quickly be able to speak evil of me. For who is not against us is for us. For whoever will give you a cup of water to drink in my name,[6] amen I say

6. P. Schmiel rightly conjectures, I think—especially in the light of Mark 8:29–31— that the phrase, "because you are of Christ," which manuscripts add at this point, is a scribal interpolation.

to you, that he will by no means lose his reward. And whoever offends one of these believing little ones, it is better for him, if a millstone, worked by donkey power, were laid around his neck and he were cast into the sea. And if your hand offends you, cut it off; it is good (that) you enter into **life** deformed than to go off into Gehenna into inextinguishable fire having two hands. And if your foot offends you, cut it off; it is good (that) you enter into life lame than having two feet to be cast into Gehenna. And if your eye offends you, cast it out; it is better (that) you enter into **the rule of God** one-eyed than having two eyes to be cast into Gehenna 'where their worm does not die and the fire is not extinguished.' For everyone will be salted with fire. Salt (is) good; but if salt becomes saltless, with what will you season it? Have salt among yourselves and keep the peace among each other!"

10:1 And arising from there he comes into the districts of Judea and the other side of the Jordan, and the **crowds** again accompany him, and, as he is accustomed, he was teaching them again.

10:2–9 And approaching Pharisees were questioning him if it is right for a man to divorce his wife, testing him. Now answering he said to them, "What did Moses command you?" And they said, "Moses permitted to write a document of divorce and to divorce." But Jesus said to them, "For your hard heart he wrote you this commandment. But from the beginning of creation 'he made them male and female! On account of this a human being will leave behind his father and mother, and the two will become one flesh.' So that they are no longer two but one flesh. What therefore God yoked together, let a human being not separate."

10:10–12 And into **the house** again the disciples were questioning him about this. And he says to them, "Whoever divorces his wife and marries another, commits adultery against her; and if she divorcing her husband marries another, she commits adultery."

10:13–16 And they tried to bring children to him so that he might touch them, but the disciples rebuked them. Now Jesus seeing (this) was indignant and said to them, "Let the children come to me, do not prevent them, for of such is **God's rule.** Amen I say to you, whoever does not receive the rule of God like a child will by no means enter into it." And embracing them he blesses (them) putting his hands on them.

10:17–27 And as he goes out into (the) **way,** one running up and kneeling before him questioned him, "Good Teacher, what shall I do so that I inherit eternal life?" But Jesus said to him, "Why do you call me good? No one (is) good except God alone. You know the commandments, 'You shall not kill,' 'You shall not commit adultery,' 'You shall not steal,' 'You shall not testify falsely,' 'You shall not defraud,' 'Honor your father and your mother.' " But he said to him, "Teacher, all these things I guarded for myself from youth." Now Jesus looking at him loved him and said to him, "You lack one thing! Go, sell all that you have and give to (the) destitute and you will have treasure in heaven, and come follow me." But he, being appalled at the word, went off grieving, for he was having many possessions. And Jesus looking around says to his disciples, "How hard it is for those having possessions to enter into **God's rule!**" Now the disciples were astounded at his words. So Jesus again responding, says to them, "Children, how hard it is to enter into **God's rule!** It is easier for a camel to go through the eye of the needle than a wealthy (person) to enter into **God's rule.**" But they were even more overwhelmed saying to themselves, "And who is able to be saved?" Looking at them Jesus says, "With human beings impossible, but not with God. For all things (are) possible with God."

10:28–31 Peter began to say to him, "Look, we left all things and have followed you!" Jesus said, "Amen I say to you, there is no one who left home or brothers or sisters or mother or father or children or fields because of me and because of the good news (who) does not receive a hundred times more homes and brothers and sisters and mothers and children and fields now in this right time—along with persecutions— and in the coming age eternal life. But many (who are) first will be last and the last first."

10:32–34 Now they were on **the way** going up into Jerusalem, and Jesus was going before them, and they continued to be astounded and those following continued to be afraid. And again taking the twelve aside he began to say to them the things about to happen to him,

"Look, we are going up into Jerusalem, and **the Human Being** will be delivered up to the chief priests and the scribes, and they will condemn him to death and they will deliver him up to the gentiles and they will mock him and they will spit on him and they will scourge him and they will kill (him) and after three days he will arise."

10:35–45 And James and John, the sons of Zebedee, approach him saying to him, "Teacher, we want that whatever we request of you, you will do for us." So he said to them, "What do you want me to do for you?" And they said to him, "Give us that we may be seated in your glory, one on your right hand and one on your left hand." But Jesus said to them, "You don't know what you are requesting. Are you able to drink **the cup** which I drink or to be baptized with the baptism with which I am baptized?" And they said to him, "We are able!" So Jesus said to them, "**The cup** which I drink you will drink, and the baptism with which I am baptized you will be baptized. But to sit on my right hand or on my left hand is not mine to give but it is for those for whom it has been prepared." And the ten hearing began to be indignant about James and John. And summoning them Jesus says to them, "You know that those supposing to rule the nations lord it over them and the great one tyrannize them. But it is not so among you! Rather whoever wants to be great among you will be your minister; and whoever wants to be first among you will be a slave of all. For **the Human Being** also did not come to be ministered to but to minister and give his life a ransom for many."

10:46–52 And they come into Jericho. And as he goes out from Jericho—also his disciples and a considerable **crowd**!—the son of Timaeus, Bartimaeus, a blind beggar was seated **at the edge of the way.** And hearing that it is Jesus the Nazarene he began to cry and to say, "Son of David, Jesus, show me mercy!" And many were trying to rebuke him that he keep silent. But he cried all the more, "Son of David, show me mercy!" And Jesus standing (still) said, "Call him." And they call the blind man saying to him, "Cheer up! Keep on being courageous! Rise, he is calling you." So throwing away his cloak he, leaping up, came to Jesus. And responding to him, Jesus said, "What do you want me to do for you?" So the blind man said to him, "Rabbouni, that I shall **gain sight.**" And Jesus said to him, "Go! Your faith has saved you." And immediately he **gained sight,** and he began following him **on the way.**

11:1–11 And when they draw near to Jerusalem, to Bethphage and Bethany, toward the Mount of Olives, he sends two of his disciples and says to them, "Go into the village opposite you and immediately (upon) entering it you will find a colt tied (up) on which no human beings ever sat; loose it and bring. And if anyone says to you, 'Why are you doing this?' say, '**The Lord** has need of it, and immediately he (will) send it back here.' " And they went off and found a colt tied (up) at a door outside in the street, and they loose it. And some of those standing there were saying to them, "What are you doing loosing the colt?" So they said to them even as Jesus said, and they allowed them. And they bring the colt to Jesus, and they throw their cloaks on it, and he sat on it. And many spread out their cloaks into **the way,** but others reeds, cutting (them) from the fields. And the ones going before and the ones following were crying:

"Hosanna!
Blessed is the one coming in the name of the Lord!
Blessed is the coming rule of our father David!
Hosanna in the highest!"

And he came into Jerusalem into the temple. And looking about at all things, as the hour is already late, he went out into Bethany with the twelve.

11:12–19 And on the next day when they came out from Bethany he was hungry. And seeing a fig tree from a distance having leaves he came (to see) whether he will find anything in it. And coming up to it he found nothing except leaves; for it was not the right time of figs. And responding he said to it, "From now on may no one ever eat fruit from you!" And his disciples were listening. And they come into Jerusalem. And entering into the temple he began to cast out the ones selling and the ones buying in the temple, and he overturned the tables of the money-changers and the chairs of the ones selling doves, and he was not allowing that anyone carry about a vessel through the temple. And he was teaching and saying to them, "Has it not been written, 'My house shall be called a house of prayer for all nations'? But you have

made it a den of bandits!" And the chief priests and the scribes heard
and were seeking how they might destroy him. For they continued to
fear him, for the whole crowd was overwhelmed at his teaching. And
when it was evening, they went out of the city.

11:20–25 And moving along early in the morning they saw the fig tree
withered from (the) roots. And remembering Peter says to him,
"Rabbi, look, the fig tree which you cursed is withered." And responding Jesus says to them, "Have God's faith! Amen I say to you, 'Whoever says to **this mountain,** "Be raised and cast into the sea!" and does
not doubt in his heart but believes that what he speaks happens, it will
be to him.' On account of this I say to you, 'All such things as you pray
and request, believe that you received, and it will be to you.' And when
you stand praying, forgive if you have anything against anyone so that
your Father in heaven also forgives you your offenses."

11:27–33 And they come again into Jerusalem. And as he walks about
the temple the chief priests and the scribes and the elders come to
him, and were saying to him, "By what authority do you do these
things? Or who gave you this authority that you do these things?" But
Jesus said to them, "I will question you one thing, and, should you
answer me, I will also say to you by what authority I do these things.
The baptism of John, was it from heaven or from human beings?
Answer me." And they argued with themselves, saying, "If we say,
'From heaven,' he will say, 'Why therefore didn't you believe him?' But
should we say, 'From human beings'?"—they feared the crowd, for all
held that John was really a prophet. And responding to Jesus they say,
"We do not know." And Jesus says to them, "Neither do I say to you by
what authority I do these things."

12:1–12 And he began to speak to them in parables. "A human being
planted a vineyard and placed a wall around (it) and dug a wine vat
and built a tower, and he leased it to tenant farmers and went abroad.
And at the right time he sent a slave to the tenant farmers, so that he
might receive from the tenant farmers of the fruits of the vineyard.
And taking him they beat (him) and sent (him) away empty. And again
he sent another slave to them; that one they struck on the head and
dishonored. And he sent another, that one they killed, and many others

whom (they) either beat or killed. One he still had, a beloved son! He sent him last to them saying, 'They will respect my son.' But those tenant farmers said to themselves, 'This is the heir! Come, let's kill him and the inheritance will be ours.' And taking (him) they killed him and threw him out of the vineyard. What will the lord of the vineyard do? He will come and destroy the tenant farmers and give the vineyard to others. Didn't you read this Scripture,

'The stone which the builders rejected,
This became (the) keystone;
From (the) Lord this happened
And it is marvelous in our eyes'?"

And they were seeking to take hold of him, and they feared the crowd; for they knew that he spoke the parable to them. And leaving him they went off.

12:13–17 And they send to him some of the Pharisees and the Herodians, so that they might catch him by a word. And coming they say to him, "Teacher, we know that you are true and are concerned about no one's (favor); for you do not look at the appearance of human beings, but in accordance with (the) truth you teach **the way** of God. Is it right to give tax to Caesar or not? Should we give or not give?" But knowing their hypocrisy he said to them, "Why do you test me? Bring me a **denarius** in order that I may see." So they brought (one). And he says to them, "Whose image and inscription (is) this?" So they said to him, "Caesar's." And Jesus said to them, "The things of Caesar give back to Caesar and the things of God to God." And they were marveling greatly at him.

12:18–27 And Sadducees who say there is no resurrection come to him and they were questioning him saying, "Teacher, Moses wrote for us that if anyone's brother dies and leaves behind a wife and does not leave a child, that his brother should take the wife and raise up seed for his brother. There were seven brothers; and the first took a wife, and dying he left no seed. And the second took her, and he died not leaving behind seed; and the third likewise. And the seven left no seed. Last of all the wife died also. In the resurrection, when they arise, whom of them will she be wife to? For the seven had her (as) wife."

Jesus said to them, "Is it not on account of this that you are deceived knowing neither the Scriptures nor the power of God? For when they arise from the dead neither do they marry nor are they married, but they are as angels in the heavens. And concerning the dead that they are raised, do you not read in the book of Moses how God said to him at the bush saying, 'I the God of Abraham and (the) God of Isaac and (the) God of Jacob?' He is not God of the dead but of the living! You are greatly deceived!"

12:28–34 One of the scribes approaching and hearing them debating, knowing that he answered them well, questioned him, "Which commandment is first of all?" Jesus answered, "First is, 'Hear, Israel, (the) Lord our God is one Lord, and you shall love (the) Lord your God out of your whole heart and out of your whole soul and out of your whole understanding and out of your whole strength.' Second, this, 'You shall love your fellow human being as yourself.' No other commandment is greater than these." And the scribe said to him, "Quite right, Teacher! In truth you said, 'There is one and there is no other except him. And, to love him out of the whole heart and out of the whole understanding and out of the whole strength, and to love the fellow human being as oneself is greater than all burnt offerings and sacrifices.' " And Jesus seeing him that he answered wisely said to him, "You are not far from **the rule of God.**" And no one dared to question him further.

12:35–37 And speaking up Jesus was saying, teaching in the temple, "How (is it) the scribes say that the Messiah is Son of David? David himself said by the holy Spirit, '(The) **Lord** said to **my lord,** "Sit at my right hand until I put your enemies under your feet." ' David himself calls him **lord,** so in what way is he his son?"

12:38–40 And the large crowd continued to hear him gladly. And in his teaching he was saying, "Keep on being aware of the scribes, who want to walk about in long robes and greetings in the marketplaces and seats of honor in the synagogues and reclining couches of honor at banquets: the ones devouring the houses of widows and for pretense pray for a long time. These will receive greater condemnation."

12:41–44 And sitting opposite the contribution box, he was observing how the crowd casts copper (money) into the contribution box. And many wealthy (people) were casting much. And one poor widow coming cast two lepta, which is a penny. And summoning his disciples, he said to them, "Amen I say to you, this poor widow cast more than all those casting into the contribution box. For all cast out of their abundance, but this one out of her poverty cast everything which she had, her whole life."

13:1–2 And as he goes out of the temple one of his disciples says to him, "Teacher, look what great stones and what great buildings!" And Jesus said to him, "You see these great buildings? Not a stone will be left on a stone which will not be torn down!"

13:3–13 And when he is seated on the Mount of Olives opposite the temple, Peter, James and John and Andrew questioned him privately, "Tell us, when will these things be? And what is the sign when all these things are going to be consummated?" So Jesus began to say to them, "Keep on being aware lest anyone deceives you! Many will come in my name saying 'I am,' and they will deceive many. But when you hear of wars and reports of wars, don't be disturbed! It is necessary to happen, but the end is not yet. For nation will rise against nation and kingdom against kingdom. There will be earthquakes in places, there will be famines. These things (are) **the beginning of the birth pains.** So you keep on being aware of yourselves! They will deliver you up to sanhedrins and to synagogues (where) you will be beaten, and you will stand before governors and kings because of me for a witness to them. And unto all nations first it is necessary (that) the gospel be proclaimed. And when delivering you up, they lead (you) away, don't be anxious beforehand what you'll speak, but whatever is given you in that hour, this speak. For you are not the ones speaking, but the holy Spirit. And brother will deliver up brother unto death and father child, and children will rise up against parents and put them to death. And you will be hated by all on account of my name; but the one holding out unto the end, this one will be saved.

13:14–23 "Now when you see the abomination of desolation standing where it should not—let the reader understand!—then let the ones in Judea flee into the mountains. Let the one on the roof not descend nor even enter to take anything from his house. And let the one out in the field not return home to take his cloak. But woe to pregnant women and to women nursing in those days! So pray that it doesn't happen in winter. For those days will be an affliction which has not happened to such an extent from the beginning of the creation which God created until now and never will be (again). And unless the Lord shortened the days, no flesh would be saved; but on account of the chosen whom he chose for himself he shortened the days. And then if anyone says to you, 'Look here (is) the Messiah!' 'Look, there!' don't believe it. But false messiahs and false prophets will rise and do signs and wonders in order to mislead, if possible, the elect. But you keep on being aware! I've told you all things beforehand.

13:24–27 "But in those days after that affliction, the sun will be darkened, and the moon will not give its radiance and the stars will be falling from heaven and the powers in the heavens will be shaken. And then they will see **the Human Being** coming on the clouds with much power and glory. And then he will send the angels, and he will gather together his chosen from the four winds from (the) end of the earth to (the) end of heaven.

13:28–29 "So from the fig tree learn the parable: when now its branch becomes tender and puts forth leaves, you know that the summer is near. So also you, when you see these things happening, you know that he is near, at the very door.

13:30–32 "Amen I say to you, this generation will by no means pass away until all these things happen. Heaven and earth will pass away, but my words will not pass away. But about that day or hour no one knows, neither the angels in heaven nor the son, only the Father.

13:33–37 "Keep on being aware! Keep on being awake! For you don't know when the right time is: like a departing human being leaving his house and giving his slaves authority, to each his work, and to the doorkeeper he commanded that he watch. Therefore keep on watching—for you don't know when the lord of the house comes, either at evening or at midnight or at cockcrow or in the morning—lest coming suddenly he finds you sleeping. What I say to you, I say to all, 'Keep on watching!' "

14:1–2 Now it was **the Passover** and the festival of Unleavened Bread after two days. And the chief priests and the scribes were seeking how they, taking him by deceit, might kill (him). For they were saying, "Not on the feast lest there will be an uproar of the people."

14:3–9 And while he is in Bethany reclining (at table) in the house of Simon the leper, a woman came having an alabaster flask of expensive pure oil of nard perfume. Breaking the alabaster flask she poured (it) over his head. Now some were indignant among themselves, "Why has this waste of perfume happened? For this perfume could have been sold for more than three hundred **denarii** and given to the poor." And they were furious with her. But Jesus said, "Leave her! Why cause her trouble? She carried out a good work on me. For the poor you have with you at all times, and whenever you want you are able to do good to them. But me you do not always have. That which she had she did. She undertook to **anoint my body unto entombment.** So amen I say to you, wherever the good news is proclaimed throughout the whole world, even **that which she did will be spoken unto her memory.**"

14:10–11 And Judas Iscariot, one of the twelve, went off to the chief priests so that he might deliver him up to them. Now those hearing were glad and promised to him silver. And he was seeking how he might conveniently deliver him up.

14:12–16 And on the first day of Unleavened Bread, when they were slaughtering **the Passover** (lamb) his disciples say to him, "Where do you want (that) we going off should prepare so that you may eat **the Passover?**" And he sends two of his disciples and says to them, "Go into the city and a human being will meet you carrying a pot of water. Follow him, and, wherever he enters, say to the housemaster, 'The teacher says, "Where is my guest room where I may eat **the Passover** with my disciples?"' And he will show you a big room upstairs furnished (and) ready; and there prepare for us." And the disciples went out and came into the city and found even as he said to them, and they prepared **the Passover.**

14:17–25 And when evening happened he came with the twelve, and while they are reclining and eating Jesus said, "Amen I say to you, one of you will deliver me up, one eating with me." They began to grieve and to say to him one after another, "Surely not I?" So he said to them, "One of the twelve, the one dipping with me into the bowl. For **the Human Being** goes as it has been written about him, but woe to that human being through whom **the Human Being** is delivered up. Better for him if that human being were not born." And while they are eating, he, taking bread (and) blessing (it), broke and gave to them and said, "Take. This is my body." And taking a cup (and) giving thanks, he gave to them, and they all drank from it. And he said to them, "This is my blood of the covenant which is being poured out on behalf of many. Amen I say to you, **I will absolutely not drink of the fruit of the vine until that day when I drink it new in God's rule.**"

14:26–31 And after singing the hymn, they went out to the Mount of Olives. And Jesus says to them, "You all will be scandalized, for it is written, **'I shall smite the shepherd,** and the sheep will be scattered.' Nevertheless, **after I'm raised I'll go before you into Galilee.**" But Peter said to him, "Even if all will be scandalized, yet not I!" And Jesus says to him, "Amen I say to you, today in this very night, before a cock crows twice, you will deny me three times." But he continued speaking excessively, "If it is necessary for me to die with you, I will by no means deny you." In the same manner also they all were saying.

14:32—42 And they come into a field whose name (is) Gethsemane, and he says to his disciples, "Sit here until I pray." And he takes Peter and James and John with him, and he began to be stunned and distressed, and he says to them, "My soul is sorrowful to death! Remain here and keep watching." And going on a little he fell to the earth, and he kept praying that if it is possible the hour might pass away from him. And he was saying, "Abba, Father, all things (are) possible for you. Remove this cup from me! Yet not what I want but what you (want)." And he comes and finds them sleeping, and he says to Peter, "Simon, are you sleeping? Aren't you strong enough to watch one hour? Keep on watching and praying so that you don't come into being tested. The spirit (is) eager, but the flesh weak." And going off again he prayed saying the same word. And coming again he found them sleeping, for their eyes were weighed down, and they did not know what they should answer him. And he comes the third time and says to them, "Are you going to sleep and rest forever? It's settled! The hour came! Look, **the Human Being** is being delivered up into the hands of sinners. Rouse yourselves! Let's go! Look, the one delivering me up has approached."

14:43–49 And immediately while he is still speaking, Judas, one of the twelve, arrives and with him a crowd with swords and clubs from the chief priests and scribes and elders. Now the one delivering him up had given them a signal saying, "Whomever I kiss, this is he. Take hold of him and lead (him) away securely." And coming immediately (and) approaching him, he says, "Rabbi!" and kissed him. So they laid hands on him and held him fast. Now one of the bystanders, drawing his sword, struck the high priest's slave and took away his ear. And speaking up Jesus said to them, "As against a bandit you came out with swords and clubs to seize me. Daily I was with you in the temple teaching, and you did not take hold of me. Nevertheless, so that the Scripture might be fulfilled!"

14:50–52 And leaving him **they all fled.** And a certain **youth** tried to follow him wearing **a linen cloth** over (his) naked (body), and they take hold of him. But he, leaving behind **the linen cloth, fled naked.**

14:53–54 And they led Jesus away to the high priest. And there come together all the chief priests and elders and scribes. And Peter followed him from a distance right into the courtyard of the high priest, and he was sitting with the retainers and **warming himself toward the light.**

14:55–65 Now the chief priests and the entire Sanhedrin were seeking testimony against Jesus in order to put him to death, and they were not finding (any). For many were testifying falsely against him and their testimonies were not in agreement. And some rising up were testifying falsely against him, saying, "We heard him saying, 'I will tear down this sanctuary made by hands, and after three days I will build another not made by hands.'" And not even so was their testimony in agreement. And the high priest arising into the middle questioned Jesus saying, "Are you answering nothing at all which these are testifying against you?" But he remained silent and answered nothing. Again the high priest questioned him and says to him, "Are you the Messiah, the son of the Blessed One?" And Jesus said, **"I am!** And you will see **the Human Being seated on the right hand of Power** and **coming with the clouds of heaven."** So the high priest, tearing his clothes, says, "Why do we still have need of witnesses? You heard **the blasphemy!** What does it appear to you?" And they all condemned him to be deserving of death. And some began to spit at him and to cover his face and to beat him and to say to him, "Prophesy!" And the retainers received him with blows.

14:66–72 And while Peter is down in the courtyard, one of the high priest's servant girls comes and seeing Peter warming himself (and) looking at him, closely says, "You too were with the Nazarene Jesus!" But he denied saying, "I don't know or understand what you are saying." And he went out into the forecourt. And the servant girl, seeing him, again began to say to the bystanders, "This is one of them." But again he denied. And after a little while again the bystanders were saying to Peter, "Surely you are (one) of them, for you too are a Galilean." So he began to **curse and swear, "I don't know this human being** whom you speak of!" And immediately for a second time a cock crowed. And Peter was reminded of the word when Jesus said to him, "Before a cock crows twice you will deny me three times." And brooding over (it) he kept on weeping.

15:1–15 And immediately early in the morning after preparing a plan, the chief priests with the elders and scribes and the entire Sanhedrin, binding Jesus, led him off and delivered him up to Pilate. And Pilate questioned him, **"You are the king of the Jews?"** But answering him he says, "You are saying it." And the chief priests were accusing him vehemently. So Pilate again asked him, "Don't you answer anything at all? See how much they accuse you!" But Jesus answered nothing more so that Pilate marveled. **Now in accord with the festival he used to release for them one prisoner** whom they asked for. And there was one called Barabbas bound with the revolutionaries who in the revolt had committed murder. And going up the **crowd** began to demand (that he do) even as he used to do for them. So Pilate responded to them saying, "Do you want (that) I release to you the king of the Jews?" For he knew that the chief priests had delivered him up because of ill will. But the chief priests stirred up the **crowd** so that he should rather release Barabbas to them. Now Pilate, speaking up again, was saying to them, "What then shall I do with the one whom you call the king of the Jews?" And they cried back, "Crucify him!" But Pilate was saying to them, "Why? What wrong did he do?" And they cried even more, "Crucify him!" So Pilate, wishing to satisfy the **crowd,** released Barabbas to them and delivered up Jesus, after having (him) flogged, so that he should be crucified.

15:16–20 Now the soldiers led him away inside the courtyard, which is the praetorium, and they call together the entire cohort. And they dress him in purple and weaving a crown of thorns, they place (it) on him. And they began to acclaim him, "Hail, king of the Jews!" And they kept striking his head with a stalk and spitting at him and bending the knees worshiping him. And when they (had) mocked him they stripped him of the purple and put on him his own clothes.

15:21–23 Then they led him out so that they might crucify him. And they press into service one passing by, Simon, a Cyrenian coming from (the) field, the father of Alexander and Rufus, so that he should carry his cross. And they bring him to the place Golgotha, which is translated, "Skull Place." **And they tried to give him wine treated with myrrh, but he did not take (it).**

15:24–27 Then they crucify him and divide his clothes for themselves, casting lots for them (as to) who should take what. Now it was the third hour that they crucified him. And the inscription of the charge (against) him was written above (him), "The King of the Jews." And with him they crucify two bandits, one on the right hand and one on his left hand.

15:29–32 And the ones passing by were reviling him moving their heads and saying. "Aha! the one tearing down the sanctuary and building (it) in three days, save yourself (by) descending from the cross!" Likewise also the chief priests, mocking among themselves with the scribes, were saying, "He saved others, he is unable to save himself. The Messiah, the king of Israel! Let him now descend from the cross so that we may see and believe!" Even the ones crucified with him were reproaching him.

15:33–37 And when it was the sixth hour, **darkness occurred over the entire earth** until the ninth hour. And at the ninth hour Jesus **shouted with a great cry, "Eloi, Eloi, lama sabachthani?"** which is translated, "My God, my God, why did you abandon me?" And hearing some of the bystanders were saying, "See, he's calling Elijah!" So running, someone filling a sponge with wine vinegar (and) placing (it) on a stalk gave him to drink saying, **"Let's see if Elijah comes** to take him down." But Jesus, letting go a great cry, expired.

15:38 And the curtain of the sanctuary was **torn apart** into two from top to bottom.

15:39 Now the centurion, the bystander opposite him, seeing he expired in this manner, said, "Truly this human being was God's son!"

15:40–41 But there were also **women** looking on from a distance, among whom also Mary Magdalene and Mary, the mother of James the Little and Joses, and Salome, who, when they were in Galilee, **were following him and ministering to him.** And (there were) **many other women going up with him to Jerusalem.**

15:42–47 And as it already was evening, since it was preparation, which is the day before the sabbath, Joseph, the prominent council member from Arimathea who himself was waiting for **the rule of God,** coming (and) being bold entered before Pilate and requested the body of Jesus. Now Pilate wondered if he had already died and summoning the centurion questioned him if he was already dead. And finding out from the centurion, he presented the corpse to Joseph. And buying **a linen cloth,** taking him down, he wrapped (him) up with **the linen cloth,** and he put him down in a tomb which was hewn from rock, and he rolled a stone at the door of the tomb. Now Mary Magdalene and Mary, the mother of Joses were observing where he has been put.

16:1–8 And when the sabbath passed, Mary Magdalene and Mary the mother of James, and Salome, bought aromatic oils so that coming they might anoint him. And very early in the morning on the first day of the week they come to the tomb, as the sun was rising. And they were saying to each other, "Who will roll away the stone from the door of the tomb for us?" And **gaining sight** they observe that the stone had been rolled up, for it was very great. And entering the tomb they saw **a youth seated on the right hand** wearing **a white robe,** and they were stunned. But he says to them, "Don't be stunned! You are seeking Jesus the Nazarene, the one crucified. He was raised! He is not here! See the place where they put him! But go, say to his disciples and Peter, 'He **is going before you into Galilee.** There you will see him, even as he said to you.' " And going out they fled from the tomb, for trembling and ecstasy possessed them; and they said nothing to any-one, for they continued to be afraid.

Actualizing the Semantic Potential of the Gospel

BEGINNING THE CONSTRUCTION OF THE WAY (1:1–11) _____

The Gospel According to Mark tells the story of the construction of "the way." It features the extraordinary career of Jesus the Jew "from Nazareth of Galilee" whose unparalleled activity establishes once and for all a new road into life. Jesus, however, is not the initiator of this engineering enterprise. Its beginning is attributed to John the Baptizer, and Jesus is the first to enter upon it. Although the narrator ascribes its ancient anticipation to the prophet Isaiah, the more immediate of the two quotations from the Septuagint translation of the Hebrew Scriptures that are cited appears to be a composite of Mal. 3:1 and Exod. 23:20,[1] which has no parallels in Isaiah but which hints at a more explicit identification of the latter's vague "voice of shouting in the wilderness." Of the two texts from which the composite of 1:2 has been constructed, Mal. 3:1 is a more appropriate parallel to Isa. 40:3 insofar as it forthtells both the coming of God and a preceding messenger. In both the Hebrew version and its Septuagint translation only two parties are specified: "Look, **I [God]** send my **messenger** to prepare [or, according to the Septuagint rendition, "to watch over"] the way before me." According to Malachi, God is coming. The day of

---

1. See Hugh Anderson, "Old Testament in Mark's Gospel," in *The Use of the Old Testament in the New and Other Essays*, ed. James M. Efird (Durham, N.C.: Duke University Press, 1972), 307ff. Anderson does not include Exod. 23:20 in his analysis of Mark 1:2. The differences between his examination of the intent and design of Mark's use of the OT and that of this study are too numerous to cite individually; they appear to be determined largely by difference in literary-critical approaches. A comparison of both works should confront the reader with the wide divergence between them.

Yahweh is at hand. Moreover, God's coming will be preceded by a messenger who is identified subsequently in 4:5–6 as Elijah the prophet. Since Elijah did not die but was taken into heaven in a whirlwind chariot drawn by fiery horses (2 Kings 2:11), he is able to return for a second career and appropriately serve as the messenger of God's imminent arrival.

At the same time, Exod. 23:20 also has a certain correspondence to the wording of Mark 1:2: "And look, I send my messenger before your face in order that he may guard you on the way so that he may lead you into the land which I prepared for you." In one respect it approximates Mark 1:2 more closely than Mal. 3:1. Both the original Hebrew text and its Septuagint translation differentiate three parties: God, who is doing the sending, the messenger or angel who will guard Israel, who is referred to in the second person "you." In contrast to Mal. 3:1, it is not God but Israel who is coming. Israel is on the way to the promised land and will be escorted safely to its destination by God's attendant messenger.

In the light of this fundamental difference between Mal. 3:1 and Exod. 23:20, how is Mark 1:2 to be interpreted? The "I" who is doing the sending can refer only to God. But who is the messenger? Is the explicit identification of Elijah that is made in Mal. 4:5 intended by Mark? And to whom does the second person singular pronoun "your" refer? Israel, as Exod. 23:20 suggests, or someone else? Finally, what does the relative clause "who will construct" signify? It is not found in either of the Old Testament texts which seem to have been conflated and may well be an innovation of the narrator.

The second of the quotations (1:3) is an almost literal rendition of the Septuagint text of Isa. 40:3. The only change is the substitution of "his" in place of the phrase "of our God." It seems to be nothing more than the elimination of a needless redundancy, but, as will be revealed in the narrative that follows, its use allows the identity of "the Lord" in 1:3 to be more ambiguous.

The more immediately critical problem is the basic contradiction between both quotations as they are juxtaposed in 1:2–3. The composite of 1:2 differentiates three individuals: God, the messenger, and the one referred to under the pronoun "your." The citation of Isa. 40:3 in 1:3, on the other hand, indicates only two: the one who is shouting and "the Lord," who, at least according to Isaiah's original signified, must be Yahweh. The second person plural pronoun "you" in 1:3 may be considered a third party, but it does not correspond to the "you" of 1:2, either in number or in function. The "you" singular of 1:2 walks on the way which the messenger constructs; the "you" plural of 1:3 prepare the way for Yahweh who will walk on it.

Who, then, is actually coming? "The Lord" of 1:3 or someone who in 1:2 is the unidentified addressee of God's pledge? The apparent contradiction between the two quotations is resolved by the narrative that follows but with a number of startling surprises.

John the Baptizer is presented as the one who "happened in the wilderness." Evidently he is to be identified with "a voice of shouting in the wilderness" of the Isaiah quotation in 1:3. His preaching of a baptism of repentance is his summons to Israel to prepare the way of the Lord. Can he also be the messenger of 1:2 sent by God to construct the way?

According to 1:5, John is astonishingly successful in his work: "And the entire Judean countryside and all the Jerusalemites were going out to him, and they were letting themselves be baptized by him in the Jordan River confessing their sins." In other words, all the Jews of Judea and Jerusalem responded to John's call by submitting to his baptism and confessing their sins. The basis for such extraordinary success is intimated in the first half of the next verse: John was wearing camel's hair and a leather belt around his waist. This description corresponds almost literally to the Septuagint translation of 2 Kings 1:8, where it refers to Elijah the Tishbite. The narrator is alluding that all the Jews of Judea and Jerusalem went out to John in order to be baptized by him and so "to prepare the way of the Lord," because on the basis of his clothing they recognized him as none other than Elijah, who, in fulfillment of Malachi's prophecy, had returned for his second career.

Later, in 9:11–13, Jesus himself hints at this identification when, in response to a question from his disciples, he asserts: "Elijah indeed coming first will restore all things! . . . But I say to you, 'Elijah in fact has come, and they did to him such things as they were wanting, even as it has been written of him.'"

If John, therefore, is Elijah, there can be only one inference: God is coming! The great event that the prophets had been announcing down through the centuries is about to happen, and Israel responds to the call en masse.[2] All the Jews of Judea and Jerusalem let themselves be baptized by John/Elijah in the Jordan River confessing their sins.

Nevertheless, while John may be Elijah on the basis of similarity of clothing, he cannot fulfill the Elijah typology on the basis of his food. His diet consists of grasshoppers and wild honey.[3] Elijah, on the other hand, did not live in the wilderness. He withdrew into it only at critical moments in his career. On one occasion bread and meat were brought to him by ravens (1 Kings 17:6); at another an angel ministered to him by baking a cake and providing him with a jar of water. John's identity therefore appears to be ambiguous. The signifiers of 1:6 simultaneously intimate that he is Elijah, because he wears identical clothing, and yet not Elijah, because he is only a wilderness ascetic who subsists on grasshoppers and wild honey. This is the contradiction of the Baptizer's identity. It corresponds essentially to the paradoxical character of Old Testament anthropology; that is, the human being as "soul" or "self" who is divinely inbreathed and therefore participates in the possibility and freedom of God *and* as "flesh" or "body" who is subject to the limitations and necessity of mortality.[4] But it is determined by his unique eschatological role as the messenger who prepares the way for God's coming.

In any case, John's clothing indicates that he is Elijah, and for the Jews that can only signify that God is coming. John himself acknowledges this apocalyptic reality in the promise that he conveys to all who come to him for baptism: "The one stronger than I comes after me, whose thong of his sandals I stooping down am not worthy to loosen. I baptized you with water, but this one will baptize you with the holy Spirit."

Traditionally, "the one stronger than I" has been interpreted to refer to the Messiah, and since the Messiah is eventually identified as Jesus, John is proclaiming Jesus' imminent arrival and his own subordinate status relative to him and his office. But in the story world of Mark's Gospel, Jesus never baptizes with the holy Spirit. Only God does that,

2. On millennial movements as mass pilgrimages, see Norman Cohn, *The Pursuit of the Millenium* (New York: Oxford University Press, 1970), 61–70.

3. For OT purity laws on eating grasshoppers and other insects, see Deut. 14:19–20 and Lev. 11:20–23.

4. See Hans Walter Wolff, *Anthropology of the Old Testament* (Philadelphia: Fortress Press, 1974), 10–25, on *nephesh*, and 26–31 on *basar*.

and Jesus is the one who is baptized. Furthermore, there is no expectation in the Hebrew Scriptures and the literature of the so-called intertestamental period and classical Judaism that Elijah will return to serve as the forerunner of the Messiah.[5] He is always and only the apocalyptic manifestation of God's imminent coming. For the Jewish people in Mark's story world John the Baptizer, dressed as Elijah, is that sign and that is the basis of his spectacular success. The Jews of Jerusalem and Judea are preparing for this eschatological event by confessing their sins as they submit themselves to John's water baptism.

Jesus also comes to John for baptism (1:9). In the story world of the Gospel he is the only Jew from Galilee to present himself for baptism at the Jordan River. Perhaps the narrator is intimating that he is the outsider, for, in contrast to the other Jews, he originates from the insignificant town of Nazareth in the rural province of Galilee.[6] What is more, he is baptized by John **into** the Jordan, and nothing is said about him confessing his sins. While the preposition "into" has generally been ignored, the absence of any reference to Jesus' confession of sins has traditionally been attributed to his sinlessness as "the Son of God." Jesus does not confess his sins, because he has no sins to confess. He is already God before his baptism by John.

However, there are no signifiers in the Gospel that denote or connote Jesus' sinlessness.[7] Furthermore, John's promise of the eschatological blessing of being baptized with the holy Spirit, which he makes to all of the Jews (1:8), would have no significance at all if the natural advantage of being the sinless "Son of God" qualified Jesus alone for its fulfillment. The assumption of 1:9 is that Jesus is simply a Jew and, like all of his contemporaries who are coming to John's baptism, a sinner. His Galilean origin may be held in contempt by the Jews of

5. See Morris M. Faierstein, "Why Do the Scribes Say That Elijah Must Come First?" *JBL* 100 (1981): 75–86. Faierstein shows conclusively, in my judgment, that Elijah is never considered to be the forerunner of the Messiah in intertestamental literature and classical Judaism.

6. There is no hint of a birth in Bethlehem in the Gospel According to Mark. Jesus simply comes from Nazareth of Galilee and is known throughout the story world of Mark as "the Nazarene." See 14:67 and 16:6.

7. That requires a standard of some kind, and, if the Ten Commandments are used for that purpose, Jesus, in view of his transgression of the sabbath, can be considered to be a sinner. However, sin as both condition and act may be involved in this repentance, since it involves a baptism of dying in the Jordan River.

Judea and Jerusalem, but that only serves to accentuate the irony of the surprise climax of the episode.

Jesus' baptism **into** the Jordan, without any reference to a confession of sins, implies that he is doing something more extreme than the Jews of Judea and Jerusalem. "They were letting themselves be baptized . . . **in** the Jordan River confessing their sins." Apparently standing in the water and therefore retaining some degree of autonomy over their lives—note the use of the middle voice in the verb *ebaptizonto* ("they were letting themselves be baptized")—they performed the verbal act of confession. But, according to 1:4, John was proclaiming a baptism of repentance. Obviously they did not submit themselves to the full depth of his baptism. They did not abandon themselves to the injunction of the voice crying in the wilderness, "Prepare the way of the Lord!" Jesus, however, without any confession of sins, immerses himself in the water: he was baptized **into** the Jordan. Surrendering himself to John's baptism, Jesus alone expresses the repentance that God's forerunner was demanding. In effect, he drowned; he died eschatologically; he embraced the reality of his death before his physical expiration. Nothing less than such a comprehensive experience of nothingness corresponds to the announced purpose of John's baptism. It is a genuine act of repentance.[8]

As such it ends Jesus' participation in the structures and values of his society. It concludes his submission to the moral order into which he was born, in which he has been nurtured, and in which he is to realize his potentiality. The entire redemptive process of Jewish society as it is maintained by the institutions through which power is ordered—the temple and its priesthood, the Great Council of the Sanhedrin and its dispensation of justice, the scribes and the Pharisees and their guardianship of the law, the Roman administration and its military forces of occupation, its political oppression and economic exploitation, indeed the totality of the Jewish-Roman social construction of reality—has been terminated by his "death" experience. All of the debts that had been incurred under this hierarchical ordering of power and its community life have been canceled: to his parents for

---

8. Further support for this interpretation of Jesus' baptism "into the Jordan" as a death experience is furnished by the episode of Mark 10:35–40, esp. 10:38–39, where Jesus utilizes the sacraments of baptism and the drinking of the cup as symbols undergoing a judgment-oriented or eschatological death.

feeding, clothing, and sheltering him; to his friends for their love, encouragement, and support; to his society for educating and civilizing him; and to the government for its maintenance of law and order. The death experience of repentance has redeemed Jesus from his comprehensive indebtedness and the prescribed ways and means of discharging his obligations. As a result, he has become wholly unobliged!

According to Kenelm Burridge, unobligedness is the redemption or salvation which orients millennial movements of oppressed and dispossessed people who reject the moral order that exists and look for a new heaven and a new earth, or, in Jesus' case, "the kingdom of God." When religion no longer orders political, economic, and social power equitably for a particular group of people and "the process whereby individuals attempt to discharge their obligations in relation to the moral imperatives of the community" has become ineffective, new assumptions about power arise "which predicate the creation of a new [human being], a new culture, society or condition of being."[9] But first participation in the old redemptive process and its indebtedness must be terminated.

> From the pen of a social scientist, 'redemptive process' seems as one of general indebtedness: a feature which we acknowledge in variations of the aphorism 'paying our debt to society.' For whether the capacities of a human being are given him by God and/or a particular combination of genes, his potential can only be realized by parents and others. Society, moreover, prescribes the attitudes and activities by which its members can pay back or redeem the debt incurred in being matured, made morally aware, and enabled to exert and realize their potential. While these prescribed activities may be thought of as "redemptive media," the media through which the debt is repaid or redeemed, the process of engaging in the activities—activities which are ordered in terms of particular kinds of obligations—is, in our idiom, the redemptive process, a process which leads on to redemption itself. But this, the payment of the debt in full, can only be realized when a human being becomes in himself completely unobliged, without any obligation whatsoever—a free mover in heaven, enjoying nirvana, or joined with the ancestors. For since existence in community, a moral order, necessarily entails existence within a network of obligations, *redemption itself can*

9. Kenelm Burridge, *New Heaven, New Earth: A Study of Millenarian Activities* (New York: Shocken Books, 1969), 10–11.

*only be realized at or after that appropriate death which brings to an
end an appropriate mode of discharging one's obligations.*[10]

Because Jesus is the only Jew who has responded genuinely to John's
call to repentance and thereby has prepared the way of the Lord, he
alone experiences the fulfillment of the Baptizer's promise. God
comes, as John had declared, but only Jesus is baptized with the holy
Spirit. As he ascends out of the water—he had been baptized **into** the
Jordan!—he sees "the heavens being torn apart and the Spirit going
down like a dove into him." The narrator's metaphor of the dove-like
descent of the Spirit may allude to the symbolism of the new creation
which the image of the dove conveys as the bearer of a freshly picked
olive leaf, a sign to Noah and his family at the subsiding of the great
flood of a new beginning. This is now the eschatological moment of re-
creation.[11] The future has become present! Jesus is resurrected by the
life-giving power of the divine Breath. A new human being has been
created! At last the expectation of Jewish millennialism has been
realized. "The one like a human being," the one who is authentically
human, the one in whom the image and likeness of God has been
restored and who therefore "is little less than God, . . . crowned with
glory and honor" and bearing a divinely bestowed sovereignty over the
creation (Ps. 8:4–6), the one whom the seer Daniel envisioned "coming on the clouds of heaven" (Dan. 7:13), has finally appeared.

While God acknowledges the re-created Jesus as "my beloved son,"
Jesus understands himself, as his subsequent use of the title indicates,
as "the Son of the human being," or, to convey its eschatological
character more obviously, "the New Human Being." Because he is the
New Human Being, in whom the image and likeness of God is reconstituted, he is also the son of God, the first new chip off the old divine
block. His re-creation is also his deification.

God comes, as the Baptizer promised. According to the millennial
expectations of Jewish apocalypticism, as they are voiced in Isa. 24:26,
Daniel, 1 Enoch, 2 Baruch, and 2 Esdras or 4 Ezra, this eschatological
event marks the reconstitution of all things. God's rule will now be

10. Ibid., 6.
11. A significant parallel to this eschatological moment of a new human being emerging from the waters of chaos occurs in 2 Esdras or 4 Ezra 13:1–4. "The human being
who comes up out of the heart of the sea" in 13:13 is identified by God as "my son" in
13:32, who "will himself deliver his creation" (13:26).

inaugurated. All of the forms and forces of injustice, exploitation, dispossession, and living death which dehumanized Israel will be destroyed and with them the wicked who have generated and perpetuated them. At the same time, the righteous people of God, the elect, will be ushered into a new heaven and a new earth, a new moral order, in which justice and peace will prevail forever.

In contrast to millennial expectations, however, no cataclysmic upheaval occurs, and there is no reconstitution of all things. Instead, the very opposite of what Jewish apocalypticism anticipated takes place: God creates a new human being before a new order of reality, the kingdom of God, is established. The New Human Being precedes the inauguration of God's rule. With this surprise reversal a fundamental myth of Jewish millennialism is shattered.[12]

God comes, as the Baptizer had promised, but instead of inaugurating the kingdom names a viceregent to reorder reality. Ironically, it is a carpenter from the insignificant town of Nazareth in rural Galilee who is called into being as God's beloved offspring and therefore also as God's surrogate. His identification by the Heavenly Voice is simultaneously his commission. The reality of God's rule must now be constituted and that task is entrusted to him as the New Human Being.

In his capacity as God's viceregent Jesus enters into a reordering of power. Through the death experience of John's baptism he has been discharged of all debts and obligations to society. He has become a freemover in heaven and on earth. At the end of his career at his trial he will disclose his self-understanding to the high priest and the Sanhedrin: as the New Human Being, he considers himself to be co-enthroned with God, indeed, to be "seated on the right hand of Power (14:62). As the New Human Being, he is the bearer of God's sovereignty over the entire creation. He has free and complete access to the infinite resources of the Creator. Nothing is impossible (10:27).

Consequently, as a result of this reordering of power, Jesus also

---

12. Howard Clark Kee (*Community of the New Age: Studies in Mark's Gospel* [Philadelphia: Westminster Press, 1977], 106–75) unfortunately fails to grasp the Gospel's eschatology clearly. Mark's addressees do not form an apocalyptic community living on the threshold of the new age waiting for Jesus to appear as "the Son of Man" and to begin to exercise the rule that God has assigned to him. The "kingdom" has been established, God's rule is a present reality, but whether this mystery is understood by "the ones around him with the twelve" (4:10) who reflect the Gospel's addressees is questionable.

becomes co-bearer of the divine title "Lord." "The Human Being is the Lord," he asserts as he suspends the sabbath law on behalf of his hungry disciples (2:28). He charges the Gerasene, whose demons he exorcised, to return to his house and report the things the Lord has done for him (5:19). Here Jesus' use of the title is more ambiguous and may refer both to God, as the source of the power that has been displayed, and to Jesus himself as the agent who has exercised it. The same ambiguity is present in Jesus' justification of his temporary appropriation of someone else's donkey for his coronation ride into Jerusalem: "The Lord has need of it" (11:3). Ironically, the only instance in which the title is used in its vocative form occurs in 7:27, where the Greek Syrophoenician woman, who plays a decisive role in opening the reality of God's rule to gentiles, addresses Jesus as "Lord."

More sensational, perhaps, is Jesus' limited employment of the divine self-identification, "I am," that echoes Yahweh's self-disclosure of Moses in Exod. 3:14 and is widely used in the Septuagint translation of *ani hu* ("I he") in Isa. 41:4; 43:10, 25; 45:8, 18, 19, 22; 46:4, 9; 47:8, 10; 48:12, 17; and 51:12. The most dramatic occurs in the episode of Jesus walking on the Sea of Galilee and identifying himself to his disciples as "I am" as he approaches them in their boat. The phrase appears again in the so-called Little Apocalypse of Mark 13, where in v. 6 Jesus predicts, "Many will come in my name saying 'I am.'" Finally, it serves as a double-edged response which Jesus makes to the high priest at his trial before the Sanhedrin: "'Are you the Messiah, the son of the Blessed One?' And Jesus said 'I am.'"

Both uses of "I am" and "Lord," as limited as they are in the Markan Gospel, convey a startling revelation of the new self-understanding that Jesus acquires as a result of his entry into a reordering of power through his death and resurrection experience at the Jordan River. He simply embraces his new divinely acknowledged identity and proceeds to live and act according to it. As the New Human Being, he is the ultimate human being, the one who is so completely and perfectly human that the image of God will become transparent in his life and activity. Because of this reflection of divine being in his re-creation and the eschatological activity of building God's rule that it will involve him in, Jesus unhesitatingly—but also with great restraint—acknowledges his divine identity by appropriating the divine epithets "Lord" and "I am" which are now his by divine ordination. If he is God's beloved offspring, he is also the heir to the fullness of all that belongs to God, and in coming of age as the New Human Being he may command and use his patrimony.

To the ruling elite who serve as the guardians of what they believe to be a divinely instituted, hierarchically ordered society, Jesus' self-understanding and its expression in his activity are blasphemous. When Jesus assumes the prerogative of God in forgiving sins, the scribes accuse him of blasphemy. When he asserts that he is the New Human Being seated on the right hand of God, the Sanhedrin condemns him to death on a charge of blasphemy.

Nevertheless, Jesus' resurrection is the culminating approbation of the one in whom God began to be pleased at his baptism. It is the supreme legitimation of Jesus as the New Human Being and his inauguration of the transformation of the world. What is begun at his baptism is established ontologically by his resurrection from the dead. History, according to the perspective of Jewish millennialism, has finally reached its destiny: the birth of a new society in which each individual is drawn into the same reordering of power and the same self-understanding of the New Human Being into which Jesus entered as he followed his forerunner, John the Baptizer, into the construction of the way. The divine sanction that is pronounced on him at the beginning of his new career, "In you I began to take pleasure," is based on his radical response to John's call to repentance. There is no indication that it reaches back to any earlier act or event in his life prior to his baptism. The Greek verb *eudokēsa* is in the past, or aorist, tense and is best identified as an ingressive aorist, an entry into an action in the recent past.

Finally, at this point in the narrative, the contradiction resulting from the juxtaposition of the introductory Old Testament quotations is resolved. John, by leading Jesus into the Jordan River for a baptism of repentance, constructs Jesus' way into death and unobligedness. The identification of the three parties of the composite quotation of Mal. 3:1 and Exod. 23:20 in 1:2 is complete:

> Look, I, God, send my messenger, John/Elijah, before your face, Jesus, and he, John/Elijah will construct your way, Jesus.

As the third party he corresponds to Israel of the exodus in Exod. 23:20. For, since he alone among his Jewish contemporaries repents in the story world of Mark's Gospel, he becomes the embodiment of Israel, who will be escorted into the promised land of the new creation by God's messenger.

By following the Baptizer, Jesus prepares "the way of the Lord." God comes, as anticipated in Mal. 3:1 and Isa. 40:3, and baptizes him with the holy Spirit. Jesus rises from the water as the New Human Being and is called to act on God's behalf in establishing God's rule. In his capacity as God's viceregent he is entitled to bear the divine epithet "Lord." Consequently he is identifiable with "the Lord" of the second quotation derived from Isa. 40:3.

> A voice of shouting in the wilderness [John the Baptizer]: Prepare the way of the Lord [God and God's viceregent, Jesus]. Make his paths straight.

The time will come when Jesus the Lord will ride into Jerusalem for his coronation on the cross, and his followers will prepare the way for him (11:8–10) as he once more by his death prepares "the way of the Lord." At his first baptism into death the heavens were torn apart and God came forth to baptize Jesus with the holy Spirit. God will come forth again when the curtain of the Holy of Holies is torn apart at the moment of Jesus' death on Golgotha, but then for divine judgment. The beginning determines the end, for the end is already present in the beginning.

TEMPTATION IN THE WILDERNESS (1:12–13)

Immediately after his baptism Jesus is driven **into** the wilderness by the very Spirit that descended into him. The wilderness is a reality of chaos and formlessness, and it is symbolic of the anarchy he now confronts as a result of his experience of nothingness and his entry into a reordering of power. For him the old order of reality, with its first principles and absolutes, its myths and the structures they constitute, its redemptive process and the rules governing the use of power, has been abolished. The new order, the reality of God's rule, has not yet been constituted. Jesus himself, as the New Human Being, has been appointed to undertake its inauguration. How he will do that, what methods and means he will employ, must be determined. Various possibilities may present themselves, perhaps with different degrees of urgency. This is the time of testing, the period of critical scrutiny when things must be sorted out, when the temptations of Satan must be clearly discriminated. The long-awaited rule of God is now to succeed the old moral order, but by what ways and means will it be constituted? If the end is already present in the beginning, if the outcome is determined by the outset, what course must be pursued? What structures must be erected? What are the new rules that will govern the use of power in the new redemptive process that is to be instituted?

Jesus' critical forty-day period of being tested by Satan in the wilderness is analogous to the ordeal that ancient Israel endured for forty years after liberation from Egyptian slavery under the leadership of Moses, and it is this parallel that the narrator may imply by the employment of signifiers that convey this literary allusion: "And he was in the wilderness forty days." Jesus continues his typological representation of Israel. Embodying the people of God as the only Jew to respond to the Baptizer's call to repentance, he is now engaged in a new exodus which will culminate in his death and resurrection.[13] Like the Hebrews of old, he has abandoned the moral order of Roman-occupied Palestine, which has become as oppressive and inhuman as the bondage that they suffered in Egypt. Like them, after their redemption from the unjust and exploitative Egyptian ordering of power and their escape into the bliss of unobligedness, he must determine which social and economic structures will reorder power and initiate a just process of redemption.

Other literary allusions are intimated by the signifiers of the two brief sentences with which the narrator concludes this episode. On the one hand, "he was with the wild beasts." The parallel of Daniel in the lions' den is one likely possibility. The heroic disobedience of Jewish millennialism's paramount sage who defies the ordering of power in a context of exile adumbrates Jesus' style of ministry and perhaps even hints at his victorious emergence from the den of death. But the more plausible resemblance that is suggested here is Adam with the beasts

13. See also Kee, *Community of the New Age*, 111–12, although he does not relate this motif to Jesus' baptism and wilderness temptation. Eduard Schweizer (*The Good News According to Mark* [Atlanta: John Knox Press, 1970], 32) acknowledges that on the basis of Isa. 40:3, which is quoted in Mark 1:3, a recurrence of the exodus was expected in the end time.

in the Garden of Eden (Gen. 2:19) and the return to that relationship between human beings and animals prophesied in Isa. 11:6–9 and 65:25. Of course, the primordial setting of the garden conflicts with the reality of the wilderness, but this may be precisely the paradox the narrator intends to connote. The garden that God had originally created for human beings has become a wilderness, a place of chaos and death. Yet it is in this context that the New Human Being begins to reorder reality. Like the first human being, he will exercise his divine sovereignty and by naming call a new world into being.

On the other hand, "the angels were ministering to him." Although the narrator has already implied a correspondence between Jesus and ancient Israel, this literary allusion bears little resemblance to the continuous divine provision of sustenance that Israel experienced during the forty years of wandering in the wilderness. A more credible parallel is the angelic ministration that sustained Elijah in the wilderness (1 Kings 19:4–8). But such an allusion would signal an affinity between Jesus and Elijah and would appear to contradict the earlier identification of John the Baptizer with Elijah. If John is Elijah, how can Jesus also be linked to him?

John's identity, however, proved to be equivocal. While his camel's hair clothing and leather mark him as Elijah, his wilderness diet of locusts and wild honey has no parallel in Elijah's career. John, as 1:6 intimated, is simultaneously Elijah and not Elijah but only a wilderness ascetic.[14]

The same contradiction holds true for Jesus. On the one hand, as the result of his re-creation, he is the New Human Being and God has acknowledged him as "my beloved son." Under this identity he will shortly begin to fulfill his viceregency and establish God's rule. His mighty works of healing, feeding, and resurrection correspond to aspects of Elijah's career that have no parallels in the Baptizer's ministry. It is this side of Elijah's activity that is manifested in Jesus' new vocation and endorses his identification with the ancient prophet. Accordingly, Jesus is not only the New Human Being, God's beloved offspring. He is also an Elijah figure who experiences the ministration of angels in the wilderness.

14. Fernando Belo, *A Materialist Reading of the Gospel of Mark*, trans. Matthew J. O'Connell (Maryknoll, N.Y.: Orbis Books, 1981), 99. Belo's reduction of John's role to "the sole function of being a voice" does not do justice to the paradox of John's identity.

Gradually, as the narrative moves toward its climactic events, this other identity will become more pronounced. Its prominence will be especially evident in 10:32: "Now they were on the way going up into Jerusalem, and Jesus was going before them." Emulating John, who conducted him into an experience of nothingness that culminated in re-creation, Jesus has undertaken the construction of the way for his disciples. As their forerunner, he is leading them into a vicarious participation in his death and resurrection.

Both John and Jesus fulfill the Elijah typology in their careers, although in different ways. Nevertheless, united in this identity together they constitute and inaugurate the full scale of Elijah's eschatological mission: preparing the people and building the way for God's coming. Because they are co-bearers of this identity, especially in their function as forerunners, Jesus is sometimes confused with John. When Herod Antipas hears about Jesus, according to 6:14, people are claiming, "John the Baptizer has been raised from the dead and on account of this the mighty deeds of power are at work in him." Others, however, maintain, "It is Elijah." Herod himself concludes, "The one whom I beheaded, John, he was raised." In the narrative world of Mark's Gospel, Jesus and John are inextricably linked together in identity and activity.[15]

ESTABLISHING GOD'S RULE
(1:14–45)

After John's imprisonment, Jesus returns to Galilee. How long he remained in Judea after his wilderness sojourn is apparently unimportant. His withdrawal is linked to John's incarceration, because, as has become evident, there is a partial coincidence of identity and activity that will be manifested when Jesus begins his new career. Jesus will continue the construction of the way that John has initiated while he also fulfills his commission as God's viceregent in establishing God's rule.

He commences his work in Galilee with an ambiguous proclamation

15. Perhaps the exodus model also provides a basis for differentiating their ministries. Moses brought the Israelites to the Jordan River but did not enter the promised land. The new generation of Hebrews that had arisen during the forty years of wandering in the wilderness were led into the land by Joshua.

of the good news of God and an attendant call to repentance: "The right time has been fulfilled and the rule of God has approached. Repent and believe in the good news." The threshold of the long-awaited reconstitution of all things has been reached. The new moral order is at hand. For Jesus, in view of his entrance into a reordering of power, God's rule is here and now. He has crossed the threshold! For his fellow Jews it is only near, but near in a sense that it never was before, for the New Human Being has finally come and by divine appointment is about to begin to establish the rule of God.

The expectations of Jewish millennialism, which already have been reversed by the arrival of the New Human Being, will now begin to be fulfilled. But in contrast to Daniel's avowal that the God of heaven will destroy all beastly powers and kingdoms of the world without a human hand (Dan. 2:44), Jesus of Nazareth, formerly a carpenter, now God's viceregent, will be the artisan whose divinely empowered human hands will build a kingdom that will never be destroyed.

Jesus, however, will not involve himself in the revolutionary violence of zealotism. Although he is an activist, he will not adopt the methods and tactics of the Galilean freedom fighters. He will not counter injustice with injustice, violence with violence, power with power, or death with death. That kind of engagement with the powerful and the privileged and the inhuman institutions that they maintain will only perpetuate the destructive cycle of action and reaction: an eye for an eye and a tooth for a tooth. It belongs to the redemptive process of the world that Jesus has left behind in his baptism of repentance. Because the outset determines the outcome, because the end is already in the beginning, a new way must be constructed for the realization of a new society in which love and justice will prevail.

Jesus will undertake this divinely commissioned enterprise as a full participant in God's rule who already has entered into the reordering of power that Jewish apocalypticism continued to anticipate and zeal-otism failed to achieve.[16] He is already free, and therefore there is no need for him to engage in a struggle for self-liberation. His ministry will concentrate on enabling others to enter into the same reordering of power, and that will eventually involve him in a confrontation with

16. Mark's Gospel probably originated soon after the destruction of Jerusalem in A.D. 70 rather than shortly before it. See below, pp. 198–99.

the systemic structures of his society and those who regard themselves to be their divine guardians. Since he embraced his death at baptism, any penalties or punitive measures threatened by the ruling elite will not intimidate him into compromise or surrender.

As he embarks on this new way, Jesus urges his fellow Galileans to join him in repentance and to believe the good news that the turning point in history has been reached. His millennial preaching evokes an immediate response from two pairs of brothers in the fishing business: Simon and Andrew, and James and John. They simply hear his summons and follow.

Simon and Andrew are net casters; they own no boat. Their fishing is limited to the use of casting nets weighted with stones which they throw out while standing waist deep in the water at those places along the shoreline where the fish swarm in shoals.[17]

Zebedee, the father of James and John, on the other hand, owns a boat and therefore can fish anywhere on the lake, dragging long seine nets through the water in those areas where schools of fish have been located. Because of his superior equipment and greater maneuverability, fishing for him has become a commercial enterprise. He can afford to hire day laborers. Consequently, James and John, who are in partnership with their father, probably enjoy a kind of middle-class prosperity and comfortability.

In responding to Jesus' call, both sets of brothers are renouncing their vocation and source of livelihood. Moreover, they are also leaving behind their families. Later in the story world of Mark's Gospel in 10:28 Simon will remind Jesus, "Look, we left all things and have followed you!" James and John, however, are relinquishing greater affluence and security as they abandon their senior partner, their father, who most likely has been setting his hopes on their taking over the lucrative fishing business he has worked so hard to establish.

Such an immediate and radical response may be intelligible only in the light of Jesus' millennial proclamation. As yet there has been no manifestation of power in works of healing and exorcism. Who Jesus is

17. See E. W. G. Masterman, *Studies in Galilee* (Chicago: University of Chicago Press, 1909), 37: "in the summer chiefly from el Bataihah, the great marshy delta of the Jordan at the northeastern corner of the Lake of Galilee" (see also 38–40). See also Wilhelm Wuellner, *The Meaning of "Fishers of Men"* (Philadelphia: Westminster Press, 1967), 39–40; and J. G. Duncan, "The Sea of Tiberias and Its Environs," *PEFQ* (1926): 19–20.

and what he proposes to do are not yet apparent to them. Simon and Andrew and James and John therefore cannot be christologically motivated to follow him. They know nothing about his baptismal experience or his entry into a reordering of power. They may be impressed by the tone of authority in his preaching, but it can be only the content of his message that attracts them. Evidently they are millennially oriented; they are waiting for the rule of God and its liberation from all injustice and oppression. While Simon and Andrew are probably victims of a great, widespread dispossession in Jewish society, James and John—along with their father, Zebedee—may be more immediately oppressed by the extortionate taxation that the Herodians imposed on the fishing industry of the Sea of Galilee.[18]

Jesus' preaching of "the good news of God" is not simply another millennial proclamation of the kind that has been resounding in Judaism for many generations. It is also more than the tidings of John the Baptizer, who appeared at the Jordan River in Elijah's clothing. Jesus' message of the imminent realization of God's rule is grounded in the actuality of a preliminary fulfillment: "The right time *(kairos)* has been fulfilled!" The threshold has been crossed; the turning point in human history has been reached: "Repent and believe in the good news!" Manifestly Simon and Andrew and James and John are ready and willing to take the risk of faith and make a radical commitment to this new possibility, in spite of any disillusionments of the past.

Together with Jesus they proceed into Capernaum; and subsequently on the sabbath Jesus enters the synagogue in order to commence his teaching ministry. What he teaches is neither conveyed nor summarized. It is the mode of teaching that is stressed. That is what makes an impact on the hearers. They were overwhelmed at his teaching, for he was teaching them as one having authority and not as the scribes. At the very outset of his career Jesus manifests an authority that is distinct, an authority that contrasts sharply with that of the elite jurists, the scribes. Precisely how it expresses itself the narrator does not indicate. Neither is it necessary, for it is the demonstration of authority that matters and not the manner in which it is displayed. It is an outward sign of Jesus' entry into a reordering of power at his baptism.

18. Wuellner, *The Meaning of "Fishers of Men,"* 43–44, 23–25, and 62–63.

But this is only one aspect of his newly gained authority. Another is immediately manifested in an encounter with a demon-possessed human being who censures him with the cry, What is there between us and you? Did you come to destroy us? In other words: Leave us in peace! Don't bother us![19] But why this rebuke? Why does this individual feel threatened? Jesus has simply been teaching, yet with an authority that the audience has not experienced before. Is this person intimidated by Jesus' teaching and the authority with which it is presented? The very same question in 1 Kings 17:18, "What is there between me and you?" presupposes some kind of connection with the preceding events of the story. In all likelihood this holds true here as well. Jesus' teaching, which, in the light of the millennial orientation of his preaching, is almost certainly focused on the reality of God's rule and which is conveyed with a distinctive authority, arouses apprehension, nervousness, and fear within at least one person in the Capernaum synagogue.

Why in the synagogue, a place that fosters the traditional values of Judaism? Is the narrator connoting a link between demon possession and the institution of the synagogue? Is the synagogue of Mark's "extratextual" world one of those institutions in society which breeds unclean spirits and generates death instead of life?

Social institutions that become oppressive and inhuman, according to Jewish apocalypticism's interpretation of the myth of Gen. 6:1–4, engender evil spirits. *1 Enoch* 6—7 and 15 identify the Nephilim of Gen. 6:4, born out of sexual union between "the sons of God" and "the daughters of human beings," as giants that transcend the flesh-and-blood realities of human existence. That is, they are institutions. "They take no food," the apocalypse declares, "but nevertheless hunger and thirst and cause offenses. They consume all the acquisitions of human beings; and when human beings can no longer sustain them, they turn against them and devour humankind" (*1 Enoch* 7:3–4). In agrarian society, systemic structures such as kingship and its exchange system of redistribution, the temple and its priesthood, which legitimated them, were dominant realities that deprived the greater majority of the people of much, if not most, of their livelihood through taxes,

---

19. Rudolf Pesch, "The Healing of a Demoniac: A Historical-Critical Analysis," *ER* 23 (1971): 357, "a formula for holding someone at a distance."

rents, and tithes. Metaphorically viewed as giants, they were too powerful to be conquered or overthrown. They breathed evil breath, unclean spirits, into society, which, although invisible, manifested itself in the loss of specifically those qualities which were considered to belong to being created in God's image and likeness: autonomy, glory, honor, freedom, and dignity (Ps. 8:4–6). According to *1 Enoch* 15:9, 11, "Evil spirits have proceeded from their [the giants'] bodies. . . . They shall be evil spirits on earth, and evil spirits shall they be called. . . . And the spirits of the giants afflict, oppress, destroy, attack, do battle and work destruction on the earth and cause trouble." In view of the location of this encounter between Jesus and a human being with an unclean spirit, it is difficult to avoid the conclusion that the synagogue as a socioreligious institution is insinuated to be one of those giants, a subversive reality which in its own way fosters necessity, bondage, destruction of individual sovereignty, and living death.[20] Having established itself in society, like so many other institutions, it is resistant to the teaching of a new moral order which the rule of God inaugurates in which human beings will begin to recover the essential attributes of being divinely human.

Jesus commences his work of restoration, as well as his teaching, in the synagogue in order to liberate a fellow Jew from its oppression and dispossession. The unclean spirit, however, resists. "I know who you are, the holy one of God!" it cries out.[21] Motivated perhaps by the magical belief that by naming an adversary it can gain the upper hand,[22] it attempts to prevent its expulsion, but without success. Mastery is thwarted, and demonic acknowledgment is censured. Jesus demonstrates his superior power by expelling the unclean spirit: "Be

20. For an analysis of demon possession in colonial situations of domination and oppression, based on various Third World writings, such as Frantz Fanon's *The Wretched of the Earth*, see Paul W. Hollenbach, "Jesus, Demoniacs, and Public Authorities: A Socio-Historical Study," *JAAR* 44/4 (1981): 575–79. Section 2 of his article explores mental illness "as a socially acceptable form of oblique protest against, or escape from, oppressions." What is developed here is applicable to the synagogue demoniac of Mark 1:23–26 but especially to the Gerasene demoniac of 5:1–20.

21. The title "the holy one of God" is also used in 1 Kings 17:18, but in the Markan episode it may belong to the language of Jewish apocalypticism and be drawn from its writings, such as Dan. 4:13, 23; 8:13; and Zech. 14:5. See also Vincent Taylor, *The Gospel According to St. Mark: The Greek Text with Introduction, Notes and Indexes* (London: Macmillan & Co., 1957), 174.

22. Schweizer *(Good News)* cites the fairy tale *Rumpelstiltskin* as an example.

muzzled and come out of him." Yet even in yielding and withdrawing, it emits a loud scream of protest as it devastates its victim with convulsions of surrender.

The synagogue audience, already stunned by the authority of Jesus' teaching, is electrified at his victory over the forces of oppression and dehumanization. As the New Human Being, Jesus has acted on God's behalf and begun to actualize God's rule. Both word and deed convey the authority he bears as a result of his entry into a reordering of power. With lightning speed, word about him reaches everywhere into the surrounding region of Galilee.

Leaving the synagogue, Jesus enters the house of Simon and Andrew, with James and John following. Their residence foreshadows the symbolic character that the "house" will bear in the story world of the Gospel, a place where the community that Jesus is building will enjoy the horizontal relationships of familyhood, perhaps also a mirror of the house churches of Mark's addressees. Simon's mother-in-law is bedridden with a fever. Having experienced his authority in word and deed, Simon and Andrew do not hesitate to intercede for her. Jesus simply takes her by the hand and raises her up. The signifier that the narrator has used, *egeirō,* is the same verb that Jesus employs when he raises Jairus's daughter from the sleep of death (5:41). She is reanimated, revivified, resurrected. As a result, sabbath rest is no longer binding. She arises and spends the remainder of the day ministering to them and their needs. Certainly more than the preparation of a meal is implied here. Her service engenders serenity, joy, comfort, well-being, and communion for them all.

In the evening when the sabbath had ended—the narrator emphasizes this by adding, "when the sun set," for it is only then that the sabbath is over—masses of people congregate at Simon's house, where Jesus and his followers are still enjoying their communion. In typical Markan exaggeration, it is said that "the entire city was gathered together at the door." Evidently the report of Jesus' activity in the synagogue has circulated throughout the community. Now at the end of the day, after he has been refreshed, he must return to his divine commission. Again he manifests his authority by healing the sick and exorcising evil spirits. God's rule is being extended to include the diseased and the demon possessed of Capernaum.

As previously, the unclean spirits recognize Jesus, but they are muzzled in order to prevent them from acknowledging him: "And he was not permitting the demons to speak, because they knew him." Jesus is not afraid of their pronunciation of his name or identity that might put him under their control. What he shuns is their public recognition of his identity that might convey the false impression of their endorsement or that might arouse unwanted publicity. The former could reinforce the charge of the scribes that by the chief of the demons he cast out demons (3:22), while the latter would interfere with the objective of his ministry: the establishment of God's rule. Jesus rejects all forms of recognition and acclamation that would promote his status or position. He knows who he is, and his identity has been affirmed by God. For the present, that is sufficient. Anything more is unnecessary and perhaps even dangerous.

Very early the next morning, while it is still dark, Jesus slips out of the city into the wilderness, and there he spends time in prayer. "The wilderness" outside Capernaum cannot be a desert place, for the city must have been surrounded by cultivated land. The signifier must refer to a lonely, uninhabited area where Jesus can be alone. His identity and commission evidently require such withdrawal for renewal and re-vitalization. The interdependent relationship with God which he enjoys must be nourished through communication and communion.

"Simon and those with him"—most likely Andrew, James, and John—pursue him in order to bring him back to Capernaum. They do not understand his sudden departure. The work that he has done must be continued, and, perhaps, the rewards that accompany it should be enjoyed. Indeed, it may be that in their hometown of Capernaum they do not want to miss an opportunity of sharing a little of the notoriety and prestige that Jesus has gained through his activity on the previous day. But he points the way to other towns and villages. His commission involves him in disseminating the good news of God and in expelling the forces of oppression and dehumanization throughout Galilee. The work in Capernaum will go on because those who have been healed will begin to minister to others.

During this campaign of preaching the good news and exorcising unclean spirits throughout Galilee, Jesus is approached by a leper for healing. No location is fixed for this encounter, probably because lepers are ostracized and therefore excluded from all human community.[23] He kneels before Jesus and begs to be cured of the terrible malady that is devouring his flesh and alienating him from his fellow human beings. In compassion Jesus reaches out to touch him, thereby making himself unclean, as he utters the command, "Be cleansed!" Once again his authority is manifested, and God's rule is actualized in a twofold restoration: the individual is healed and simultaneously returned to society.

Jesus dismisses the person with a fury that stands in stark contrast to the compassion with which he received, touched, and cured him: "And being furious *(embrimaomai)* with him he immediately cast him out." This sudden change of conduct is explicable only in the light of his accompanying charge: "Keep on seeing to it that you say **nothing** to **no one!**"[24] In Greek—in contrast to English—the second negative reinforces the first. Jesus is in earnest about his insistence on silence. He wants no publicity, no public testimony, no propaganda. His work of healing has achieved its purpose in the restoration of a human being. It does not aim at anything beyond that.[25] The only kind of demonstration that is necessary is: "Show yourself to the priest and offer up for your cleansing the things which Moses prescribed for a witness to them."

Healed in body and restored to society, the former leper refuses to be intimidated by the blazing anger or the forceful expulsion he has experienced. Defying Jesus' command, he goes out and proclaims all the more vigorously the word of his marvelous cure. As a result, Jesus' popularity grows to such proportions that he is no longer able to enter a city or town openly. Surrounded and jostled by the crowds, he is obliged to withdraw to the wilderness. Yet even there he is pursued by the people who are coming from everywhere to experience his healing and liberating power. The beginning of Jesus' ministry in Galilee is an

23. See Lev. 13:45–56.

24. Against Schweizer, *Good News*, 8. Schweizer concludes that Jesus' anger is directed at "the horror of the misery which accompanied the disease." But see Walter Grundmann, *Das Evangelium nach Markus*, THKNT, 8th ed. (Berlin: Evangelishe Verlagsanstalt, 1980), 69. Grundmann correctly recognizes that Jesus' fury has nothing to do with the healing that has occurred but is intended to prevent the dissemination of publicity of Jesus as a miracle worker.

25. Compare Mark's presentation of Jesus as a healer with Philostratus's *Life of Apollonius of Tyana* 7.31–36 and 8.22–26. Jesus appears to be the opposite of the Hellenistic wonderworkers; there is not self-promotion or self-aggrandizement.

instantaneous and smashing success. The millennial rule of God is being actualized for the masses of the poor, oppressed, diseased, and dispossessed people of Galilee.

REORDERING THE WORLD AND CONFLICT WITH
THE GUARDIANS OF SOCIETY
(2:1—3:6)

After an itinerant ministry in the rural areas of Galilee, Jesus returns to Capernaum.[26] The authority he manifested over unclean spirits and displayed in teaching on a previous sabbath has not been forgotten. Word of his arrival spreads quickly through the community, and before long the house in which he is staying, perhaps that of Simon and Andrew, is bursting with people who are eager to hear what he has to say. Their number is so large that they spill through the doorway out into the street.

While Jesus is teaching them, four men arrive bearing a paralyzed human being on a mat, but they are unable to present him to Jesus for healing because the way is completely blocked. Undaunted, they lift the paralytic up onto the roof of the house and, after digging through the tile construction that covered the wooden beams, lower the person directly in front of Jesus.[27] Such deliberate faith, evident in their determination to reach him at all costs, induces Jesus to attend to the paralytic who suddenly has appeared before him. "Child," he declares, "your sins are forgiven." In view of the apparent need, such a response is completely unexpected, perhaps especially for the addressees of the Gospel.[28] Up to this moment Jesus has said nothing about the forgiveness of sins to any of the diseased and demon possessed he has healed.

26. Joanna Dewey ("The Literary Structure of the Controversy Stories in Mark 2:1—3:6," *JBL* 92 [1973]: 394–401) in her analysis of the literary construction of this section of Mark isolates a chiastic pattern but does not examine it in the light of the theme of the reordering of world provided by the central pericope of 2:21–22.

27. Josephus (*Antiquities* 14.459) describes an incident in the career of Herod the Great when, during a battle in Jericho, he tore open the roof of houses in order to expose the soldiers who were hiding in them. However, S. Krauss ("Das Abdecken des Daches, Mc 2,4—v. Lc 5, 19," *ZNW* 25 [1926]: 307–10) locates Jesus in the loft of the house and believes the healing occurred there before the eyes of all present.

28. This is especially true, if the author is responsible for the incorporation of this part of the tradition (2:5b–10) into the story, thereby transforming an ordinary so-called miracle into a conflict episode. See Kee, *Community of the New Age*, 54–55.

Furthermore, the objection of the local scribes who happen to be present is ostensibly well founded. Who does Jesus think he is, pronouncing forgiveness on someone who apparently has not sinned against him? If personal injury or injustice had been involved, his forgiveness would be appropriate. But what right does Jesus have to forgive all of the sins that the paralytic has ever committed and concomitantly to open up a new future in which the past with all the consequences that it transmits is abolished?

As the scribes clearly recognize, Jesus is assuming a prerogative that belongs to God: "Who is able to forgive sins except God alone?" But what they do not know and what Jesus must subsequently enunciate is that he as the New Human Being has the authority on earth to forgive sins. By his entry into a reordering of power, Jesus is acting on God's behalf and fulfilling the commission that was bestowed on him at his baptism. Nevertheless, according to these professional interpreters of the law, this is a perpetration of blasphemy, a charge that will be leveled against him again. A new aspect of Jesus' ministry is manifest here: a negation of sacred tradition, a reordering of the world, a restructuring of reality in which the verticality or transcendence of the reality of God begins to express itself horizontally in and through the activity of a human being, a New Human Being.

Jesus seems to have perceived that this condition of paralysis is the consequence of all the injustices, injuries, and wrongs that have been done *to and by* this individual. Not simply to *or* by, but both *to and by*. The narrator's use of the noun *hamartiai* ("sins") is significant in this respect, for it bears the connotation of being flawed by entrapment in the cycle of action and reaction.[29] Evidently this condition of helpless entanglement has engendered a paralysis that has prevented growth into adult maturity. For Jesus is constrained to address this person as "Child." What is needed is a total cancellation of the past that will remove the destructive effects of the action and reaction cycle of sin. That kind of renewal is God's work, and the effective power that is required to penetrate into the depths of the human psyche in order to restore its freedom and autonomy can come only from God.

---

29. *Hamartia*, as it is used elsewhere, especially in the writings of Paul, is sin understood as a condition. See Rom. 3:9; 5:12ff. It is a condition of action and reaction or cause and effect which the prophet Jeremiah characterized with a proverb, as he expressed his anticipation of its termination in the future (Jer. 31:29).

To prove that the New Human Being has been ordained to act for God in such matters, Jesus proceeds to demonstrate his divine authorization to bring about human emancipation. "What is easier," he inquires of the scribes, "to say ... 'your sins are forgiven,' or to say 'Arise and take your mat and walk'? But so that you know that the Human Being has authority to forgive sins on earth,"[30] he legitimates the pronouncement of the New Human Being as the re-creating word of God with the resurrection command, "Arise *(egeire)*, take your mat and go to your house." When the person stands up and exits through the crowd with the mat under arm, a roar of ecstasy explodes in praise to God and in mutually exchanged attestations: "We never saw anything like this."

Jesus not only proclaims and teaches the good news of God; he makes it present through concrete deeds by actualizing God's rule for the dispossessed, the sick, the diseased, and the ostracized. Moreover, he redeems life by canceling the debts and obligations of the past that continue to determine human existence in the present. Structures, traditions, principles—any realities that thwart or prevent the realization of God's will for the fullness of life are abolished. If the glory of God is to become incarnate in human beings created in God's image and likeness, the old order must be subverted.[31]

The narrator's change of setting that follows in 2:13 is natural in this context. Jesus resorts to the edge of the Sea of Galilee. In the story world of the Gospel it is the borderland between two realms: the land, which is defined, limited, and secure, and the sea, which connotes chaos, the unlimited, the uncontrollable.[32] Under the order of the old covenant the two were separated by divine fiat (Gen. 1:9–10). The former became the environment of human beings, while the latter

30. Mark 2:10 presents the first use of the title "the Son of Man." That it appears here for the first time is not necessarily to be attributed to tradition. This is the very first time Jesus is challenged, and, in legitimating his word by a deed, he has occasion to disclose his self-understanding as "the Son of Man" or the New Human Being.

31. Analyses of Mark 2:1—3:6 concentrate one-sidedly on the conflicts and controversies of these five pericopes without including the radical aspects of Jesus' activity and teaching that emerge here. It is no wonder that the section ends in 3:6 with the plot of the Pharisees and the Herodians to kill Jesus.

32. For a more extensive analysis of the symbolism of the Sea of Galilee and Jesus' relationship to it, see Elizabeth S. Malbon, "The Jesus of Mark and the Sea of Galilee," *JBL* 103/3 (1984): 363–77. Malbon, however, does not link the new sovereignty over the sea to Jesus' identity as the New Human Being.

stood under the sovereignty of God (Job 9:8). For Jesus, however, the realms are not binary oppositions that must be maintained in eternal separation by impermeable socially erected barriers. In the new order that is emerging, the relationship between the two will become pliable and fluid, and the jurisdiction over the sea and all that it symbolizes, which God alone formally exercised, will be shared with the New Human Being.

Here, at the edge of the sea, "the entire crowd was coming to him." The New Human Being, who has entered into a reordering of power and therefore participates in the Creator's sovereignty over chaos, magnetizes the masses of the poor, the oppressed, and the dispossessed and draws them to himself in order to link them to the possibilities of God. What he teaches them at the edge of the sea is not indicated, but the setting expresses the orientation of his mission both socially and existentially: to bring the disadvantaged and the dehumanized to that point where order and chaos and limitation and possibility meet and can begin to interact.

Later, when he moves on, he comes across a tax collector, Levi the son of Alphaeus, seated at the revenue table, possibly engaged in the collection of the fish tax imposed by the Herodians on all fishing in the Sea of Galilee, and he calls him to discipleship. Obviously Jesus is not operating according to a purity code. The despised trade that Levi practices, indeed, one to which "the greatest social stigma was attached,"[33] does not prevent him from inviting the tax collector to join his following. The binary oppositions of the Jewish pollution system do not determine his associations and relationships. He does not acknowledge any structures that separate the clean from the unclean, the good from the evil.

Levi enters into discipleship and celebrates this transition in his life by throwing a party for Jesus and those who already have attached themselves to him. He also invites his fellow tax collectors and other "sinners," for many of them "were following him." Although the latter group, the sinners, is not identified more explicitly by the narrator, the demurral of "the scribes of the Pharisees" indicates that they are the impure and unclean of Jewish society. Because they do not measure up

---

33. Joachim Jeremias, *Jerusalem in the Times of Jesus: An Investigation Into Economic and Social Conditions During the New Testament Period* (Philadelphia: Fortress Press, 1975), esp. 310 but also 303–12.

to the ethical standards set by the professional jurists of the Pharisaic movement, they are excluded from the religious, social, and even economic privileges that are awarded by these guardians of law and order.

The tax collectors, on the other hand, who work as retainers for the rich and the powerful by preying upon the poor and the weak, are trapped in a vertical relationship of symbiotic dependency. They are dispossessors, but they are also dispossessed; oppressors, but also oppressed. Exploited by those above them, despised by those below them, they are reduced to a life of inhumanness by their daily practice of extortion and its resulting experiences of contempt and self-hatred.

Jesus has no scruples about being friends with such people and enjoying their company. He refutes the charge of self-pollution, directed at him by the scribes, by comparing his calling to that of a physician. His work is to serve and care for the sick: "I did not come to call the just but sinners." He is committed to drawing all the dispossessed and oppressed, who, according to the pollution system of the religious elite, belong to the realm of the unclean and therefore are regarded to be sinners, into the freedom and unobligedness of God's rule. By dining with them he communicates to them its realities of family-like horizontality, intimacy, acceptance, love, and life. The structural dichotomization of Pharisaic ideology has no place in the orientation of the New Human Being and the community he is building.

Traditional piety is also affected by this emerging new life style. While Jesus subverts the pollution system by eating with tax collectors and sinners, his disciples do not practice fasting. Whether it results from vocational limitations or some other circumstance is not stipulated and is probably of no import. Jesus does not defend his disciples by arguing from economic or social necessity. He offers three metaphors which convey conditions that demand new responses. First, he meets the challenging question with a counterquestion that appears to be rhetorical: "Are the groomsmen able to fast while the bridegroom is with them?" Obviously the answer is, "Of course not!" Nevertheless Jesus follows the interrogatory response with an affirmative declaration: "As long as they have the bridegroom with them, they are not able to fast."[34] Evidently it is not simply a matter of whether they will or will not. They cannot! The circumstances of the celebration are such that they are unable to fast. Fasting connotes repentance, but the disciples have already turned around to follow Jesus into the reality of God's rule. Therefore this is a time that demands its own appropriate response. Like the new beginning of a marriage, the arrival of God's rule interrupts all continuities and elicits a new way of living.

"But the days will come," Jesus continues, "when the bridegroom will be taken from them, and then they will fast on that day." It would seem that the narrator at this point has Jesus convert his metaphor into an allegory by alluding to himself as the bridegroom who will be separated from his followers in the future. How is the phrase "when the bridegroom will be taken from them" to be construed? It is doubtful that it hints at the time of the passion. Jesus was taken away from his disciples in the field of Gethsemane, but there is no indication that they returned to the practice of fasting.[35] According to the narrator, they all forsook him and fled (14:50). It is even more doubtful that it refers to the exaltation of Jesus' resurrection, for that is in fact the ontological establishment of God's rule and legitimates the continuation of the celebration of the new beginning that Jesus has inaugurated. An allegorical identification of Jesus with the bridegroom appears to be invalid. The metaphor must remain what it is, simply a comparison: it is the case with Jesus' disciples as with the groomsmen of the bridegroom. Its concluding sentence, "But the days will come when the bridegroom will be taken from them, and then they will fast on that day," is not intended to signify a time in his own career when his removal will induce the disciples to resume the practice of fasting.[36] It simply conveys the openness of the new style of life that is alive under God's rule. Every new situation or circumstance con-

34. Mark 2:19b, which is omitted by various manuscript witnesses, is almost certainly authentic. Not only is it supported by the text critical principle of the preferability of the more difficult reading, it conveys the striking note of the disciples' inability to fast under this circumstance.

35. Perhaps, as various commentators suggest, this eventually became the basis for fasting on Fridays in late Christianity. See Schweizer, *Good News*, 68; and Grundmann, *Markus*, 87.

36. Grundmann (*Markus*, 87–88) recognizes that the metaphor carries no christological significance but nevertheless interprets the verb "will be taken away" to bear a connotation of violent removal and to imply Jesus' passion.

stitutes an opportunity for a new response. Arbitrary continuity determined by tradition not only enslaves; it obliterates the possibility of living creatively and responding in a fresh way to the experience of God's coming in each new moment of the present.

The same anarchy is conveyed by the other two metaphors, but in a different way. "No one sews a patch of unshrunk cloth on an old garment; otherwise the patch [in Greek actually "the fullness," which refers back to the patch and raises the question whether this signifier intimates the superiority of the new over the old] takes away from it, the new part from the old, and the tear becomes worse." A worn piece of clothing cannot be mended with a new and unsanforized piece of material. But what does that imply? That unshrunk cloth should not be used to repair old garments? That old clothing should be maintained only with old material? The third metaphor, which is similar in structure, facilitates the construction of meaning. "No one casts new wine into old skins; otherwise the wine tears the skins, and the wine and the skins are lost." In both cases, the old and the new are incompatible. The old garment and the old wineskins are representative of the old order of reality, the order of the old covenant. On the other hand, the new untreated cloth and the new wine connote the reality of God's rule which Jesus is inaugurating. The new cannot be accommodated to the old! The result is loss! This does not imply that the old should be retained in favor of the new. The new is here, but the old traditions which established identity and security cannot be maintained by making adjustments and adaptations. In the face of the new, the continuity of patterns of habituation and institutional structures perpetuates existing injustices and incurs the loss of an open and vibrant future and with it human creativity and self-determination. Not reformation but revolutionary transformation is being advocated here.

Two concluding episodes of this narrative section illustrate the reconstruction of world or the reordering of reality to which Jesus is committed. Once again it is sabbath, and on this occasion Jesus is proceeding through fields of grain. His followers, who are with him, leave the path and begin "to make a way plucking the heads of the wheat." What this denotes is unclear. Are they threshing a path through the field or are they harvesting grain for eating? The objection raised by the Pharisees offers no elucidation: "Look, why are they doing on the sabbath that which is not lawful?" Clearly there is an infringement of the sabbath law, but what it is is not explicit. The Greek text states that "the disciples began to make a way"; and Jesus' response to the Pharisees' complaint intimates that they are eating grain. The compound verb "to proceed alongside" *(paraporeuesthai),* followed by the prepositional phrase "through the grainfields," suggests that Jesus is scrupulously following a path. His followers, however, have left the path and are trampling into the grain seemingly to do more extensive reaping in order to satisfy their hunger. Yet more than a destructive act of making a path through the grainfields is implied. Here is another of the sixteen occurrences of the word "way" that first appeared in each of the Old Testament quotations that the narrator placed at the head of the Gospel. It would seem that the disciples have begun to take part in the reordering of power which Jesus is initiating. Making a way through the grain while plucking and eating the kernels on the sabbath is activity forbidden by the law in the Jewish process of redemption. But hunger must be satisfied! It is a human need that cannot be determined by rigid patterns of habituation.

In his defense of their conduct Jesus poses the example of David. Although it had nothing to do with the transgression of the sabbath, David's audacious act of entering the holy place and appropriating for himself and those with him the sacred loaves of the Presence reserved strictly for the priests is juxtaposed alongside the disciples' activity. In making a way, the followers of Jesus have the right of sovereigns. They are not subordinate to the law of the sabbath—even as David was not subject to the law of the loaves—but are free to decide when and how the sabbath is to be observed. Genuine human needs always have priority over regulations and institutions. For, as Jesus continues, the institution of the sabbath was not established for its own sake but for the benefit of human beings. Under this principle which, it is important to note, the rabbis also acknowledged,[37] the New Human Being determines when and how the sabbath is to be discharged, for the New Human Being is sovereign even of the sabbath.

The climax of this narrative section is reached in an episode of healing, a counterpart to the opening incident of the restoration of a paralytic. It is still the sabbath, and Jesus enters a synagogue. On this

37. See Mechilta on Exod. 31:14.

occasion, however, he takes the offensive and raises the challenge. A human being with a withered hand is lurking in the shadows, "and they were watching closely if he would heal him on the sabbath, so that they might accuse him." Who "they" are is not immediately evident. The nearest antecedent of the pronoun is found in the previous story of the harvesting of grain on the sabbath. "They" must refer to the Pharisees who have been aroused by Jesus' scriptural justification of his disciples' infringement of the sabbath law, and they have followed him into the synagogue.

Without hesitation Jesus summons the individual with the withered hand into the middle of the synagogue and calls them to account with the critical question: "Is it lawful to do good on the sabbath or to do evil, to save a life or to kill?" This is the criterion which Jesus raises for personal and social activity on the sabbath. For if the New Human Being, who has entered into a reordering of power, is sovereign also of the sabbath, no laws or patterns of habituation can be imposed to regulate his practice of justice. His identity determines his ethical conduct and commits him to a life of doing good and working on behalf of those who continue to suffer injustice and oppression.

The Pharisees refuse to respond to Jesus' question. They could have objected that this was not really a matter of life or death and that therefore to wait until the following day to heal this person was not necessarily evil. Instead, they remain silent. Obviously something more fundamental is at stake here, and it is not merely the benevolent act of restoring a withered hand on the sabbath. The formulation of Jesus' question addressed to the Pharisees implies a suspension of the unique status that the sabbath has traditionally held in Judaism. For if doing good and saving life are as valid for the sabbath as for any other day of the week, the singularly sacred character of the sabbath is negated, and there is no longer any valid basis for differentiating it from the rest of the week.

Good is done, a life is saved, the withered hand is restored. As a result, a human being recovers the use of a limb and is enabled to enter into a fuller and richer life—on the sabbath! The Pharisees, however, who have witnessed this, have become conscious of the ultimate consequences of Jesus' activity and show an unyielding determination to preserve their world and the power and privilege they possess as its guardians. Joining with the secular politicians, the Herodians, they begin to plot Jesus' destruction.[38]

FOUNDING A NEW ISRAEL
(3:7–35) _____

As earlier, after the encounter with the scribes over the pronouncement of forgiveness at the healing of the paralytic, Jesus withdraws to the edge of the sea with his disciples. In view of the growing hostility of the religious and the secular elite at the anarchic character of his activity, the narrator's use of the verb "to withdraw or take refuge" *(anachōrein)* may intimate a retreat in the face of danger. Once again the border between the land and the sea becomes the location of his ministry to the crowds. It is another opportunity to draw them into the ambiguous demarcation between the two realms in order to experience the possibility of God.

The great multitude of people who follow Jesus appear to be displaced persons; they come from many different places: Judea, Jerusalem, Idumea, Transjordan, the regions around Tyre and Sidon, as well as Galilee. Undoubtedly they are members of the dispossessed lower classes: unemployed artisans and peasants, unskilled laborers of various kinds who drift from place to place looking for work.[39] Undernourished and sickly, all are eager to experience his healing; and as they press upon him in order to touch him, Jesus proposes to his disciples that a small boat be kept ready for him for a hasty withdrawal to prevent himself from being crushed by the people. At the same time, unclean spirits, when confronted by him, fall down in apparent submission, crying out, "You are the son of God," perhaps once again

38. See Etienne Trocmé, *The Formation of the Gospel According to Mark*, trans. Pamela Gaughan (Philadelphia: Westminster Press, 1975), 88–93. Trocmé is typical of many scholars who analyze the Markan Gospel as though it were a window providing direct and immediate access to the historical realities that the text seemingly narrates. In his discussion of the Pharisees and the Herodians of 3:6 he focuses on the question why the evangelist harbors an aversion to these people and searches for an answer in history rather than the story world of the Gospel.

39. Wolfgang Stegemann, *The Gospel and the Poor*, trans. Dietlinde Elliott (Philadelphia: Fortress Press, 1984), 18–21. See also Gerhard E. Lenski and Jean Lenski, *Human Societies: An Introduction to Macrosociology*, 4th ed. (New York: McGraw-Hill, 1982), 189–93, 197–98, and 212.

to try to render his authority ineffective. But they fail. As before (1:34), Jesus rejects their acknowledgment and silences them. He neither needs nor desires this kind of publicity even when their recognition echoes his call into being by the Heavenly Voice at his baptism.

There is irony in these contrasts. While the Pharisees and the Herodians are conspiring to kill Jesus, a multitude of displaced persons are oppressing him physically in order to regain their health and autonomy. At the same time, the destructive forces of the systemic institutions of society acknowledge him as "the son of God." And Jesus, who withdrew to the edge of the sea, is obliged to keep a boat waiting for him in order to avoid being trampled by the crowd.

The narrator's summary of Jesus' ministry reveals a society in which the process of redemption has broken down. The use and the control of power by the ruling class are self-serving, oriented toward the preservation of the existing structures and institutions without regard for the mutuality of coordinated interests and obligations which they were originally commissioned to order and supervise. The system has no integrity. Economic, political, and social conditions engender greater impoverishment among the masses of people. Mounting pressure drives individuals to desperate action, and repression from above increases. Laws are enforced without regard for justice in order to stabilize the existing status quo. Order has become the obsession of the governing classes, and the power they exercise and the institutions through which they rule generate more virulent demons and unclean spirits.

In this social turmoil and chaos Jesus proceeds to establish a new community. Like Moses of old, he ascends "into the mountain" and constitutes a new Israel. In contrast to Sinai, however, this mountain is not named, perhaps because it is not to be identified; more likely, however, it is not named because it simply serves as the *axis mundi* of the story world of Mark's Gospel. This is the mountain of Jesus' Galilean ministry; it stands in contrast to Jerusalem's Mt. Zion, and in its mythical significance it marks the birthplace of a new people of God.[40] In contrast to the Old Testament traditions of Exod. 19:20–24, where Moses ascends Mt. Sinai alone, and Exod. 24:9–11, where

---

40. On mountains as navels or architectonic centers, see Mircea Eliade, *Cosmos and History: The Myth of the Eternal Return* (New York: Harper & Brothers, 1959), 12–17, and idem, *The Sacred and the Profane* (New York: Harper & Row, 1961), 20–42.

Moses went up into the mountain with Aaron, Nadab, Abihu, and seventy elders representing the people, all of Jesus' followers gather on the mountain with him. Here "he summons whom he wanted," and from them he selects twelve to serve as the patriarchs of the new Israel that he is constituting. Unlike the twelve sons of Jacob, however, they are not linked to one another by family ties or blood relationships. Moreover, by endowing them with the same authority he bears as the New Human Being to preach the good news and to exorcise demons, Jesus establishes the egalitarian character of this new people of God. For if he does not subordinate the twelve to himself or organize descending levels of power and authority among them, they are not to order themselves above the other disciples. They serve only as representatives of the community at large in which there are to be no vertical structures or hierarchical rankings. Related to Jesus, to the twelve, and to one another horizontally, all are to participate equally in the power, sovereignty, and freedom of the New Human Being.

New names are bestowed on the twelve, and therefore representatively on all of the disciples, to signify their entrance into a new Israel and its distinctive process of redemption. Simon is to be called Peter; and James and John, the sons of Zebedee, are renamed Boanerges, or "sons of thunder." The remaining nine are enumerated but whether by their old or new names is not clear. Striking is the absence of Levi the son of Alphaeus, who was called by Jesus as he sat at the customs table (2:14). He appears to have been replaced by James the son of Alphaeus. Perhaps this is the new name that Levi receives as a patriarch of the new Israel.[41] The old name may be too easily identified with the patriarchal family of the priesthood, set apart to carry the ark of the covenant and to minister on behalf of the people before Yahweh. In the new Israel, no single representative is to assume the obligations of the ancient Levites "to stand before Yahweh to minister to him and bless in his name" (Deut. 10:8–9). All of the members of Jesus' new community partake of this privilege equally. As the last to be named, Judas Iscariot is identified as the one who betrayed him.

Nothing is said of Jesus' descent from the mountain where the new Israel has been born. The narrator moves the story forward by relocat-

---

41. It is also speculated that Matthew may be the new name that Jesus gave Levi and that James, the son of Alphaeus, is his brother. So Grundmann, *Markus*, 104.

ing Jesus in a house (3:20). Which one or where it is located is unimportant. There is no indication that this is his home. In the story world of Mark's Gospel it is the symbol of the family-like character of the new Israel that he has constituted, and it stands in contrast to the hierarchical institution of the synagogue where leaders have begun to reject him and even plot his death. The new people of God will express its familyhood by meeting in house churches.[42] Its growing membership will strain the limitations of space: "they are not even able to eat bread." But the house will nevertheless retain its symbolic character as the family of God's rule. Those who are in the house with Jesus are simply identified as "the crowd." No differentiation is made between the twelve chosen as the representative patriarchs of the new Israel and the crowd. All who are with him belong to the family of God.

In contrast to this household of the New Human Being there are "those alongside him" *(hoi par' autou)* who, when they hear about him and his activities, "come out to take hold of him." Most likely these are his relatives from Nazareth, specifically his mother, brothers, and sisters who subsequently arrive at the house church where Jesus is meeting with his followers (3:31). Convinced that he is mad, they have come to take him away, perhaps in order to save him from himself. But more likely they are scandalized by the things they have heard about him, and they want him to return to his ancestral home.

Besides these outsiders—Jesus' own family!—there are those who have a more malicious perspective. Elite jurists, who have come down from Jerusalem, maintain that he is a tool of the devil. He is possessed by Beelzebul and is performing his exorcisms in the name of the chief of demons. Evidently Jesus' activity has captured the attention of the Jerusalem ruling class, and they have journeyed to the province for an inquiry.

The narrator suspends the scene in the house temporarily while Jesus turns to these two groups of outsiders for a response. By utilizing parables—the first time in Mark's story world that this word is employed by the narrator—Jesus exposes the absurdity of the scribes' point of view. If a nation is divided against itself or if a household is

---

42. At this point the reader may "see through" the story into the extratextual world of Mark's Gospel. On "house churches," see Abraham J. Malherbe, *Social Aspects of Early Christianity*, 2d ed. enl. (Philadelphia: Fortress Press, 1983 [1977]), 60–91.

torn apart from within, neither is able to survive. Consequently, if Satan rises up against himself and is disunited, his end is imminent.

Anyone who wishes to break into the house of a strong individual in order to plunder his possessions must first bind him before he can fulfill his purpose. Analogously, this is precisely what Jesus has begun to do in the household of Satan. By his entry into a reordering of power he has overpowered the strong one and is now engaged in the liberation of the possessed and the dispossessed.

In general, outsiders who offend and blaspheme will be excused. As Jesus puts it, "All offenses and blasphemies will be forgiven." His relatives, therefore, who regard him to be insane, will be pardoned. There is one blasphemy, however, that will not be, indeed cannot be, absolved; and that is the judgment of the Jerusalem scribes that Jesus' liberation activity is to be attributed to the agency of Satan. As long as this perspective is maintained and the work of God's holy Spirit is identified with Beelzebul and the forces of darkness, there can be no forgiveness. Only a complete change of mind that recognizes the creative and re-creative action of God's Spirit in the ministry of Jesus will reverse this condemnation and open up the possibility of divine absolution.[43] But ironically in the meantime, the elite jurists of Jerusalem are the ones who are on the side of Satan.

At this point Jesus' relatives arrive at the house where he has been meeting with the crowd of his followers. They have come in force: his mother, his brothers, and his sisters. Preferring to wait outside—the narrator hints at this point in the story that Jesus' relatives do not belong to the new Israel—they send word to him that they are there.

Earlier his reply to the accusation of the Jerusalem scribes had been initiated with a question charged with incredulous astonishment at the absurdity of their logic: "How is Satan able to cast out Satan?" In a similar vein but with apparently shocking heartlessness he now asks, "Who is my mother and brothers?" And looking at those seated around him, he declares, "See, my mother and my brothers!" This is not a rejection of his nuclear family in reaction to their assessment of his mental stability. It is, rather, a declaration of a new familyhood which is constituted in a house. The Israel that Jesus formed on "the

---

43. See Schweizer, *Good News*, 86–87. He writes eloquently on these verses of 3:28–30.

mountain" is based on a horizontally structured human interconnect-edness, that is, sister and brother relationships with all people, not on blood, ethnic, or racial ties. The community of the New Human Being encompasses all who attach themselves to it for the recovery of their freedom and autonomy, their health and integrity, without any ranking of class or achievement, without any permanent levels of power and privilege.

TEACHING IN PARABLES
(4:1–34)

Once again Jesus returns to the edge of the sea and begins to teach a newly assembled crowd, now the largest of his career.[44] The setting, the border between the land and the sea, and symbolically between the defined and the undefined, order and chaos, is also appropriate for this context, for his teaching will be conveyed in the form of parables, stories that subvert world.[45] The masses of people surrounding him are so overwhelming that he is forced to address them from "the boat," which allows him to be "seated on the sea," while they stand on the beach facing him. Subsequently this will be the starting point for him to cross the sea in order to bring his ministry of establishing God's rule to the other side (4:36). His disciples are also present, as 4:10 indicates, but as yet there seems to be no clear-cut differentiation between them and the crowd.

"Listen!" he charges his hearers. "Look, the sower went out to sow." Intensive hearing and seeing are to be engaged as Jesus tells of the typical events that encompass an entire agricultural season after the

44. Norman R. Petersen, "The Composition of Mark 4:1—8:26," *HTR* 73 (1980): 194–96. Petersen marks off this narrative segment on the basis of the roles that the sea and the boat play in it. He rightly argues that the actions of Jesus "repetitively disclose the ignorance of the disciples." As ingenious as his literary analysis and reconstruction of three cycles is, it tends to be arbitrary, for when a segment breaks his pattern and he is unable to explain it, he regards it as an anomaly (p. 199). The sea and the boat motifs may not determine the framework of this section after all. As important as they are, they do not constitute the internal structure and boundaries of this "composition." There are other themes to which the sea and the boat motifs are subordinate.

45. So John Dominic Crossan, *The Dark Interval: Towards a Theology of Story* (Niles, Ill.: Argus Communications, 1975; E. Sonoma, Calif.: Polebridge Press, 1988), 54–77. Crossan defines parable according to a narrative spectrum that locates this type of story at the opposite pole of myth. While the latter builds world, parable subverts world or explodes world-building myths and images.

seed has been sown. His similitude conveys pictures of what happens to the seed.[46] Already at the beginning the first loss occurs: "It happened in the sowing some fell at the edge of the way." Evidently the plow does not turn the earth over to cover the seed that has fallen alongside the path, and, lying exposed, it is eventually gobbled up by the birds.[47]

"Other fell on the rocky ground where it did not have much earth." Seasonal wind and rain may erode a portion of the field where a rocky substratum lies, and, unperceived by the peasant, the covering earth may be reduced to a thin layer of topsoil. The seed is sown upon it, and the scratch-plow turns it under. It sprouts immediately because of the shallow earth, but its roots are unable to penetrate into deeper ground for moisture, and consequently it is scorched by the fierce heat of the sun.[48] As a result, the second loss occurs.

Other seed fell into thorns, and the thorns grew up and choked it, and it did not give fruit. Still later in the agricultural season the weeds begin to compete for moisture and sunlight, and where they have sprung up in abundance they succeed in overwhelming the grain. In this manner the peasant suffers the third loss of the season.

The seed also falls into good earth, growing up and increasing, but it is not until the end of the agricultural year that the extent of the yield can be determined. Only at harvesttime can the quantity of the grain be measured: in some parts of the field there will be a yield of thirty kernels for every seed planted, in others sixty, and in still others an astonishing one hundred fold.[49] The three kinds of gain more than counterbalance the three kinds of loss!

But what meaning are the addressees intended to produce from

46. The parable of the sower may be more technically classified as a similitude, a comparison based on a typical situation, which, because of its correspondence to experience, would be entirely convincing. See Eta Linnemann, *Jesus of the Parables: Introduction and Exposition* (New York: Harper & Row, 1967), 3–4, 8–12.

47. The phrase "at the edge of the way" *(para tēn hodon)* will be encountered again in 10:46. Blind Bartimaeus was seated "at the edge of the way," in Jericho; and after Jesus restored his sight he followed him "on the way." In the light of this wordplay, it would appear that the author is also using the phrase metaphorically to allude to the earliest Christian self-identification as the people of "the way."

48. For a careful structural analysis of this similitude which also identifies Markan redaction, see John Dominic Crossan, *In Parables: The Challenge of the Historical Jesus* (New York: Harper & Row, 1975), 39–44.

49. One hundredfold was truly an astonishing harvest. Today with chemical fertilizers and irrigation, farmers reap five hundredfold.

their living through this similitude that more or less corresponds to
their experience of an agricultural season? Although the object of
comparison is not stipulated, the parable is almost certainly to be
juxtaposed alongside the eschatological reality of God's rule that Jesus
is constituting. What disclosure emerges when his hearers consider the
reality of God's rule in the light of their experience of an agricultural
season? For them this is more than new information. On the one hand,
it is a shattering of their own millennial expectations, for the myths of
Jewish apocalypticism foresee an imminent end of the present moral
order that is sudden, unexpected, cataclysmic, and by divine agency.[50]
However, in comparing the reign of God to the entire process of
growing grain—from sowing to harvest—Jesus is not only exploding
myths of Jewish millennialism and subverting the world that they
build, he is also unveiling a new vision of God's rule which can
constitute a new symbolic world and its attendant self-understanding.

For if the rule of God is like an agricultural season, it is a process
reality that has a clearly defined beginning analogous to the sowing of
the seed. In fact, the parable of the sower as the very first parable of
Jesus in the story world of Mark's Gospel, and perhaps the one on
which the others depend (4:13), also appears to serve as the representative metaphor of Jesus' ministry. Jesus is like the sower broadcasting
seed without prejudging the soil in terms of its potentiality. In his
ministry of preaching and teaching, liberation and restoration, God's
rule is being sown. Some of the seed has already germinated; some,
however, has been devoured by the birds or has been withered by the
fierce heat of the sun. Yet there is the promise of a harvest, but how
extensive its yield will be cannot be determined until the end of the
agricultural season. The loss that has already occurred is not the last.
The peasant knows there will be more, perhaps much more, before the
harvest takes place.

Obviously, therefore, in the light of this comparison the reality of
God's rule and its beginnings in Jesus' ministry are not to be judged
prematurely. There will be loss, probably a great deal of it. Three of the
four sentences of the similitude concentrate on loss from the time of
sowing to harvest. But there will also be gain, indeed, in some instances mind-boggling gain. In the present the extent of the harvest

50. See Isaiah 24—27 and Mal. 3:1—4; Daniel 2 and 7; 2 Baruch 53—74; *1 Enoch.*

cannot be anticipated. Loss may appear to be predominant, but the end of the agricultural season has not yet arrived and indeed may not for a long time. Meanwhile, human beings can live in hope—as peasants do—because the seed has been sown, the reign of God has begun, and there will be a harvest.

After Jesus has spoken the parable of the sower to the great crowd, the narrator unexpectedly changes the scene. The teaching of the masses through parables is temporarily interrupted; Jesus will return to them with more similitudes a little later. More immediately, however, the focus is fixed on "the ones around him with the twelve," an ambiguous phrase that differentiates a particular group of people from the crowd that has been following Jesus and has been identified by him as his new family (3:32–34). Most likely these unnamed individuals who are around Jesus—along with the twelve from whom they are distinguished—have attached themselves to him more closely than others. At this point, perhaps, a circle of disciples is beginning to emerge from the larger crowd and, in view of 15:40–41, it includes women as well as men.

Privately they approach Jesus and proceed to ask him the parables. The narrator's grammar is crude here; two direct objects follow the verb "they were asking": "him" and "the parables." The expected preposition between the two, "about," is absent. As a result, what the disciples are asking is not clear. Moreover, why is the plural, "parables," used? Jesus has told only one similitude. Evidently an anticipation of other forthcoming parables is being expressed here, and this is supported by the narrator's change of setting which introduces this episode. The ambiguity of what the disciples are asking may include both the purpose and the meaning of Jesus' parables.

Jesus' response, especially in the light of 4:13, conveys a sense of surprise at their question. They have been with him, they have heard his teaching, they belong to his new family, they are "insiders." To them, therefore, he affirms, "To you the mystery of the rule of God has been given." Consequently they should have no difficulty grasping his similitudes. If the eschatological reality of God's rule is perceived in his ministry, his parables should be perspicacious to them. For, as 4:33 indicates, he is concerned about the crowd's ability to understand, and therefore "with many such parables he was speaking the word to them, even as they were able to hear." If, unlike the crowd, which also belongs to Jesus' family, they cannot comprehend his comparisons, it may be necessary for them to scrutinize their discipleship.

To be sure, they are not like Jesus' relatives (3:21) or the professional jurists of Jerusalem (3:22) whose vision is so distorted that they consider him to be insane or a tool of the devil. Such assessments belong to the perspective of outsiders to whom "all things happen in parables." Jesus characterizes them in the words of Isa. 6:9–10: "Looking they look and they do not see, and hearing they hear and they do not understand." True seeing and hearing are essential, but they depend on perspective; and perspective is determined by the ideology of socioeconomic position and its concomitant existential self-understanding. For the time being, at least, the outsiders are trapped in a vicious circle. Predetermined by their traditions—like Jesus' family—or by their socioeconomic power and privilege—like the Jerusalem scribes—they are victims of their erroneous perspective and false consciousness. For them, Jesus' entire ministry is an enigma: "All things happen in parables." Consequently, because they are unable to see and understand, they are prevented from repenting and experiencing divine forgiveness. At the same time, however, they are not simply the victims of a faulty perspective. Because of their attachment to the past or because of their elitist orientation, they refuse to see and understand. Their own willful and deliberate choice eliminates their openness to the truth of God's involvement in Jesus' iconoclastic life style and ministry of liberation.

Therefore the adverbial conjunction "so that" (hina) at the beginning of 4:12 is deliberately ambiguous; that is, it is both consequential and purposive. As a result of being on the outside looking in, they are unable to see, understand, repent, and be forgiven. Simultaneously, however, because they also choose to be outsiders, all things are intentionally parabolic in order to prevent them from seeing, understanding, repenting, and being forgiven. They must bear the responsibility of their own judgment.

Parables, therefore, are ambiguous stories and images. They are not simply riddles! For "insiders," those to whom the mystery of God's rule has been given, particularly the oppressed and the dispossessed, they are transparent pedagogical devices[51] which mediate greater par-

---

51. Crossan, *In Parables*, 15.

ticipation in God's rule and simultaneously facilitate a brighter illumination of the divine intention for human existence in society. On the other hand, for "outsiders" they are opaque metaphors that preclude participation, the production of new configurations of meaning and therefore also a new understanding of the self in relation to the world. There are, of course, instances when they do understand, as 12:12 indicates, but that is because they are able to identify themselves with particular referents and therefore also able to participate in the story. If "the ones around him with the twelve"—in contrast to the crowd!— are having hermeneutical difficulties with his parables, the question of the character of their discipleship becomes critical.

Jesus' second response addresses itself to this conditional possibility: "Don't you know this parable, and how will you understand all the parables?" If they do not comprehend the similitude of the sower, they may also be incapable of construing his other metaphors. As he ostensibly proceeds to interpret the parable, he does not explain the comparison to them. Instead, he utilizes the metaphor allegorically in order to create a mirror for the self-examination of discipleship.

In place of the contrast between three kinds of loss and three kinds of gain, he focuses on the fourfold outcome of the sowing of seed which reflects four types of response to the proclamation of the word. First, there are those "who are at the edge of the way." They hear the word, but it is never planted in them: Satan "comes and takes the word sown into them," and from the outset discipleship never germinates. Then there are those who are like the seed sown on the rocky places. When they hear the word, they immediately embrace it with joy. But their discipleship is temporary, because it is withered by the heat of stress and persecution. There are also those who are like the seed that grows up among the thorns. Eventually they are overcome by the cares and concerns of their sociocultural environment, and their discipleship is neutralized by the seduction of wealth and the craving of material things. Finally, there are those who are like the seed falling on good earth. Hearing leads to assimilation and eventually to a discipleship that is fruitful and productive. Now, in critical self-examination vis-à-vis these four diverse results of sowing seed on different kinds of soil, "the ones around him with the twelve"—and, of course, the addressees of Mark's Gospel!—are to determine the character of their discipleship.

The repeated employment of the phrase "and he was saying to them" in 4:11, 13, 21, and 24 contributes to the general structure of 4:1–34 and indicates that the disciples continue to be the addressees of Jesus' admonitions and exhortations. Since the pronoun "them" refers back to "the ones around him with the twelve" in 4:10, it may be assumed that the same holds true for all of these instances. The disappearance of the pronoun at the beginning of 4:26 and 30 suggests that the narrator has returned to the original setting of 4:1–2 and Jesus is resuming his teaching of the crowd in parables.

First, however, more instruction seems to be required for the disciples. The interrogatory formulation of 4:21 conveys a sense of rebuke: "Does the lamp come in order that it should be placed under a peck measure or under the reclining couch? Not in order that it should be placed on the lampstand?" The first question, of course, presupposes a negative answer. Indeed, it would be nonsensical to place a lamp under a peck measure or a reclining couch. Its proper function is to give light. The second question offers the commonsense reply: the appropriate place for a lamp is the lampstand. Such rhetoric communicates a note of dissatisfaction, a tone of faultfinding. Since this interrogatorily composed metaphor of locating the lamp is addressed to the disciples—and therefore also the addressees of Mark's Gospel—there must be a deficiency in their function as illuminators. Giving light visibly and openly is as inherent to discipleship as it is natural and logical for a lamp to be placed on a lampstand. What is at stake is nothing less than the exposure of false consciousness, the unmasking of all illusions. "For," as Jesus continues, "nothing is secret that will not be disclosed; neither did (anything) happen hidden but that it will come into the open." Accordingly, the disciples are engaged in hermeneutical pursuits: on the one hand interpreting what they hear and on the other hand penetrating the facades of society and demystifying the illusions that they foster.[52] Senses and sensibilities must be sharpened and employed critically: "Keep on being aware of how you hear!" Examine what is perceived. Judgments and evaluations have consequences! "With the measure you measure, it will be measured to you." Perceptive hearing determines the extent to which authentic existence

---

52. For a hermeneutic of demystification and the exposure of false consciousness, see Paul Ricoeur, "The Critique of Religion and the Language of Faith," *USQR* 28/3 (1973): 205–12.

is gained or lost. Critical discernment in living life and unmasking false values not only bears personal rewards but it may also have far-reaching consequences for society that will ultimately return benefits to the individuals. Jesus therefore can append, "and it will be added to you." For it is proverbially true that a capital stock of critical awareness and insight will produce further dividends. But where it is lacking, even the little that may exist will be lost (4:25).

As Jesus resumes his teaching in parables, he also returns to his original audience, the crowd, with the disciples of course included. Both of the similitudes that he speaks to them explicitly refer to the same object: "Thus is the rule of God!"

God's rule is like the activity of a peasant. At the beginning of the agricultural season the peasant sows seed. As the subsequent weeks and months pass, the daily routine of sleeping at night and working during the day continues, while the seed at the same time sprouts and grows, how the peasant does not know. Rain, of course, is essential; and even weeding may be done from time to time. But Jesus does not include these details in his extended metaphor. His emphasis is on the mystery of germination and growth: the earth bears fruit by itself, first grass, then ear, then full grain in the ear. Throughout this time there is nothing the peasant can do to hasten or help this wonderful ripening of the grain. Only at the end of the process, when at last "the fruit allows," that is, when the grain is ripe, is the peasant drawn into new involvement with that which was initiated by the sowing of the seed: "he sends for the sickle, for the harvest has come."

If God's rule is like the activity of a peasant during an agricultural season, a collaboration is implied between human beings and the Creator that is comparable to the partnership between the peasant and the earth. Their interdependent activities will eventually produce a harvest of the realities that the reign of God brings: justice, freedom, autonomy, health, and the fullness of life. As in agriculture, the human side of this collaboration requires actors, like Jesus, in whom the image of God has been restored and who, by having entered into a reordering of power, are fulfilling the divine commission of reconstituting all things. As members of the new Israel they work as the peasant does: they sow the seeds of God's word through the activities of preaching, teaching, and liberation. But, like the peasant, they also allow the seed to germinate and grow in its own mysterious way without violating it, forcing it to mature, or periodically digging it up in order to measure its rate of growth. Even as "the earth bears fruit by itself," so the dynamic reality of God's rule that is at work in the world will realize the harvest of global salvation.

Jesus' parable of the seed growing secretly may be both antizealot and antimillennial. On the one hand, it explodes the myth of violent revolution as a completely human enterprise to achieve world transformation. Zealot activity can succeed in tearing down systemic structures that oppress and dispossess human beings, and there may be times when it is necessary. But the reconstruction of a society in which justice and love prevail requires the kind of human-divine cooperation that occurs during an agricultural season. On the other hand, Jesus' similitude also subverts the orientation of millenarians who consider themselves to be too frail and powerless to transform the seemingly invincible institutions of society that dominate and dehumanize their lives. Accordingly, while they can engage in resistance activities—as did Daniel and his companions[53]—they must wait for "the most high God" to act on their behalf and deliver them from their dispossession. Their perseverance will eventually be rewarded. God's rule will arrive, but "without a human hand,"[54] and, like the great stone of Dan. 2:35, it will destroy all the imperialistic nations and kingdoms and grow into a universal reality of justice and peace. In antithesis, Jesus' metaphor substitutes practical, peasantlike interdependent partnership with the wonderful and mysterious processes of God's activity in the world— from sowing to the time of harvest.

At the same time, God's rule is like a grain of mustard, proverbially the smallest of all seeds. Indigenous to Galilee and seemingly ubiquitous, it springs up to a height of eight to ten feet,[55] or, as Jesus says, "it becomes greater than all the vegetable bushes and makes big branches." The final clause of the metaphor, "so that the birds of the sky are able to nest under its shade," parallels the climax of two eschatological visions of Old Testament prophecy. According to Ezek. 17:22–24, God will break off "a sprig from the lofty top of the cedar"—a tree not indigenous to Palestine—and will plant it "on the

53. Dan. 1:8–16; 3:1–39; 6:1–28.
54. Dan. 2:34, 44–45; 8:25.
55. Joachim Jeremias, *The Parables of Jesus* (New York: Charles Scribner's Sons, 1966), 148.

mountain height of Israel . . . that it may bring forth boughs and bear fruit, and become a noble cedar; and . . . in the shade of its branches birds of every sort will nest." In Dan. 4:10–12, King Nebuchadnezzar recounts his dream of a cosmic tree to Daniel: "I saw and, look, a tree in the middle of the earth, and its height was great. The tree grew and became mighty, and its top reached to heaven. . . . The beasts of the field found shade under it, and the birds of the sky dwelled in its branches." Both of these prophetic images, the cedar and the cosmic tree, convey elitist realities of an imminent new moral order. Ezekiel's royal ideology is oriented toward the restoration of the Davidic dynasty, which will be as mighty and noble as a cedar.[56] For Daniel, "the saints of the Most High," the remnant of Israel that has remained faithful to God, perhaps specifically the scribes, will succeed the beastly empires that "devour much flesh" and be elevated to the top of the world pyramid by receiving "dominion, glory, and kingdom."[57]

The currency of these images and their attendant expectations is attested by Jesus' employment of the clause that climaxes the visions of both prophets: "so that the birds of the sky are able to nest under its shade."[58] Indeed, he deliberately concludes his similitude with this sentence which is more or less identical to Ezek. 17:23 and Dan. 4:12 in order to compel his listeners to juxtapose his image of the mustard bush alongside the cedar and the cosmic tree. Which order of reality will they choose? Will it be the one, like the mustard, that is tiny in its beginnings but eventually becomes ubiquitous and in its indigenous and ordinary character is essentially egalitarian? Or will it be the one, like the cedar, that reaches upward and is fundamentally hierarchical?

The narrator concludes Jesus' teaching by accentuating his distinctive pedagogy of teaching the crowds of people assembled on the seashore by speaking in parables: "And with many such parables he was speaking the word to them, even as they were able to hear. And without parables he was not speaking to them." Jesus adjusts himself to his audience's level of perceptivity. He utilizes similitudes that convey a familiar experience. Although his metaphors are subversive, exploding myths that build or maintain structures, values, and expec-

56. See Ezek. 34:23–24; 37:24–25.
57. Dan. 7:14–27.
58. Crossan, *The Dark Interval*, 93–96.

tations that thwart the actualization of God's rule, they do not alienate or devastate his hearers. While on the one hand they negate realities that have become traditional and even sacred, on the other hand they offer a glimpse of a superior order of social and individual being. As comparisons of God's rule, his similitudes have their own power and compulsion. Nevertheless his hearers are at liberty to make their own response between the worlds he has brought into view. His pedagogy of speaking in parables respects their integrity and freedom.

Ironically, however, while the crowd apparently grasp his parables—for "he was speaking the word to them, **even as they were able to hear**—Jesus, according to the concluding sentence of 4:34, is compelled to explain "all things to his own disciples." Certainly these must be "the ones around him with the twelve," who, according to 4:10, were asking about the parables. Can it be that they are more dull-witted than the crowd?[59] Evidently they are having great difficulty in hearing, and Jesus' earlier admonition, "Look to how you hear!" has not yet had its effect on them. A scrutiny of their discipleship is critical. At the same time, how will the reader disciples, the addressees of Mark's Gospel, interact with this episode?

GRADATIONS OF THE AUTHORITY OF THE NEW HUMAN BEING (4:35—5:43)

A new phase of Jesus' ministry is opened in the following narrative segment as gradations of the authority of the New Human Being are disclosed by a series of four momentous events. The first and also the most threatening, the storm on the Sea of Galilee, is encountered as a result of his determination to expand his ministry. "Let's cross over to the other side," he urges his followers. Since he has been teaching from "the boat," they simply "take him as he was in the boat" and set

---

59. T. A. Burkill (*Mysterious Revelation: An Examination of the Philosophy of St. Mark's Gospel* [Ithaca, N.Y.: Cornell University Press, 1963], 108) recognizes that the disciples do not understand but identifies them in this respect with "the uninitiated multitudes." This, however, is not supported by 4:33—34. Moreover, the multitudes are not the outsiders of 4:11—12, and the parables are not designed to conceal the truth from them (p. 100). Also against, Petersen ("The Composition of Mark 4:1—8:26," 214), who claims that neither the words nor the deeds of Jesus are understood by the people "and deliberately so." Petersen has not identified the outsiders correctly.

out for the opposite shore.[60] "And other boats were with him," probably filled with "the ones around him" of 4:10, both women and men,
while the twelve representatives of the new Israel accompany him in
the boat. Soon after they are under way "a great storm of wind" arises
which covers Jesus' boat with waves, and most likely the others as well.
It is as though the furies of chaos mean to destroy Jesus and the new
Israel, which he has constituted, in the same way they wrecked "the
boat of Jacob," as narrated in the Testament of the patriarch
Naphtali.[61]

In the latter episode the grand patriarch Jacob inexplicably disappears in the middle of the tempest; and since he is no longer holding
the steering paddle, the boat is tossed about on the sea and soon
destroyed by the pounding waves. Israel has been victimized by the
forces of chaos, and the twelve patriarchs, divided between a tiny skiff
in which Joseph escapes and the wreckage of the boat which the others
grasp to save themselves, are "scattered to the ends of the earth." At
the conclusion of Naphtali's story, after Levi, clothed in sackcloth, has
prayed, the hull of the boat of Jacob is wondrously reconstituted, the
twelve patriarchs find themselves aboard, and, sailing back to the land
of Israel, are welcomed by Jacob, who has been awaiting their return.[62]

60. Werner H. Kelber (*Mark's Story of Jesus* [Philadelphia: Fortress Press, 1979],
36–42) concludes that, in view of the disappearance of the boat after 8:22, its significance is to provide the transportation for Jesus to minister to "the other side" and
thereby to bind Jews and gentiles together into one.

61. For this earlier story, see *T. Naph.* 6:1–6, in *The Old Testament Pseudepigrapha*,
vol. 1, ed. James H. Charlesworth (Garden City, N.Y.: Doubleday & Co., 1983), 813.
For those to whom it is unavailable, I offer my own translation of the Greek text.

And again after seven days I saw my father Jacob was standing at the sea of
Jamnia, and we were with him. And behold a boat was coming, sailing without
sailors and pilots. Now there was written on the boat, "the Boat of Jacob." And
our father says to us, "Come, let us embark onto our boat." And as we went
aboard a violent storm happens and a great whirlwind; and our father, who was
holding the handle of the steering paddle was withdrawn from us. And we being
storm driven were carried over the open sea, and the boat was filled with water,
being wrecked by great waves until it was smashed. And Joseph set out in a little
boat, but we were separated on nine boards, and Levi and Judah were together.
So we all were scattered to the ends of the earth. Now Levi clothed in sackcloth
entreated the Lord. And as the storm ceased, the hull arrived at land, as it were,
whole. And behold our father came, and we all rejoiced with one accord.

Both stories, *T. Naph.* 6:1–6 and Mark 4:35–41, built world for their respective communities.

62. The Naphtali story is not cited under the assumption that Mark was familiar with
the story, but because it offers a contrast that contributes to the elucidation of Mark
4:35–41.

In contrast to Jacob, Jesus does not disappear as the storm intensifies; he is not bound to the land of Israel. But while he is seated "on the pillow" in the stern evidently holding the steering paddle, he falls asleep. Alarmed and perhaps even panic-stricken at the disaster that threatens them, the disciples arouse Jesus: "Teacher, is it no concern to you that we are perishing?" What they expect of him is not immediately clear unless it is recognized that "the pillow" in the stern is where the pilot sits. In sleep, Jesus' hand has slipped off the tiller! The disciples have awakened him in order that he resume his piloting of the boat.

Arising without delay, he censures the wind and commands the sea, "Silence! Be muzzled!" When the forces of chaos have abated, and a great calm prevails, he turns to reprimand them for their cowardice and lack of faith.[63] What expectations he has of his disciples are not immediately transparent. Obviously, however, turning to him in child-like dependency for the relief of adversity and misfortune is not considered to be an act of faith. In their discipleship they have heard Jesus defend their act of making a way through a field and plucking grain on the sabbath as the right of royalty. They have learned about the authority of the New Human Being to act on behalf of God. On the architectonic center of the mountain in Galilee where Jesus established a new Israel they received authority to cast out demons. Since he is building a new moral order in which relationships are family-like and power and privilege are shared, he must be expecting his disciples to appropriate and exercise the authority of royalty that is rightfully theirs. At least they could have assumed responsibility for the boat, gripped the tiller, and weathered the storm. Perhaps his rebuke that they have no faith also insinuates that they might have confronted the forces of chaos as he did and, in their self-understanding as members of the new Israel, exercised their sovereignty to reprimand the wind and calm the sea. But they are too overcome by their awe to grasp the scope of the reordering of power in which they too may participate as members of his community. Instead, they begin to ask the

---

63. See Petersen, "The Composition of Mark 4:1—8:26," 205. Petersen proposes that the disciples' fear of the storm in Jesus' presence is a sign of "their continuing lack of faith." But where did their first expression of lack of faith occur prior to this incident? Their lack of faith and their cowardice have to do with their inability to take action by taking over the steering paddle to guide the boat through the storm.

christological question for the first time: "Who then is this, for even the wind and the sea obey him?" Although they may not be aware of it, their sudden realization that they do not after all know who he is simultaneously throws their own identity into question. For the self-understanding that they had been developing as his disciples does not appear to have the limits and boundaries they had fixed, either for him or for themselves. As they enter into this new crisis and confront the chaos inside them, they are deluged by fear.

The second momentous event occurs in gentile territory when Jesus and his disciples—including those in the other boats!—reach their destination on the eastern shore of the Sea of Galilee and begin to enter "the country of the Gerasenes."[64] Geographically the boundary of Gerasa and its surrounding countryside did not reach to the edge of the lake; the city itself is approximately thirty miles away from the sea. Evidently, however, that is of no consequence for the story. Although this tradition bears the marks of a miracle story, it is more than an account of a miraculous cure. It is a narrative of the destruction of demonic powers of living death and dehumanization. As such it is most appropriately interpreted as a world-building myth in which the meaning underlying its figurative language is to be construed rather than its geographical and literary difficulties resolved through a form-critical analysis of its various stages of oral transmission.[65]

Upon entry into the territory of the great provincial city of Gerasa on the frontiers of the Roman Empire, Jesus is "met" by a human being with an unclean spirit who has come out of the tombs. The individual appears to be a male. The narrator's employment of the verb "he met"

64. For a literary-critical analysis of these spatial indications in the story, see Jean Starobinski, "An Essay in Literary Analysis—Mark 5:1–20," *ER* 23 (1971): 382–84.

65. See Pesch, "The Marcan Version of the Healing of the Gerasene Demoniac," *ER* 23 (1971): 349–76. Pesch treats the narrative as a miracle story and ingeniously traces it through four individual stages of tradition before it was adopted by Mark. Yet Pesch himself acknowledges its unusual features. The combination of the plea for a concession and the sending into the swine is unusual. Usually the demoniac pleads for a sending forth and the demons for a concession in exchange for a strict sending forth. The amalgamation of the two constitutes the distinctiveness of the Markan narrative (p. 367). It is also the combination of both that leads to the story's unusual climax of the destruction of the swine expressing Jesus' final victory over the demoniac forces of Legion in the present, thereby adding a new dimension to his authority as the New Human Being over all the powers of chaos and evil. On myth and its use of figurative language, see Crossan, *In Parables*, 15. See also Geoffrey S. Kirk, *Its Meaning and Functions in Ancient and Other Cultures* (Berkeley and Los Angeles: University of California Press, 1970), 252–85.

in the opening scene may imply a hostile confrontation. Jesus as he attempts to extend his ministry into the gentile world of the Decapolis is challenged by an incarnation of uncleanness emerging from Gerasa's cemetery. Not only does he come out of the tombs, places of uncleanness, according to Jewish tradition, where demons dwell; the tombs are his home, while he himself is the home of unclean spirits. A complete necrophile, he is the embodiment of living death, and he is distinguished by the narrator's rather redundant description of his condition as the most dehumanized and wretched individual whom Jesus has yet encountered. But he is incredibly powerful, for "even with a chain no one was able to bind him, because he had been bound often with shackles and chains, and the chains were torn apart by him and the shackles broken in pieces, and no one was strong (enough) to subdue him." Gerasene society has been unable to restrain or control him, even by resorting to extreme measures. Indeed, the efforts to subdue him, to impose greater limitations beyond those which he already has been subjected to and victimized by, probably have intensified his alienation and stoked the fires of his already burning rage. He appears to be a violent schizophrenic devastated by a fragmented psyche and deeply estranged from himself and his society. Abandoning his fellow human beings, he has taken up residence with the dead, but his despair has not been alleviated. In his desolation he continues to be tormented by self-hatred and impelled to self-destruction: "and through every night and day in the tombs and in the mountains he was crying out and bruising himself with rocks."

Seeing Jesus from a distance, he runs to him and worships him. Instead of confrontation, there is submission. While the opening scene hints at a challenge, the continuation of the narrative in v. 6, which follows the diagnostic description of the demoniac's condition, conveys his recognition of Jesus as the superior antagonist. Like the demoniac of 1:23–24, therefore, he meets Jesus with the defensive formula, "What (is there) between me and you?" Any contest between them would clearly result in Jesus' victory. Consequently his act of worship and his christological acknowledgment of Jesus as "son of the most high God" are a wily defensive strategy to counter the threat that confronts him. That is, by taking the offensive in naming Jesus and acknowledging his identity with an exalted title, he may be attempting to gain the upper hand, not by rendering Jesus powerless but by convincing him that he recognizes his superiority and has no desire for a confrontation. What is more, in an effort to ensure a standoff he attempts to place Jesus under oath: "I adjure you by God that you do not torment me." Although this is a formula that exorcists employ to drive out unclean spirits,[66] the demoniac has no illusions about exorcising Jesus. He has already acknowledged Jesus' superiority, and his adjuration not to be tormented is both an admission of his own weakness and his desperate entreaty to be spared immediate expulsion.

In this encounter with Jesus, the demoniac has moved through a series of attitudinal changes: from confrontation to defensive maneuvers to a plea of no contest. Only then, as awkward as it is, does the narrator cite Jesus' expulsion command, introducing it with the adverbial conjunction "for" in order to indicate that it had been issued at the beginning of the encounter: "For he was saying to him, 'Come out, unclean spirit, from the human being!' " Jesus had taken charge of the scene from the outset. His response to the demoniac's pathetic adjuration is not acquiescence but a startling question: "What is your name?" Such a disclosure, of course, would subject the demoniac more completely to Jesus' domination, for the knowledge of the name implies mastery over an adversary.[67] But no resistance is offered. Jesus' superiority is not in doubt. "My name is Legion," he replies, "for we are many."

As a signifier the name "Legion" seems to bear several layers or levels of meaning. First, it is a Latin military term and links the demoniac to the institution of the Roman army. But what is the nature of the relationship between the two? Most likely it is colonialism! By its economic exploitation and political suppression, its social disruption and systematic denial of all attributes of humanity to its subjugated people, colonialism creates an atmosphere of living death which fosters a systemic breakdown of the human personality. People who

66. Walter Bauer, *A Greek-English Lexicon of the New Testament and Other Early Christian Literature*, 2d ed. rev. and aug. by F. Wilbur Gingrich and Frederick W. Danker, from Bauer's 5th ed. of 1958 (Chicago and London: University of Chicago Press, 1979), 581.

67. That is why in Rev. 2:17 the promise is made to the one who conquers: "a white pebble and on the pebble a new name written which no one knows except the one who receives it." That is, an eschatological promise of sovereignty without subjection to the domination of others.

are dominated by colonialism are continuously forced to ask themselves the question, "In reality, who am I?"[68] Situations of social tension such as class antagonisms rooted in economic dispossession, breakdowns in society's process of redemption, colonial domination, and revolution are the causal context of possession and mental derangement.[69] Roman colonialism was no different, as Revelation 18 dramatically testifies. Merchants and business entrepreneurs in collaboration with the local upper class were reinforced by the occupation of Roman legions who were stationed in or near Gerasa in order to maintain the lucrative trade routes to both southern Arabia and India.[70] The aggravating presence of the Roman army would foster "the atmosphere of total war."[71] Moreover, where severe deprivation prevailed in the lives of the people, specifically the lower-class masses—without any possibility of sublimation—the symbol of social control, the Roman legions, would be "at one and the same time inhibitory and stimulating." Yet the message that would be transmitted would be a declaration of war. Paul W. Hollenbach quotes Frantz Fanon:

> The native will strengthen the inhibitions which contain his aggressiveness by drawing on the terrifying myths that are so frequently found in underdeveloped communities. These are maleficent spirits which intervene every time a step is taken in the wrong direction, leopard-men, serpent-men, six-legged dogs, zombies . . . which create around the native a world of prohibitions, of barriers and of inhibitions far more terrifying than the world of the settler.[72]

68. Hollenbach, "Jesus, Demoniacs, and Public Authorities," 547.

69. See Franz Fanon, *The Wretched of the Earth* (New York: Grove Press, 1968–82), 55–61 and 249–310, whose analysis of mental illness in the colonialism of French-occupied Algeria provides equivalencies for Hollenbach's interpretation of the gospel accounts of Jesus' exorcism.

70. See A. H. M. Jones, *The Cities of the Eastern Roman Provinces*, 2d ed. (Oxford: Clarendon Press, 1971), 289–90. See also Carl H. Kraeling, ed., *Gerasa: City of the Decapolis* (New Haven: American Schools of Oriental Research, 1938), 35–45. In view of the Parthian threat it would seem that a Roman presence would have to be stationed in Gerasa in order to guard both the frontier and the trade routes from the east and the south. Such in fact appears to have been the case, for Kraeling refers to a Roman garrison stationed in the city (p. 40). Perhaps the *stratēgos* placed over the "free" cities of what had once been Coelesyria by the Romans under Pompey, as Josephus indicates in *Antiquities* 14.74, may have resided in Gerasa. Certainly at least by Mark's time after the destruction of Jerusalem, because Vespasian had established a garrison there.

71. Hollenbach, "Jesus, Demoniacs, and Public Authorities," 575.

72. Ibid., 573.

Such restraints had been imposed on the demoniac: "he had been bound often with shackles and chains." The figurative language of this myth should not be construed literally. The shackles and chains may simply represent different types of social control. But the greater the repression, the more volcanic the reaction: "and the chains were torn apart by him and the shackles broken in pieces, and no one was strong (enough) to subdue him." The vicious cycle of restraining and releasing aggression, of being suppressed and throwing off restraint, eventually reached the breaking point and swept him away into the total possession of manic-depressive spirits: "And through every night and day in the tombs and in the mountains he was crying out and bruising himself with rocks."[73]

"Legion" therefore also hints at "a maximum of demon concentration."[74] The demoniac is possessed by many unclean spirits. As such, he is *the representation* of gentile "(dis)order" and (dis)integration,[75] and there are many more like him who are afflicted with the same derangement. Their number is "legion." And this too is one of the meanings of the name by which the demoniac identifies himself.

Realizing his imminent expulsion, in spite of his adjuration, the demoniac, in typical fashion, proceeds to beg for lenience.[76] Indeed, he pleads for two concessions: "that he [Jesus] not send them away out of the country" and that he send them into the swine. Since their nature is to possess, a host is needed to survive. Moreover, like the military giant that helped to spawn them, they are determined to persist in the country they have occupied.

The location of the substitute host, the swine, according to 5:11, is "at the mountain." Like the prepositional phrase in 3:13, "into the mountain," it is a feature of "the implied reader" which must be construed by the addressees. This place, evidently, is intimated to be an *axis mundi,* a sacred center of transcendent power. Perhaps it is a mythical substitute image for Gerasa, a center of Roman administra-

73. See Hollenbach's conclusion, "Jesus, Demoniacs, and Public Authorities," 581: "His possession is at once both the result of oppression and an expression of his resistance to it." Hollenbach treats the demoniac as an example of social accommodation until Jesus' healing disturbs the equilibrium between the individual and the community. The equilibrium, however, already seems to have been broken.

74. Pesch, "The Marcan Version of the Healing of the Gerasene Demoniac," 360.

75. Ibid., 361.

76. Ibid., 363.

tion and trade, as already noted, where Vespasian had established a military garrison to safeguard Roman interests.[77]

Jesus permits the transference to take place, as though both concessions are simultaneously being granted: to remain in the country and to enter into the swine. Unexpectedly, however, but as a result of the transference of the self-destructive frenzy of the demons from the human being to the swine, "the herd rushed down the cliff into the sea, about two thousand, and they were drowned in the sea." The demoniac possession of the swine produces a profound change in their character; instead of scattering in different directions, they violently stampede as a herd plunging off the cliff into the sea.[78] The torment that they had dreaded has been inflicted on them: they meet their eschatological doom by being banished to the realm of the abyss, symbolized by the sea, but ironically by the very hosts by which they had expected to remain in the country of the Gerasenes. The swine, the prototype of uncleanness, have become the "scape-pigs" of the demoniac and, by returning the demons to their place of origin, have rendered them ineffective.

As a result, a human being has been liberated and restored, while the countryside of the gentile city of Gerasa has been exorcised. But at the same time a disastrous economic loss has been incurred: two thousand swine have been destroyed. Such a large herd would most likely belong to a cooperative of the wealthy elite of Gerasa involved in agribusiness. Grazed by swineherds hired from the local peasantry, this unusually large number of animals was probably destined to be sold at a good profit to the Roman army in order to furnish the tables of the legionnaires with pork. By consenting to the entreaty of the unclean spirits to enter into the unclean swine, Jesus has not only eliminated them from the countryside of Gerasa, he has also destroyed the food supply of the Roman legions stationed in the territory.

The fleeing swineherds, after circulating the news of the event in the city and its surrounding fields, return with the owners, who undoubtedly are anxious to determine exactly what happened. "They come to Jesus, and they observe the demoniac seated, clothed and being of sound mind, the one having had the legion, and they were frightened."

77. Kraeling, *Gerasa*, 45.

78. See J. Duncan M. Derrett, "Contributions to the Study of the Gerasene Demoniac," *JSNT* 3 (1979): 5–6.

What further losses might be sustained if Jesus continues his ministry among them? He could ruin their economy! Consequently they beg him to withdraw from their country. The demons had implored him to be permitted to remain within the country; the wealthy elite request him to leave. The humanization of one individual is too costly for them.

Jesus leaves quietly, without challenge or resistance. This is not his country, and if he is not wanted, he will not insist on staying. There is someone, however, who can represent him, the former demoniac who is now clothed and of sound mind. Instead of allowing him to attach himself to his Galilean group of followers, as he desires, Jesus commissions him to return home to his family and friends: "Report to them how much the Lord has done for you and how he showed you mercy."

Jesus' employment of "the Lord" appellation is another instance of its ambiguous use throughout the Gospel. Co-bearer of the divine title and collaborator with God in this extraordinary victory over the forces of death, Jesus has once again revealed the power and the sovereignty he has received by his co-enthronement with the Creator. By proclaiming the things Jesus did for him, the restored demoniac is acknowledging the relationship between Jesus and "the Lord."[79] In antithesis to his strict Galilean policy to forbid the publicizing of his deeds of healing and restoration—at least until the revelation has been completed by his resurrection from the dead—Jesus charges the individual to make public the liberation he has experienced.[80]

Crossing the sea with his disciples, Jesus returns to Galilee. While he is still at the edge of the sea, he is surrounded by a great throng of people, but before he can resume his ministry among them he is approached by the chief officer of a synagogue. His name, Jairus, is omitted in several manuscripts and, because it is also missing in Matthew's Gospel, may be a later scribal insertion derived from Luke

79. See Petersen, "The Composition of Mark 4:1—8:26," 213–14. Petersen concludes that "the demoniac healed by the Lord through Jesus misunderstood the source of his well being." But the demoniac has not misunderstood it at all! The ambiguity of the appellation is consistent throughout the story world.

80. Burkill (*Mysterious Revelation*, 95) suggests that "the action of the healed man at the end would be seen as a sort of anticipation of the work of the apostolic missionaries." Perhaps this is an aspect of "the implied reader," which would be meaningfully construed by the addressees of the Gospel living in the rural countryside of southern Syria.

8:41.[81] In a surprising display of humility he falls at Jesus' feet before the crowd of people and earnestly begs him to accompany him to his home in order to lay his hand on his deathly ill daughter "so that she is saved and may live." The ruler of the synagogue, whose household is threatened with the death of his daughter, poses a significant contrast to the elite of Gerasa who prefer living death to the life that Jesus brings.

As Jesus begins to follow, the crowd moves with him, squeezing and crushing him. Among them is a menstruating woman who has been suffering from a continuous hemorrhage of blood for twelve years. Apparently she is in middle age but has been unable to reach her menopause. The narrator reveals his lower-class bias with the bitter indictment that she had suffered many things by many physicians and had spent everything she had and had been benefited nothing. Moreover, throughout the twelve years of her hemorrhaging she has been stigmatized as unclean, for, according to the Mosaic legislation of Lev. 15:25–27,

> If a woman has a discharge of blood for many days, not at the time of her impurity, or if she has a discharge beyond the time of her impurity, **all the days of the discharge she shall continue in uncleanness;** as in the days of her impurity, she shall be unclean. Every bed on which she lies, all the days of her discharge, shall be to her as the bed of her impurity; and everything on which she sits shall be unclean, as in the uncleanness of her impurity. And whoever touches these things shall be unclean, and shall wash his clothes, and bathe himself in water, and be unclean until the evening.

Consequently she has been forced into an oppressive confinement within her home, isolated from society and even physical contact with her family. As a wife, she has been barred from sexual intercourse with her husband.

Having heard about Jesus' reputation as a healer, she takes the risk of leaving her home, to which she has been restricted for twelve years. Perhaps as a final hope she seeks to make some kind of contact with him. Evidently she has convinced herself that a simple, unobtrusive touch will be enough to cure her condition. But her very presence in society exposes her fellow Jews to defilement; and direct physical contact with Jesus will make him unclean. In desperation she conceals

81. Schweizer, *Good News*, 117.

herself in the jostling crowd and stealthily reaches out to touch his garment.

Immediately sensing an emission of his charismatic power, Jesus turns toward the crowd and asks, "Who touched my clothes?" While his disciples insist that he has felt nothing more than the jostling of the crowd, Jesus scrutinizes the people around him in order to detect the individual who tapped his power. No longer able to hide, the woman steps forward to identify herself and with fear and trembling to reveal before all of the people the nature of her act. Instead of rebuking her for her violations of the law, Jesus commends her for risking vulnerability in order to be liberated from her oppressive condition: "Your faith has saved you." At last she has attained the salvation that had eluded her for so many years. Through the risk of faith she has finally reached her menopause; and now set free from the bondage of uncleanness and its accompanying isolation, she is at last able to enter into a full new life in the circle of her family and friends. Jesus' charge, "Go into peace and be restored from your scourge" marks her entry into God's rule.

However, this unexpected event with its happy ending has delayed Jesus and prevented him from hurrying to the home of the synagogue ruler in order to heal his daughter. In fact, while he is still speaking to the woman, word arrives that the girl is dead. It is now too late. Because Jesus allowed himself to be detained, the child of twelve years dies. She had lived as long as the middle-aged woman had been moving toward menopause. But now, on the verge of puberty, the girl dies. The restoration of the one who is no longer capable of bearing children has resulted in the death of the other who was approaching sexual maturity.

"Don't be afraid! Only keep on believing!" is Jesus' response to this ironic coincidence. To witness what will take place he selects Peter, James, and John from among the twelve. As they enter the synagogue ruler's house they encounter weeping and loud wailing. The mourners have already arrived to initiate the conventional ritual of moaning and shrieking. When Jesus interrupts them to declare that the girl is not dead but only sleeping, they reply with ridicule and mockery. After expelling them from the house, he takes the parents and his three disciples and proceeds into the room where the corpse of the girl is lying. Taking the child's hand, he summons her out of death: "Talitha koum!" The narrator cites the original Aramaic words, perhaps in order to convey a sense of the historical authenticity of this momentous event, and translates them into Greek in order to draw the addressees of the Gospel into it: "Little girl, I say to you, rise!"

As she stands up and begins walking about, the five, who have witnessed the event, "went out of their minds with ecstasy." But the matter is to remain confidential; there is to be no publicity. Jesus forbids them to divulge the secret to anyone. His objective has been achieved: the girl has been raised from the sleep of death. All that is necessary at the moment is to give her something to eat. Resurrection is a bodily reality involving the total person and therefore physical sustenance is essential to life.

At the end of the story the narrator observes that the girl is twelve years old (5:42). Added as though it were an afterthought, this seemingly insignificant note generates the irony of these coincidental episodes: because Jesus is delayed by healing the woman who has been menstruating for twelve years, the twelve-year-old girl who is on the verge of puberty dies. Although these intertwined narratives may originally have been transmitted as independent miracle stories, in their present interlocking—which is probably the work of the author[82]—they constitute a world-building myth. The number twelve links the two women to each other and to the ethnic reality of the twelve tribes of Israel which the number intimates. The older woman, who has been moving toward menopause for twelve years, represents tradition-bound mother Judaism. Unclean, isolated from the world and oppressed by the law, she is saved and her life is redeemed by her risk of reaching out to make contact with the New Human Being. The young girl embodies the new Israel, offspring of the synagogue and its Pharisaic heritage, who is on the verge of bearing children and bringing new life to the world. By resurrecting her from the dead, Jesus redeems her life and, as a result, enables her also to fulfill her destiny.

The boat journeys across the Sea of Galilee, in spite of the risks and hazards encountered, particularly during the initial crossing, have enabled Jesus to establish his mission on both sides of the lake. However, extraordinary gradations in the exercise of authority were necessary in order to overcome the different kinds of death, constitute

82. Ibid., 16.

God's rule, and open the future to both gentiles and Jews for the realization of a new destiny.[83]

REJECTION IN NAZARETH AND THE RISING NEED TO PREPARE THE DISCIPLES FOR THEIR OWN MINISTRY IN THE FUTURE (6:1–56)

After demonstrating through two mighty works how the future can be opened to these people, Jesus, followed by his disciples, travels to his hometown. Although the town is not named, the content of the story, particularly the reference to his mother, brothers, and sisters, indicates that it is to be identified as Nazareth. He enters the synagogue on the sabbath and begins to teach. Many of the folk are present, perhaps to satisfy their curiosity and find out for themselves what has become of their former townsman about whom they have heard so many rumors. His teaching startles them, and they react with apprehension. They are unable to account for his wisdom, much less his works of power. His present activities are so discontinuous with the past in which they have imprisoned him that they are uncertain that this is the same person who grew up among them: "Is this not the carpenter?" They have stereotyped him, and they are unwilling to be open to the changes that have occurred in his life. Scandalized because they are unable to bridge the past and the present, since what they remember of him cannot explain what they have heard, they close their doors to him. Their alienation expresses itself in their insulting reference to him as "the son of Mary." Conventionally Jesus, like any other male in Jewish society, would be identified in relation to his father, that is, as "the son of Joseph." But Joseph is never named in the story world of the Gospel.

Jesus marvels at their closedness and observes, "A prophet is not without honor except in his hometown and among his relations and in his house." A few, however, experience the health that his touch effects; but the narrator prefers to put it negatively: "He was unable to

---

83. Werner H. Kelber, *The Kingdom in Mark: A New Place and a New Time* (Philadelphia: Fortress Press, 1974), 62–63; and Malbon, "The Jesus of Mark and the Sea of Galilee," 373. This is not really a bridging of the gulf between Jewish and gentile Christians. Rather, these are episodes of defeating and eliminating the realities of death by overcoming the separation symbolized by the lake, between Jews and gentiles. The future is now open for both groups of people.

do any mighty work there, except putting his hands to a few sick people he healed (them)."

Leaving Nazareth, Jesus resumes his teaching in the surrounding villages. At the same time, however, he sends out the recently appointed twelve in companies of two in order to enter into his commission. Earlier, after withdrawing to the edge of the sea in the face of a plot to kill him (3:6), Jesus had summoned them for the purpose of founding a new Israel. Now, in view of his rejection in Nazareth and its implications for the future, he authorizes them to collaborate with him as apostles in the work of driving out demons and preaching repentance. Through their own practical experience they are to be trained for a ministry in the future when Jesus, as a result of a greater rejection, will no longer be with them.

Jesus' mission instructions are simple and explicit. The twelve are to take no bread, money, or traveling bag. Evidently nothing is to be stored up for any contingency. Consequently, there is no need for a knapsack or traveling bag. A staff is permitted, perhaps to facilitate walking on treacherous roads in mountainous regions. They should wear sandals, but they are not to carry an extra pair of underwear. Their mission life style is to be austere but not ascetic. Such unpretentious outfitting not only would differentiate them from preaching mendicants who begged from door to door and perhaps used their traveling bag to carry what they collected[84] but it would serve especially to identify more closely with the people they are evangelizing, specifically the lower-class masses of peasants and artisans residing in the rural countryside. Their identification with the poor is to be so intimate that they are to live with them in their homes during the time they are ministering in a particular place. "Wherever you enter into a house," Jesus says, "remain there until you go out from there. And whatever place does not receive you nor hear you, departing from there shake off the dust under your feet for a testimony to them." The gesture is to be a sign to those not ready to repent "so that they might recognize the seriousness of their action and perhaps repent even yet."[85]

Venturing forth on their own for the very first time, the apostles, as

84. Kee, *Community of the New Age*, 103.
85. Schweizer, *Good News*, 130.

they are designated in 6:30, carry out their commission with notable success. They preach repentance, they exorcise many demons, they anoint the sick with oil—an action that probably reflects the activity of the addressees, and therefore a feature of "the implied reader"—and so they set free and restore many people.

While the twelve, as representatives of the new people of God, are engaged in their brief internship, the narrator turns to the fate of John the Baptizer, who has been imprisoned since Jesus commenced his ministry in Galilee (1:14). The story of his martyrdom is a dramatic interlude; its arbitrary placement is emphasized by its easy omission without any apparent mutilation of the plot. Verse 30 picks up where 6:13 left off without any loss of continuity. Yet the insertion of the story into this context reinforces Jesus' foreboding sense of a more dreadful rejection and his consequential motive for equipping his followers for their own future ministry. John the Baptizer, by initiating the construction of the way, which led Jesus into repentance and a reordering of power, became his forerunner in life. Now he will also become his forerunner in death.

An extraordinary congruence unites them in the existential ambiguity of their individual identity. John is both Elijah and not Elijah: he is dressed like Elijah, but he does not eat Elijah's kind of food. Therefore, while on the one hand he is God's forerunner, he is on the other hand only a wilderness ascetic. In a similar vein, Jesus is both God's son and not God's son. By death and re-creation in the Jordan River he has become God's beloved son and is "seated on the right hand of Power." At the same time, as he himself acknowledges in 14:62, he is only coming to co-enthronement with the Creator, and therefore is only a forerunner of his disciples, whom he will lead into Jerusalem for a vicarious death experience.

It is this role of forerunner which John and Jesus share; each of them bears certain features of the Elijah typology. Consequently it is possible for an outsider like Herod Antipas, the tetrarch of Galilee—and others—to confuse them or even consider the one to be a reincarnation of the other: "And King Herod heard, for his name became manifest and they were saying, 'John the Baptizer has been raised from the dead and on account of this the mighty deeds of power are at work in him.' But others were saying, 'It is Elijah.' And others were saying, 'A prophet like one of the prophets.' Now Herod hearing was saying, 'The one whom I beheaded, John, he was raised!' "

The narrator's recounting of the legend of John's martyrdom shows marks of a lower-class origin. A comparison with Josephus's brief account of the Baptizer's death in *Antiquities* 18.116–19 poses alternate viewpoints. According to Josephus, Herod Antipas had John killed for political reasons, fearing that his influence with the masses might lead to open revolt. Mark's version, on the other hand, attributes his death to the injustices of a decadent ruling class and particularly a vicious upper-class woman.

While Josephus's account is probably more historically accurate, the specific contradictions within the Markan tradition that are often cited in order to establish its factual questionability indicate quite another intention. It is Herod himself who, "sending forth, took hold of John and bound him in prison." Yet, according to the narrator, "Herod feared John, knowing him (to be) a just and holy man, and he was protecting him, and hearing him was greatly disturbed, and yet he was hearing him gladly." Evidently Herod is not the villain, although he had John imprisoned. He acted "on account of Herodias, the wife of Philip, his brother, because he married her. For John was saying to Herod, 'It is not right for you to have your brother's wife.' " Whether Herod committed this injustice because of Herodias's influence or because his conscience was stung by John's ethical imperative is not clear. In any case, he is implicated in spite of his veneration of John. The real adversary is Herodias, who had a grudge against him and wanted to kill him and was not able. Like Elijah versus Jezebel, John has gained the enmity of an unscrupulous woman of the ruling class. Herod succeeds in defending John for a time, but he is basically a weak-willed, self-indulging profligate. When his scruples are overwhelmed by carousing and an erotic dance performed by Herodias's daughter, he foolishly promises the young girl, "Whatever you request, I will give you up to half of my kingdom." Such an incredible offer seems doubtful. It was not Herod's kingdom to give; it belonged to the Romans, and he was only their surrogate ruler. Moreover, an erotic dance by a young upper-class girl also appears to be highly unlikely. Banquets were restricted to men, and upper-class children, particularly young girls, were kept in discrete seclusion.[86] Nevertheless, ac-

86. Gideon Sjoberg, *The Pre-industrial City: Past and Present* (New York: Free Press, 1960), 176.

cording to the story Herod was overpowered by his intoxication and sexual excitement, and Herodias used this moment of weakness to gratify her hatred. Through her direction her daughter requests the head of the Baptizer. Herod, although grieved, is obliged to order the execution in order to avoid losing face; and the head of John is brought into the banquet on a platter, as though it were a piece of meat, and is given to the girl, who in turn hands it over to her mother. His corpse was entombed by his followers. All of these components of the legend, many of which are historically suspect, dramatize the injustices and the cruelties that the lower classes and their heroes suffer at the hands of their degenerate corrupt ruling elite.

The narrator resumes the account of Jesus' ministry by observing the return of "the apostles" from their mission: "They reported to him all the things which they did and which they taught." After they have shared their stories and experiences with him, Jesus invites them to accompany him into a desert place and rest awhile. For, as a result of their work, more people were being drawn into the orbit of Jesus' movement: "Many were coming and going, and they did not even have time to eat."

Going aboard "the boat"—the boat of Jesus!—they sail to a desert place to be alone. But there is no time for solitude. Many had noticed their departure, and guessing their destination, they were running by land from all cities, and they arrived ahead of them. Stepping out of the boat and observing the large crowd, Jesus "was moved with compassion for them, because they were like sheep not having a shepherd." Although weary with fatigue, "he began to teach them many things." What that included the narrator does not say.

Late in the day Jesus is reminded by his disciples that the people need food. "Dismiss them," the disciples urge, "so that, going off into the surrounding fields and villages, they may buy for themselves something they may eat." In response Jesus surprises them with the charge, "You give them (something) to eat!" In view of their remarkable fulfillment of the commission he had entrusted to them, his charge is natural and spontaneous. On their first mission they had enjoyed phenomenal success in driving out demons and healing the sick. Such outstanding participation in his power and sovereignty should also enable them to resolve this problem.

The level of their thinking is revealed by their reply, "Going off shall

we buy bread for two hundred denarii and give it to them to eat?"
Whether two hundred days' wages could purchase sufficient bread for
five thousand men, not to mention the women and children who may
be present, the narrator does not speculate. For Jesus the critical
situation provides an opportunity to demonstrate to his disciples the
extent of their participation in his authority. First, they must determine
how much food is actually available. Somehow, as if they had already
anticipated his inquiry, they know: five loaves and two fish. While the
disciples are organizing the crowd to recline on the grass in groups of
fifty and one hundred, Jesus multiplies the meager resources of bread
and fish. Looking up into heaven where, as he later reveals, he understands himself to be "seated on the right hand of power," he pronounces the blessing and begins to break the bread for distribution by
his disciples to the people. He repeats his eucharistic ritual with the
two fish. When all have eaten and have been satisfied, the leftovers are
gathered and twelve baskets are filled. Not only is there sufficient food
for this crowd; there is enough for all the tribes of Israel.

As soon as the meal is over, Jesus **compels** his disciples to embark
into the boat and to set out across the lake to Bethsaida. Evidently a
new area is to be opened to Jesus' ministry, for the destination he
prescribes is Bethsaida, a place that has not been named before by the
narrator. The disciples are to precede him and prepare the way for
him. For the first time they are going to cross the Sea of Galilee
without him. That is probably the reason why it is necessary for Jesus
to force them to embark into the boat. Previously he had always
accompanied them, and, when a storm arose, he exercised his authority to calm the wind and the sea. What will they do without him,
especially if their lives should be threatened again by the forces of
chaos?

While the disciples begin to row across the sea, Jesus dismisses the
crowd and ascends "into the mountain" in order to pray. This feature
of the implied reader is identical to that of 3:13. The mountain is not
named, even though the definite article is used in the prepositional
phrase. Perhaps this is the architectonic center on which a new people
of God was constituted by the New Human Being. Like this one, that
mountain was located near the sea. What Jesus is praying about or for
is not indicated, but it would seem appropriate for him to ascend the
Sinai-like mountain on which the new Israel was born in order to

intercede for his disciples who are crossing the sea without him and his fortifying presence. His concern for them is manifested in his descent from the mountain and his surveillance from the shore at dusk. The disciples have succeeded in reaching the middle of the lake, but their rowing against an adverse wind has exhausted them.[87] During the fourth watch, the darkest time of the night, Jesus approaches them walking on the sea; "and he was wanting to pass them by." In spite of all the difficulties that they are continuing to encounter, he does not wish to interfere. He is anxious about them, but he refuses to be paternalistic.[88] They must be trained for the future when he will no longer be with them, and their exercise of sovereignty and power as members of the new Israel will be essential for the continued expansion of God's rule. They have already engaged in independent action in his mission, they have proclaimed repentance, they have exorcised demons, they have healed the sick. Now it is imperative for them to learn the limits or boundaries of the authority Jesus wants to share with them as members of the new Israel.

The disciples, however, see Jesus walking on the sea and, imagining him to be a ghost, cry out in fear. According to Job 9:8 and 38:16, only God tramples the waves of the sea.[89] Obviously, in spite of all their experiences with Jesus—the stilling of the storm, the defeat of a legion of demons, the raising of the synagogue ruler's daughter, and the feeding of the multitudes—they are still unprepared for this ultimate manifestation of sovereignty.

Jesus immediately responds to their alarm: "Keep on being courageous! I am. Stop being afraid!" In his self-disclosure he does more than identify himself. The phrase *egō eimi*, usually translated "It is I" or "I am he," literally means "I am." The combination of the personal pronoun *egō* and the first person singular of the copula *eimi* indicates a moment of epiphany. In performing an act that traditionally is

---

87. Unfortunately the positive achievements of the disciples are too easily overlooked. If they did not cross the sea with the aid of a boat, at least they managed to reach the middle of the lake. Earlier they did succeed in their mission by exorcising demons and healing the sick with oil. Their failures may outweigh their successes, but the picture is not entirely negative, as Petersen ("The Composition of Mark 4:1—8:26," 209–14) and Malbon ("The Jesus of Mark and the Sea of Galilee," 377) convey it.

88. Compare Malbon, "The Jesus of Mark and the Sea of Galilee," 367 n. 14, for other interpretations.

89. See also Sir. 24:5–6.

limited to deity, Jesus reveals the identity and destiny of the New Human Being in whom the image of the Creator has been restored. To be divine offspring means nothing less than full participation in the limitless possibilities of God. This incredible realization of incarnation is articulated by Jesus in the divine affirmation, "I am." Walking on the sea, like Yahweh, he makes himself known to his followers with the same words of self-identification that Yahweh employed in the epiphany to Moses at the burning bush of Sinai in Exod. 3:14.

When Jesus climbs into the boat, the wind ceases. His reunion with his disciples as the bearer of God's presence effects both an inner and an outer calm. At the same time, this extraordinary experience leaves them profoundly unsettled: "They went absolutely out of their minds." But they do not grasp the significance of what they have witnessed, because, as the narrator explains by breaking into the story world (6:52), "they did not understand about the loaves, but their hearts had been hardened." Of course, the connection between the two is not immediately apparent, but evidently there is a relationship that the disciples have not grasped. The supreme sovereignty that Jesus demonstrates in one episode accounts for the other. His walking on the Sea of Galilee is not intended to prove his messiahship but to display the capabilities of God. If it is possible to feed many thousands by multiplying five loaves and two fish, it is equally possible to trample the waves of the sea; and conversely, if it is possible to trample the waves of the sea, it is equally possible to feed many thousands by multiplying five loaves and two fish. For the disciples the limitations by which they and their society define human existence have not yet been shattered.

Incompetence is added to the incomprehension of the disciples when they make for shore. Jesus had stipulated Bethsaida as their destination, but instead they arrive at Gennesaret and drop anchor there. Although they went off course, they did succeed in crossing the lake and reaching land. As they disembark, Jesus is quickly recognized by the local populace, and soon the whole region is electrified by the news of his unexpected appearance. Streaming from the surrounding countryside, the people bring their sick to him for healing and restoration. Sensing their needs, he remains among them, moving about from village to city to marketplace in order to make himself available to them. They present their sick to him or beg that they might simply touch the fringe of his cloak, "and as many as touched him were saved." In spite of the failure of his disciples and the miscarriage of his intentions, Jesus is able to continue his ministry in actualizing God's rule among the poor and the dispossessed.

UNDERMINING THE POLLUTION SYSTEM
(7:1—8:11) _____

Against this background of Jesus' popular ministry in and around Gennesaret the narrator reintroduces "the Pharisees" and "some of the scribes coming from Jerusalem." Both have manifested malevolence toward Jesus. The former joined in counsel with the Herodians in order to plot his destruction. The latter judged him to be an agent of Beelzebul in driving out demons. Now together they track him into the countryside for further investigation. The disciples' lack of ritual observance, eating bread with unwashed hands, provides the occasion for another direct confrontation. But before recounting the details of this controversy, the narrator enters the story to explain the Pharisaic observance of "the tradition of the elders" in the practice of ritual washing.

Not only the Pharisees but in fact all the Jews, it is noted, do not eat unless they first wash. To be Jewish means to wash! Indeed, cups, jugs, and kettles as well as hands are all subject to ritual cleansing. Whether the prepositional phrase "with fist" means what it says: to wash by turning the fist in the palm of the hand, or whether it is a textual corruption for "plunging the hand into water up to the wrist,"[90] or simply washing "properly,"[91] seems indeterminable. The criticism of their conduct, in any case, implies that the disciples are in grave danger of losing their Jewish identity, at least as it is being defined by the religious elite and their development of tradition.

The actual question, however, that the Pharisees and the scribes address to Jesus moves away from the specific infraction of ritual washing to the general issue of the oral law: "Why do your disciples not walk according to the tradition of the elders?" Although their query includes their initial objection, "but eat bread with impure

90. Matthew Black, *An Aramaic Approach to the Gospels and Acts*, 2d ed. (Oxford: Clarendon Press, 1954), 8–9.

91. Hermann L. Strack and Paul Billerbeck, *Kommentar zum Neuen Testament aus dem Talmud und Midrash* (Munich: C. H. Beck, 1922–28), 2:13–14.

hands," the real thrust of this controversy has become their nonobservance of the oral Torah. This body of tradition, maintained and developed alongside the Pentateuch, by the Pharisees—and after the destruction of Jerusalem by their heirs, the Tannaitic rabbis—was considered to be equally binding, because, like the written law, its origins were attributed to God, who had delivered it to Moses on Sinai.[92]

It is this fundamental issue of the oral law, the tradition of the elders, to which Jesus responds in 7:6–13. The particular incident that evoked this question, the disciples eating with unwashed hands, is not addressed until 7:14.

First, Jesus takes the offensive by quoting Isa. 29:13 for a bitter denunciation of their religious leaders:

> This people honors me with lips,
> But their heart remains far away from me.
> And they worship me in vain
> Teaching teachings (which are) commandments of human beings.

In Jesus' judgment the oral law, which was intended to serve as a fence around the written Torah and thereby to keep a human being far from transgression, annuls God's will. The korban institution of the Pharisaic tradition is cited as a specific example: "Moses said, 'Honor your father and mother,' and 'Let the one who speaks evil of father or mother surely die.' But you say, 'If any human being says to father or to mother, "Korban"—which is gift, whatever you are owed from me,' you no longer allow him to do anything for his father or mother." By declaring a particular possession to be dedicated to God, an individual is able to circumvent the material support of parents. In consequence Jesus concludes: "You make void the word of God by your tradition which you handed down." Moreover, this is not an isolated instance of nullifying God's law which the tradition of the elders perpetrates. "And you do many similar things," Jesus adds as a final censure. Their subversion of God's will invalidates both their authority and that of their tradition. Service to God cannot be disengaged from commitment to the fulfillment of genuine human need.

For a reply to the original criticism of the scribes and the Pharisees against the disciples' neglect of ritual washing Jesus summons the

---

92. Mishna, *Pirque Aboth* 1:1–2.

crowd. Again his concern for the masses is apparent. They too must hear the liberating word which he will speak on purity and pollution. Indeed, they especially must hear his manifesto because they are denigrated by the religious elite as the *am haaretz*, the polluted people of the land:

> Hear me all and understand.
> Nothing is outside a human being which, entering
>   into him is able to defile him.
> But the things coming out of a human being
>   are the things defiling the human being.

Subsequently, when Jesus is alone with his disciples in the privacy of a house, a setting somewhat similar to 4:10, they inquire about the meaning of "the parable" he has spoken. Once again their lack of understanding is evident, and he reproves them for it: "So you also are without understanding?" But clarification may be necessary in order to enable them to comprehend his startling invalidation of the pollution system which has defined their Jewish identity. His fundamental differentiation between the things that defile and the things that do not defile calls into question all casuistry on ritual and cultic purity. Participation in God's rule is not based on the religious observances of any kind, for they have no effect on the realities engendered by the human heart: evil thoughts, fornications, thefts, murders, adulteries, greed, wickedness, deceit, debauchery, an evil eye, blasphemy, arrogance, foolishness. All these evil things came out from within and defile the human being. Therefore, obligedness to any process of redemption that fosters an indebtedness to forms of piety and righteousness, erected and controlled by a religious hierarchy, in order to maintain a relationship with God is effectively canceled. The divine objective is to expunge the impurities of the heart in order to restore individual wholeness and social integration and transform the world of binary oppositions—constituted by pollution systems—into a new creation of the one and the many.

Jesus' subsequent departure from Galilee and his self-concealment in a house in the regions of Tyre should not be construed as a withdrawal in the face of renewed hostility from the religious establishment provoked by his radical teaching.[93] The verb "to withdraw"

---

93. This, however, is not the case in Matt. 15:21, where the verb *anachōrein* ("to withdraw") is used to denote withdrawal under threat.

(anachōrein) is not used in 7:24 as it was in 3:7, and there is no hint that Jesus is afraid of his enemies.[94] This entry into gentile territory is simply another attempt to find seclusion. Since he has not been successful in Galilee (6:31–33), the countryside of Tyre may provide the retreat he is seeking. Because it has been outside his sphere of activity—although people from Tyre and Sidon have been in the crowds to which he has ministered (3:8)—he may believe that he can remain unrecognized and enjoy a period of solitude. No mention is made of his disciples, although on the basis of 8:1 it would appear that they are accompanying him. However, the focus of the narrator is on Jesus alone.

"And entering into a house he was wanting no one to know, and he was unable to escape notice." Even in the regions of Tyre he is unable to hide and be alone. He is sought out by a Greek mother, a Syrophoenician by birth, who throws herself at his feet in order to intercede for her demon-possessed daughter. Jesus' response to her is proverbial in character: "First let the children be satisfied, for it is not good to take the bread of the children and throw (it) to the house dogs." A mother must care for her children before any considerations can be given to household pets.

In view of Jesus' earlier crossing of the Sea of Galilee in order to extend his ministry into gentile country and his exorcism of the Gerasene demoniac, his response to the Greek woman is unexpected and surprising. Why should he now be so concerned about "the children," that is, God's own people, the Jews? Is their need more acute and urgent than that of the gentiles? If the Jewish pollution system is no longer valid for him, then the benefits of God's rule belong equally to both Jews and gentiles. Moreover, if he is hesitant to dispense its benefits to gentiles, why enter into gentile territory even if it is to seek seclusion?

Jesus' proverb of satisfying the needs of the children first does not exclude the Greek woman and her daughter. Indeed, his words hint that they will have their turn.[95] Nevertheless, as a metaphor the

94. As T. A. Burkill (*New Light on the Earliest Gospel* [Ithaca, N.Y., and London: Cornell University Press, 1972], 67–68) says, "[This] is not the forced exile of a refugee who has dealings with a foreign woman because he is no longer able to serve his own people in Galilee." See also pp. 68–69.

95. Ibid, 78.

proverb conveys a Jewish perspective of the gentiles that Jesus utilizes in this context in order to express the priority of his ministry in spite of his earlier and later efforts to include the gentiles in his establishment of God's rule. As racist as it is, it conveys the reality of "the Jews first," which the apostle Paul also acknowledged in his gentile evangelization.[96] However, it is not a racism that is to be ascribed to Jesus, for it does not arise out of a pollution system. His previous encounter with the religious elite and his emancipation of his disciples and the crowd from the purity code of Judaism make it quite clear that he does not espouse any kind of Jewish racial superiority. Historically speaking, however, they are first. The promises of God's coming reign were first communicated to them, and they have been waiting for their fulfillment for a long time.[97]

The Greek mother, however, refuses to be put off or turned away by Jesus' passionate dedication to the fulfillment of Jewish need. She affirms the validity of his proverb by acknowledging Jewish priority.[98] She does not want to deprive the children of their bread. But her daughter can also share in the benefits of God's rule immediately— without waiting for her turn—because the house dogs eat the crumbs that fall from the table while the children are eating.[99]

She has prefaced her remarkable response with the title "Lord," and thereby she becomes the first and only person in the Gospel to address Jesus with this epithet.[100] Neither Jesus' disciples nor the Jews whom he insists on ministering to first and foremost ever acknowledge him in this manner. While this appellation may be typical of the gentile world to which she belongs, it is not simply to be translated as "Sir." Its

96. See Rom. 1:16; 2:9–10; 3:1–2.

97. Burkill (*New Light*, 78) has recognized that "Jesus remained consistently in harmony with his messianic vocation to his own people, ever recognizing that the mission was exclusively a mission to them." For Mark's Gospel this may be somewhat exaggerated, but it certainly holds true for Matthew.

98. I.e., if the word "yes" *(nai)* is genuine. In the manuscript tradition it is omitted by P45, W, the Koridethi, D, and others; and it is not found anywhere else in the Gospel. See Burkill, *New Light*, 72 n. 3.

99. The woman's response employs the present tense which also denotes linear action and may be translated into English by using the periphrastic: "The house dogs under the table are eating from the crumbs of the children."

100. A number of ancient manuscripts, especially in the Italian family, include "Lord" in the address of Blind Bartimaeus to Jesus in 10:51, probably as a substitute reading to interpret "Rabbouni."

employment here is determined, of course, by the narrator and therefore should be construed according to its usage and meaning in the story world of the Gospel. In contrast to the disciples, she alone appears to grasp the distinctive sovereignty of Jesus as the New Human Being who is simultaneously God's offspring. Used sixteen times in the Gospel, the title, as already noted, is ambiguous. In 11:9; 12:9, 11, 29–30, 36; and 13:20 it clearly refers to God, but in 2:28; 7:28; and 12:36–37 it designates Jesus. All of the other occurrences are equivocal and may be interpreted to refer to both, especially in 1:3; 5:19; and 11:3. The New Human Being who comes "in the name of the Lord," who is "seated on the right hand of Power," participates in the Lord's sovereignty and therefore also bears the Lord's title.

Jesus is obliged to yield to this Greek mother in view of the logic of her response: "Because of this word go! The demon has gone out of your daughter." His declaration is enough for her. She has acknowledged his lordship, and she believes it. She does not demand that he accompany her. With confidence in his word she leaves him and "returning to her house she found the child lying on the couch and the demon gone out."

The travel that Jesus subsequently undertakes has been misconstrued by many interpreters who have raised the question of the accuracy of the author's knowledge of Syro-Palestinian geography. According to 7:31, "Coming out again from the districts of Tyre he went through Sidon to the Sea of Galilee up into the middle of the districts of the Decapolis." Jesus is returning to his home province by way of an extensive detour which, in fact, takes him in the opposite direction, that is, farther north, and then leads him through the gentile cities of the Decapolis around to the eastern side of the Sea of Galilee and eventually across the lake into the regions of Dalmanoutha (8:10). His objective can only be deeper penetration into gentile territory.[101] As a result of his encounter with the Syrophoenician woman, he is motivated to expand his mission more extensively among the pagan gentiles.

Somewhere in this area of southern Syria—no precise location is given—Jesus is confronted with a deaf-mute. They bring to him a deaf

---

101. See Burkill, *New Light*, 73–74. Burkill recognizes that Mark's knowledge of geography is not deficient but believes that the author "had apostolic missionaries in mind."

person with a speech impediment, and they beg him to put his hand on the person. Even among pagans Jesus continues his practice of avoiding publicity: "And taking him away from the crowd alone he cast his fingers into his (her) ears and spitting he touched his (her) tongue, and looking up into heaven he groaned and says to him (her), 'Ephphatha.'" In his private treatment of applying saliva to the tongue, inserting his fingers in the ears and uttering a command, Jesus acts like a physician utilizing the technique of healing that seems to have been common and widespread among the lower classes. But two actions are included in his treatment that do not appear to be characteristic of the general practice of medicine: "looking up into heaven" and "groaning," and they are especially meaningful in this context. The latter discloses Jesus' emotions as he ministers to this gentile. In earlier episodes he had been moved with compassion to heal, to teach, and to provide food. Here his "groaning" or "sighing" is an expression of anguish evoked by the reality of the moment and linked to his attendant acts of "looking up to heaven" and uttering the command, "Be opened!" But what is to be opened? The ears of the deaf-mute, of course, into which he has thrust his fingers! But the indirect object of the verb "he says" is a pronoun that may refer back to the deaf-mute or more immediately to "the heaven." Since therefore the antecedent of the pronoun is ambiguous, Jesus appears to be addressing his command "Be opened!" to heaven, into which he is peering. For, overcome with distress at the gentile predicament of defective hearing and speaking and therefore also a deficiency of genuine communication, which is represented by this deaf-mute, he summons God's rule to come to the gentiles, as it has for the Jews and the distinctively human capacities of hearing and speaking to be restored to this individual for the beginnings of new communication and community.

Ironically, however, both the healed deaf-mute and his or her companions are admonished to maintain silence. This, of course, is in keeping with Jesus' general policy of no publicity. No disclosure of his mighty works is to be made until his ministry has culminated in his resurrection from the dead. At Easter the imperatives "Go and tell!" will finally be issued.

But new capacities for speaking and hearing are not to be stifled. Jesus' injunction to remain silent is ignored. Those who have been involved in this incident find it impossible to restrain themselves. "The more he ordered them, even more they were proclaiming. And they were overwhelmed beyond measure saying, 'He has done all things well, and he makes the deaf hear and the mute speak.' " It is only here in the Gospel that the narrator employs an adverb in the superlative degree, *hyperperissōs*, meaning "beyond all measure," or, more literally, "superabundantly." Such is the intensity of the gentile response to Jesus' work; and the accompanying affirmation, "He has done all things well" is a confession of faith that seems to be based on more extensive activity among these people.

That may be intended to include the event that follows, the feeding of the four thousand. Once again Jesus is in—or, more literally, on—a desert (8:4) with a large crowd, which, in view of this context, must be gentile. The distinctive word *spyris*, which signifies a "mat-basket"[102] and sometimes, as in Acts 9:25, is large enough to contain a human being, supports this identification, for it stands in contrast to the *kophinoi*, or wickerwork baskets that were used by the Jews and, according to 6:43, served as the containers for the leftover morsels of the first feeding. The intensity of the gentile response, which the narrator noted in 7:37—"they were overwhelmed beyond measure"— has expressed itself in their continuation with Jesus for three days without food. "And some of them," as he acknowledges, "are from far away."[103] Evidently they have accompanied him on his return to his home province. The location of this desert where the feeding takes place is not given. Previously Jesus had demonstrated his compassion for the Jewish masses who had followed him into the wilderness by providing them with a meal. On this occasion he expresses his compassion for a gentile crowd by multiplying bread and fish for them: "because they continue with me already three days and they have nothing they might eat. And if I dismiss them hungry into their homes, they will give out on the way; and some of them are from far away."

Why does Jesus wait three days in order to provide a meal for these enthusiastic and devoted gentiles? Earlier he had fed the Jewish multitudes on the very day they had joined him in the wilderness. Is there any particular significance attached to the time reference "three days," which does not occur in the previous feeding story? Perhaps Jesus'

---

102. Taylor, *St. Mark*, 360.

103. See F. W. Danker, "Mark 8:3," *JBL* 82 (1963): 215–16. Danker also relates the phrase "from far away" to gentile followers of Jesus.

forthcoming threefold announcement to his disciples that the New Human Being will be resurrected after three days may throw some light on the meaning of this time period.

In this feeding, after three days of accompanying Jesus without food, the gentiles will experience a foretaste of the eschatological reality of Easter. They will be renewed by the bread and the fish for their continuation "on the way." The employment of this phrase, "on the way," corresponds to its use in 10:52 where it is linked to the discipleship of Bartimaeus. The gentiles, by attaching themselves to Jesus, will become involved, no less than the Jews, in a new exodus and, by continuing on the way, will eventually be drawn into the construction of the way.

To feed these thousands of people Jesus once again utilizes the resources at hand, this time seven loaves and a few small fish. As in his earlier manner, which he will repeat at the celebration of the Passover, he takes the bread and the fish and with a thanksgiving breaks them and gives them to his disciples for distribution to the people. When the people have eaten and been satisfied, the morsels that are left over are gathered into seven "mat-baskets." The seven here, in contrast to the twelve of the Jewish feeding, may symbolize eschatological completeness. For now, in representative fashion at least, by the inclusion of the gentiles in the new exodus, the fullness of God's rule has been realized.

CRISIS IN DISCIPLESHIP
(8:11—9:50)

After dismissing the crowd, Jesus leads his disciples into the boat and with them crosses the Sea of Galilee to the district of Dalmanoutha on the west shore of the lake. Once again both sides of the Sea of Galilee are joined together by his activity of constituting God's rule.[104] But no ministry is possible in this particular region. Here he reencounters the Pharisees whose "tradition of the elders" and its pollution system he had rejected in a previous confrontation. They not only want to continue their debate with him, they demand a sign from heaven for his

104. Once again see Kelber, *The Kingdom in Mark*, 62–63; and Malbon, "The Jesus of Mark and the Sea of Galilee," 373.

self-validation. Jesus, however, refuses to legitimate himself or his ministry with a token of divine endorsement. If his works and his words are not already a heavenly affirmation of the arrival of God's rule, how can the test of a special sign be convincing or conclusive? "And groaning deeply in his spirit he says, 'Why does this generation seek a sign? I'll say "Amen" to you if a sign will be given to this generation!'"

Once again Jesus' emotions have surfaced. The anguish that he feels in this encounter with hostile unbelief, however, is greater than his earlier distress among the gentiles (7:34), because of the apparent hopelessness of the condition he perceives. He is being tempted to authenticate his deeds and words which already bear witness to their heavenly origin. If such a token were granted, it would abolish the humanly indispensable necessity for vulnerability and faith. Moreover, he would be acknowledging the authority and superiority of these religious elite; and his fulfillment of their need for certification and control would destroy any humanness they still retained. An unusual grammatical construction in which the apodosis or consequent clause of the conditional sentence is deliberately omitted: "Amen [I say to you], if a sign will be given to this generation!" expresses Jesus' emphatic denial of a sign. C. F. D. Moule offers an example of how such a conditional sentence as this might be completed: "I'm damned if I will . . . give a sign to this generation."[105] All that he can do is to leave them to their own reflection. He reembarks and recrosses the lake to the other side with his disciples.

If these guardians of religion continue to be unrepentant outsiders, his disciples, on the other hand, pose little contrast by their own inability to see, hear, and understand. When Jesus charges them to beware of "the leaven of the Pharisees and the leaven of Herod," they reason among themselves that he is reprimanding them for their negligence in remembering to take along a supply of bread. They are unaware, as the narrator observes, that they already have "one loaf" in the boat with them. Although the identification is not made explicit, the signified of the verbal sign "one loaf" or "one bread" connotes Jesus himself.[106] This allusion is already implicit in the eucharistic

---

105. C. F. D. Moule, *An Idiom Book of New Testament Greek*, 2d ed. (Cambridge: Cambridge University Press, 1960), 11.

106. So also Burkill, *New Light*, 84–85.

character of the previous feeding episodes. As the dispenser of bread to the multitudes, he also is the bread, and those who partake of this one loaf are joined together to form one body. The disciples' failure to recognize the "one loaf" in the boat with them simultaneously prevents them from grasping the meaning of Jesus' warning to look out for the leaven of the Pharisees and the leaven of Herod. Previously they had not comprehended the sovereignty that Jesus had exercised in walking on the sea, because, as the narrator commented, "They did not understand about the loaves, but their hearts had been hardened." Their lives are circumscribed by their obsession for control and self-sufficiency. Enslaved to necessity, their fear of contingency and death limits their openness to the possibilities of God. Unaware, they submit themselves to the boundaries of human existence as they are defined by their society and particularly those who are advantaged by them, Herod and the Pharisees.[107] Their leaven, the very opposite of the one loaf and all that it means, signifies the forces of necessity and the forms of dependency that imprison human beings and prevent them from realizing their divine-human potentiality.

Astonishingly, in spite of their continuation with Jesus, the disciples seem to have learned very little: "Don't you remember when I broke the five loaves for the five thousand? How many full wickerwork baskets of crumbs did you take up? . . . When the seven for the four thousand, the fullness of how many mat-baskets of crumbs did you take up?" At this point Jesus' aggravation with his disciples reaches its highest pitch. Although they are insiders to whom the mystery of God's rule has been given (4:10), there appears to be little difference between them and the Pharisees. "Don't you know yet or understand?" he asks them. "Do you have your heart hardened?" And in the words of Isa. 6:9, which previously he had applied to the outsiders, he confronts them with their own blindness and deafness: "Having eyes don't you see? And having ears don't you hear?" And he kept on saying to them, "Don't you understand yet?"[108]

---

107. If this is what Petersen ("The Composition of Mark 4:1—8:26," 211) means when he construes "leaven" as a metaphor for understanding things in human terms, I would assent. But he is too vague. What is the meaning of "human terms"?

108. Petersen ("The Composition of Mark 4:1—8:26," 208 n 48) is probably right when he says that "when the dust has settled on the discussion of the theme of the disciples' incomprehension, we will probably find that it, not the 'messianic secret,' is the fundamental theme of the gospel."

This lack of perspicuity, of genuine seeing, is mirrored in the following story of Jesus' restoration of sight to a blind human being in two stages. The earlier healing of a deaf-mute in gentile territory, which intimated the opening of heaven for pagans, had culminated in an overwhelming response of affirmation: "He has done all things well." This incident, somewhat parallel in structure, signals the necessity of a second round of treatment in order to enable the disciples to see clearly, while at the same time it anticipates the inadequacy of Simon Peter's confession in 8:29.

Ironically they have arrived at Bethsaida, the destination Jesus had prescribed immediately after the feeding of the five thousand. It is a fitting context in which to display the incompetence and inadequacy of the disciples, specifically their inability to see clearly and the consequences that result from it. In this humorous episode, an unidentified individual, whose sexual identity is not disclosed, is presented to Jesus for healing. As before, he leads the person out of the village in order to ensure privacy. In view of the condition of blindness, it is necessary to guide him or her by hand. The same treatment of applying saliva and laying on hands is used. Spitting into his (her) eyes, placing his hands on him (her), he asks, "Do you see anything?" The sight, however, that is gained is imperfect. Looking up, he (she) was saying, "I see human beings, like trees I see them walking." The awkward grammar and syntax of the Greek text makes a literal translation impossible. Perhaps they are intended by the narrator to express the excitement and confusion that is being experienced by the one whose vision is being restored. The conjunction *hoti*, which stands at the beginning of the second clause, may be causal, meaning "for," or it may introduce a second response as direct discourse, especially if the imperfect tense, "he (she) was saying," is considered to be iterative. While the excitement of seeing is verbalized in the announcement, "I see human beings," a disturbing but also amusing disorientation is disclosed in the additional utterance, "Like trees I see them walking." Trees do not walk! That human beings could look like walking trees is an indication of the absurdity of this intermediate stage of seeing.

Jesus therefore must place his hands on these eyes again, and only then, as the narrator indicates in a somewhat redundant manner, he (she) opened his (her) eyes widely and was restored, and he (she) began looking at all things clearly. It is this capacity of sight resulting from a second round of treatment—looking at all things clearly—that the disciples need, especially as the issue of Jesus' identity and concomitantly their own self-understanding becomes more critical.

The individual who has gained this clarity of vision is sent home but forbidden to enter the village. Again, Jesus wants to ensure secrecy. The village folk, of course, will learn of this healing soon enough without immediate publication. But for the story world of the Gospel the work of Jesus must first be consummated before the prohibition to speak will be lifted.

Jesus leaves the area and with his disciples proceeds into the villages of Caesarea of Philip. While they are "on the way" in the vicinity of this citadel of political power, constructed under the Herodian king Philip and named in honor of the Roman emperor, Jesus inquires about the popular views of his identity: "Who do human beings say I am?" The beliefs that the disciples cite are identical to the three posed earlier in the context of John the Baptizer's martyrdom (6:15). The resemblance between Jesus and John has led some to believe that he is the Baptizer raised from the dead. Others consider him to be Elijah, who has returned for a second career. Still others regard him simply as a prophet. These are the views of those who have observed him and his work from a distance.

More important, however, is the judgment of those who have been close to Jesus, who have attached themselves to him as his disciples, and finally the addressees of the Gospel who have been interacting with this story world: "But who do you say I am?" Although Jesus has been addressed with various titles—"the holy one of God," "the son of God," "teacher," "son of the most high God," "Lord"—he has made no effort to elicit a christological identification of himself from his followers. He has revealed his self-understanding by referring to himself as "the son of the Human Being" or "the New Human Being," who has authority on earth to act on behalf of God.

At the beginning of his ministry those whom he called were not attracted to him for christological reasons. There is no evidence that they had any knowledge of his distinctive identity as the New Human Being, God's beloved son. The only appellation they have used to address him so far has been "teacher" (4:38). Originally they responded to his millennial proclamation of the good news of God and his invitation to become "fishers of human beings." Throughout their discipleship they have witnessed the actualization of God's rule: demons have been exorcised, the sick have been healed, the dead have been raised, and multitudes of poor and hungry people have been fed. Word and deed have been joined together by Jesus. Indissolubly linked to the good news of God both as its proclaimer and its fulfiller, Jesus embodies both the eschatological and the christological expectations of Israel.

But to what extent have the disciples become aware of this, both those in the story world and those outside the story world whom the omniscient narrator is addressing? How do they associate Jesus with the millennial dreams which he has aroused within them and which he has been actualizing before their eyes? Who do they think he is, and what is their attendant self-understanding as his followers? They had raised the christological question for the first time as a response to his awesome display of sovereignty in stilling the storm: "Who then is this, for even the wind and the sea obey him?" Now they appear to have an answer, and Peter steps forward as their spokesperson to articulate it: "You are the Messiah."

Jesus' immediate response is censure, not only of Peter but of all the disciples on whose behalf he has spoken: He rebuked them that they speak to no one about him. The force of the verb "rebuke *(epitiman)* is illuminated by its earlier use in the exorcism stories in which the unclean spirits and demons were rebuked to prevent them from making him known. Here, however, Jesus is not concerned about concealing his true identity. Instead, he is exercised about a fundamental misunderstanding of who he is and what he is doing. Such an erroneous perspective must not be publicized.

The Messiah or Christ title, as its history indicates, is essentially elitist. Throughout the Old Testament and into the so-called intertestamental period it expressed both the popular kingship of the lower classes and the royal ideology of the ruling class.[109] It denotes a king who is seated at the pinnacle of the socioeconomic pyramid over which he rules. To perpetuate his reign he maintains an army, collects taxes, and supports a temple that is serviced by a priesthood committed to the preservation of the divine order of his rule.[110] Like David, who is

109. Richard A. Horsley, "Popular Messianic Movements Around the Time of Jesus," *CBQ* 46/3 (1984): 471–95.

110. See 1 Sam. 8:10–18; 2 Sam. 7:12–13.

the prototype, he may be a divinely anointed regent dedicated to social and economic justice. But the structures of the society that he governs are vertical and therefore, because they foster oppression and dispossession, are dehumanizing.

The rule of God that Jesus is establishing as the New Human Being is a new moral order, horizontal in structure and therefore essentially egalitarian, in which human destiny will be realized both individually and corporately. If, therefore, Peter's confession is to be retained, it must be filled with new content.

Jesus began to teach them that it is necessary for the New Human Being "to suffer many things, and to be rejected by the elders and the chief priests and the scribes and to be killed and after three days to rise up." Up to this point in the narrative world of the Gospel, Jesus has linked the New Human Being to lordship and authority (2:10, 28). Now, however, in response to his disciples' messianic confession, he introduces a polarity that is intrinsic to the identity of the New Human Being: "It is necessary for the Human Being to suffer many things." On the one hand, the New Human Being is co-enthroned with the Creator and therefore is co-bearer of the Creator's sovereignty. On the other hand, the New Human Being is subject to suffering and death, because he is vulnerable to all the realities of human existence, both good and evil, both happiness and pain, as they may be experienced in genuinely open relationships with other human beings. Nevertheless, life, not death, is supreme, because its source is the Creator to whom the New Human Being is horizontally joined. And even if he is killed, he will rise again. The destiny of the New Human Being therefore is irrevocable. Nothing and no one can prevent the fulfillment of this New Humanity and its attendant reality of God's rule in the world.

Therefore, if Jesus is the Messiah, as Peter and his fellow disciples have confessed, he is the Messiah only equivocally. He has divine sovereignty as God's surrogate, but his immediate destiny is suffering and dying, not the splendor and glory of a king. Moreover, his suffering and death will occur at the hands of the ruling elite who occupy the positions of power and privilege at the summit of the Jewish pyramid: the elders, the chief priests, and the scribes. They will reject him and deliver him to the Romans for execution precisely because the rule of God which he is establishing will eventually abolish the moral order which they attribute to divine origin and which they safeguard with the power of capital punishment.

Jesus' recognition of the elitist character of the disciples' confession proves to be unmistaken. Suffering and death do not belong to their understanding of messiahship. Peter especially rejects it. Reaching vigorously and independently, he draws Jesus aside and rebukes him. He may be aware of Jesus' relationship to the eschatological reality of God's rule, but his conception of the kingship that Jesus will exercise as the Christ is grandiose. In view of the sovereignty that Jesus has displayed, his destiny must be unequivocally glorious.

It is necessary therefore for Jesus to neutralize Peter's censure with an open and forceful counterrebuke that all the disciples are to hear: "Get away from behind me, Satan, for you do not think the things of God but the things of human beings." This is not the kind of discipleship to which Peter has been called. The Messiah Christology that he confesses and that simultaneously informs his self-understanding cannot be correlated with God's will. It is of human origin, and Jesus considers it to be equivalent to a temptation of Satan. As long as Peter insists on this definition of the Christ, he is representing the evil lord; and there is no place in Jesus' following for him.

The only kind of messianic confession that is acknowledged here is that which leads the disciples to an appropriation of a self-understanding that corresponds to the distinctive character of God's rule and its correlate Christology. Jesus proceeds to articulate it clearly for his followers, but, because of its fundamental importance for authentic discipleship, he summons the crowd to hear it as well: If anyone wants to come after me, let her (him) deny herself (himself) and take up her (his) cross and follow me. The way into the reality of God's rule begins with death, as it did for Jesus himself. And it is as complete a death experience as his was, inclusive of the social, economic, political, cultural, and religious realities of human existence in society. It is a death experience that terminates all participation in the "activities, moral rules and assumptions about power"[111] which belong to the redemptive process of society. Like crucifixion, therefore, it is a death experience that is slow, painful, and ostensibly full of shame, for it

---

111. Burridge, *New Heaven, New Earth*, 6.

involves the negation of values that are propagandized by the upper class.

But whoever loses her (his) life "on account of me and the gospel will save it." In these words the identification between Jesus and the good news of God's rule is explicit, but it is Jesus in his fundamental identity as the New Human Being, as 8:38 indicates, who leads the way into a reordering of reality where "being" and not "having" determines human self-worth. Life prevails beyond the death experience of taking up the cross and following Jesus, indeed, life that is eternal because it is attained through re-creation by God's Breath and incorporation into the never-ending life of God's ultimate offspring, the New Human Being.[112]

Therefore the kind of response that human beings make to the New Human Being, and concomitantly to the new order of God's rule which he inaugurates, will determine their destiny: For whoever is ashamed of me and my words in this adulterous and sinful generation, the Human Being will also be ashamed of him (her) when he comes in the glory of his father with the holy angels. In effect, they will be their own judge, for the decisions they make in the present will govern their fate in the future when the **parousia** of the Human Being will take place.[113]

More immediately, however, the rule of God will be established "in power" (9:1). Throughout Jesus' ministry this eschatological reality exists only insofar as it is linked to his career as the New Human Being, and when he dies in crucifixion it will cease to exist. The phrase "the rule of God in power" stands in contrast to the simple use of "the rule of God" which the narrator uniformly employs throughout the Gospel

112. Perhaps it is time to say that the excellent survey of "The Use of *Bar Enosh/Bar Nasha* in Jewish Aramaic," by Géza Vermès, Appendix E in *An Aramaic Approach to the Gospels and Acts*, by Matthew Black, 3d ed. (Oxford: Clarendon Press, 1967), 310–28, as comprehensive as it is, is thoroughly positivistic in its analysis. A sociological perspective on the various texts he examines is lacking. In Dan. 7:13–27 the employment of *Bar Nasha* is both eschatological or more precisely millennial *and* corporate (as 7:27 indicates). Both dimensions are expressed in Jesus' appropriation of the phrase as a title in Mark's story world. Unfortunately the same holds true for Barnabas Lindars in his comprehensive study of "the Son of Man" in *Jesus Son of Man: A Fresh Examination of the Son of Man Sayings in the Gospels in the Light of Recent Research* (Grand Rapids: Wm. B. Eerdmans, 1983). Lindars also does not utilize sociological theory, especially drawn from the sociology of millennialism, in order to perceive the distinctive millenarian character of the title as the reality of "the One and the Many." See Burridge, *New Heaven, New Earth*, 104–14.

113. This reality is the focus of Jesus' teaching in Mark 13. See below, pp. 196–202.

and must refer to the realization of a new level or more intense degree of this reality, specifically its ontological or objective establishment at Easter. Because of its intimate connection with the person of Jesus as the New Human Being, his transcendence in and by his resurrection from the dead will constitute God's rule in power forever. And it will happen in the lifetime of his disciples and the crowd who have been listening to him. To both, Jesus says, "Amen I say to you that there are some of these standing here who will by no means taste of death until they see the rule of God having come in power."

This is the significance of the story of the transfiguration which follows. The unveiling of the apotheosis of the New Human Being through a metamorphosis is an anticipation of Easter and its consolidation of the new creation. "After six days," or, in other words, on the seventh day, a time reference that intimates completion or fulfillment, Jesus selects three disciples, Peter, James, and John, to represent his community of followers and to accompany him up into a very high mountain privately alone[114] in order to share his glimpse of the future. No new covenant is to be enacted on this Sinai-like architectonic center. Higher than the earlier mountain on which the new Israel was called into being (3:13), it serves as the site of the revelation of the deity of the New Human Being that has been concealed in the "clay pot" of Jesus' flesh-and-blood body.[115] In view of the forthcoming passion, which Jesus has just announced, a preview of the future must be disclosed: "And he was transformed before them, and his clothes became very shining white such as a bleacher on earth is unable to make so white."

In this momentary metamorphosis the essence of Jesus' identity is unveiled: what he is now, but also what will be revealed more fully in the future. He is the offspring of God! After his re-creation by God's Spirit at his baptism, the Heavenly Voice had called him into being as "my beloved son." His mighty works have manifested the sovereignty that belongs to him as the New Human Being who has transcended his Adamic origin. Now for the first and only time in the story world of the Gospel three of his disciples finally capture a glimpse of who Jesus

114. Mark is deliberately redundant here to emphasize the exclusiveness of this event.

115. See Paul's understanding of metamorphosis in 2 Cor. 4:7–12.

is and what destiny awaits him, in spite of all that he will endure during his passion.

To provide additional affirmation, Moses and Elijah, the two great representatives of the Law and the Prophets, join them on this mountain summit. In their careers both of them had ascended the original architectonic center of Israel in order to be in the presence of God. Since they had not died but, according to tradition,[116] had been assumed into heaven, they are able to return and by their presence testify to the authenticity of the one whom the Law and the Prophets anticipated. Although they speak with Jesus, nothing of the conversation among them is reported. Evidently it is their appearance that is of consequence, and in and of itself it must signify their confirmation of Jesus and the New Human Being.

Astonishingly, however, Peter does not seem to grasp the meaning of what he has been witnessing. In spite of Jesus' metamorphosis and its disclosure of his apotheosis, he thoughtlessly volunteers the construction of three booths. "Rabbi," he exclaims,[117] "it is good for us to be here, and let us make three tents, one for you and one for Moses and one for Elijah." By placing Jesus alongside these giants of old Israel, Peter, whose earlier confession of Jesus as the Messiah had been repudiated, is insinuating a new christological identification. If Jesus is not the Christ he and his fellow disciples had envisioned, the validation of Moses and Elijah must indicate that he is in their company and of their stature. Indeed, perhaps he is the one anticipated as the last prophet of history, God's immediate forerunner who fulfills the predictions of Deut. 18:15 and Mal. 3:1 and 4:5–6.

In order to avoid any new misunderstanding of Jesus' identity, the omniscient storyteller interrupts the narrative in order to inject a comment for the benefit of the addressees of the Gospel: "For he did not know what he was speaking for they had become terrified." Peter's incompetence persists, but now as the result of fear.

For final clarification and, at the same time, for ultimate legitimation, God intervenes. It is the second divine acknowledgment of Jesus'

116. See 2 Kings 2:11; *Assumption of Moses*; and Josephus, *Antiquities* 4.326.

117. In Mark's story world only the two disciples who renounce Jesus, Peter and Judas, address Jesus as "rabbi." See 11:21; 14:45. Other disciples and the ruling elite of Jerusalem use "teacher."

heavenly origin: "This is my beloved son, hear him!" While the first
was communicated to him alone during his baptism in the Jordan
River, this one is addressed to Peter, James, and John in their capacity
as witnesses and representatives of the body of disciples. The auditory
experience of divine endorsement is added to the sight of Jesus' transformation. Perhaps this more immediate apprehension of his identity
and its heavenly authentication will remove their deficiencies of seeing
and hearing.

To ensure transparency, Moses and Elijah withdraw: "And suddenly
looking about they no longer saw anyone except Jesus alone with
them." The unveiling of the cloud, perhaps an allusion to the coming of
one like a human being on the clouds of heaven of Dan. 7:13, reveals
only Jesus as the object of the Heavenly Voice's certification. For the
disciples and especially Peter, there can be no misconstruction: Jesus
transcends their classification of him with the greatest prophets of
Israel. His teaching therefore also transcends that of these two representatives of the Law and the Prophets, and the disciples are exhorted
to "Hear him."

During their descent from the mountain Jesus gives strict orders not
to share this experience of his transfiguration until "the Human Being
rises up from the dead." His admonition reinforces the significance
that his metamorphosis has for his resurrection and its attendant
establishment of the rule of God in power. The divine enthronement of
Jesus as the New Human Being, unveiled in the transfiguration, will be
reflected on Easter morning by the youth inside the tomb, seated on
the right hand and wearing a white robe (16:5).

The discussion of what "to rise from the dead" means, initiated by
the disciples, generates no clarity for them. Jewish millennialism links
the resurrection of the dead to the apocalyptic event of God's coming;
and the latter, according to the interpretation of the scribes, must be
preceded by the messenger or forerunner, Elijah. How, then, can Jesus
speak about the New Human Being rising from the dead when, as far
as the disciples can discern, Elijah has not yet appeared? He affirms
this aspect of the eschatology of the scribes: "Elijah indeed coming
first will restore all things!" "But," he continues, "I say to you, Elijah
in fact has come, and they did to him such things as they were wanting,
even as it has been written of him."

No further elucidation is offered to clarify this enigmatic assertion.

Elijah has come! Consequently, therefore, the prophecies of Mal. 3:1 and 4:5–6 have been fulfilled, and the viewpoint of the scribes has been corroborated. But precisely how and when this happened Jesus does not specify. His vague characterization of that event, however, alludes to an identification with the career of the Baptizer. John, as the addressees of the Gospel already have become aware, is Elijah, who has returned for a second career to serve as God's forerunner. His clothing of camel's hair and leather belt identifies him with the great prophet. Yet at the same time the congruence is ambiguous. For John is also not Elijah but only a wilderness sojourner who eats grasshoppers and wild honey. Consequently, in view of his equivocal identity, Jesus can only offer his disciples an allusion to the Baptizer: "They did to him such things as they were wanting, even as it has been written of him." But it is enough to indicate that their millennial expectations are being fulfilled and the end is at hand.

In this context of millennial eschatology Jesus reintroduces his recently formulated teaching of the suffering and dying of the New Human Being. What relevance does it have for the termination of the old order of reality and the reconstitution of all things? Why does Jesus refer to it in the middle of the discussion of "rising from the dead" and the necessity of Elijah's preparatory appearance? The punctuation of the Greek text is problematic. Jesus seems to be raising a critical question in the light of his transfiguration which the disciples have witnessed: "And how has it been written of the Human Being, that he suffers many things and is made nothing?" If Elijah precedes and forthtells God's coming, an event that is followed by the resurrection of the dead and "the rule of God in power," where in this millennial eschatology is there a place for the suffering and dying of the New Human Being?

Jesus does not offer a direct reply. He does not cite any particular scriptural references that point to the more immediate destiny of the New Human Being. Instead, he extrapolates from the second career of Elijah, which in its ambiguous fulfillment in the life and activity of the Baptizer, is a mirror reflection of the first: "They did to him such things as they were wanting, even as it has been written of him." Persecution and suffering are not attendant features of Elijah's second career in the literature that focuses on his future activity as the

eschatological prophet who serves as God's forerunner.[118] Jesus therefore must be referring back to the record of Elijah's first career in 1
Kings 17—2 Kings 2. Although he was not martyred, he endured
opposition and adversity from the ruling elite, and these are aspects of
his life that provide another basis for associating him with John.

What has been written of Elijah and how it has "been written of the
Human Being, so that he suffers many things and is made nothing" are
attendant features that unite Jesus and John in establishing the rule of
God in power. If Elijah has come and they did to him such things as
they were wanting, then Jesus, who also participates in the eschatological activity of his second career, must also undergo similar persecution and suffering before God's coming occurs. Indeed, he and the
Baptizer together fulfill the mission of the eschatological prophet. The
latter inaugurates the construction of the way by preparing the people
of Israel for God's coming and in the process repeating the suffering of
Elijah's first career. Jesus continues John's work and encounters similar
opposition and adversity. But it is especially through his suffering and
death on the cross that he prepares the way for God's coming (1:3). At
that point in his career he unites his identity and activity of the New
Human Being with that of the eschatological prophet and makes
possible the enactment of divine judgment on history: "How has it
been written of the Human Being, that he suffers many things and is
made nothing?" Joined with John in the enterprise of preparing the
way for God's coming, as well as constructing the way for a new Israel,
Jesus will not realize the destiny of transcendence which the transfiguration unveiled until Easter morning. Accordingly, then, when the
revelation has been completed, the mandate to silence will be ended
and the three men will be at liberty to publicize the reality of Jesus'
metamorphosis.

When Jesus and his three companions rejoin the larger community
of disciples, they find many of them disputing with the scribes, surrounded by a large crowd which evidently is watching and listening.
What the issue of the debate is and what evoked it are not indicated. It
is the setting that is important, and here, perhaps more than in some of
the episodes of Mark's story world, it is possible to see "through" the

118. See the review of Faierstein, "Why Do the Scribes Say That Elijah Must Come
First?" 75–86.

incident rather than merely "in" the incident, to the situation of the Gospel's addressees.[119]

Jesus' arrival diverts the attention of the throngs: "Seeing him the whole crowd was stunned and running up they were greeting him." Their shock at Jesus' presence seems inexplicable. The verb *ekthambein*, which is used here and in two other places in the Gospel, occurs nowhere else in the New Testament. It expresses an unusually strong sense of being astounded, exceeding the force of such earlier verbs as "being overwhelmed" (1:22) and "being amazed" (1:27). Jesus himself will be staggered, dumbfounded, when he is alone in the field of Gethsemane confronting his imminent passion. The three women who on Easter morning find a youth in the tomb but not the corpse of Jesus as they had anticipated experience the same sense of paralyzing shock.

What causes it in this instance is not clear. Perhaps, as many have suggested, Jesus' person still reflects something of the splendor that was disclosed in his transfiguration.[120] A corresponding parallel often cited is Exod. 34:30. The skin of Moses' face shone when he descended from Mt. Sinai, "because he had been talking with God. And when Aaron and all the people of Israel saw Moses . . . they were afraid to come near him." But Jesus' **garments** became very shining white; nothing is said of the skin of his face glowing. Moreover, Jesus had been talking with Moses and Elijah, not with God. And perhaps even more significant, the crowd is not afraid of him but runs to him in greeting. Can it be that the lower-class masses—in contrast to the disciples—recognize him as the New Human Being and, although stunned by this perception, are naturally attracted to him? It should not be forgotten that the three disciples, Peter, James, and John, were *ekphoboi*, or terrified during their experience of Jesus' metamorphosis.

When Jesus asks his disciples why they are disputing with the scribes, one of the crowd approaches and intercedes for his possessed

119. For the literary critical differentiation between seeing "through" and seeing "in," see Dan O. Via, Jr., *The Parables: Their Literary and Existential Dimension* (Philadelphia: Fortress Press, 1967), 82–85, esp. 83: "The literary work as an autonomous focus of attention means (has meaning) in itself and, as a pointer, means through itself."

120. Taylor (*St. Mark*, 396), along with others, rejects this notion, maintaining that the situation in Exod. 34:29–30 is different. That it is different is certainly true. Yet why should such a strong verb be selected by the narrator to express "amazement" at "the unexpected appearance of Jesus"?

son: "Teacher, I brought to you my son having a mute spirit; and whenever it seizes him, it tears him and he foams and grinds his teeth and becomes stiff." The symptoms, which are recited here, indicate that the boy is afflicted with epilepsy and suffers grand mal seizures. For the father, however, who is voicing popular belief, they are the work of "a mute spirit." "And I spoke to your disciples," he continues, "that they might cast it out, and they were not strong enough."

Jesus' anguished response, "O unbelieving generation! How long shall I be with you? How long shall I put up with you?" expresses his distress at the incompetence and ineffectiveness of his disciples. Not only have they been unable to cure the boy; apparently they have also sublimated by redirecting their energies into a dispute with the scribes. Having reached the limit of their powers, they have transmitted their discipleship into intellectualizing and theological debate. Words have been substituted for deeds.

Once again the failures and defects of the disciples have been exposed, not simply those inside the narrative but particularly the addressees to whom it is being told. In their interaction with the narrative world they have not yet reached the ironic climax of the story which the transfiguration has momentarily disclosed. But, on the other hand, they themselves—in contrast to the followers of Jesus in the narrative world of Mark—are post-Easter disciples. Accordingly, their knowledge and understanding of Jesus' resurrection from the dead should enable them to recognize the reality which the transfiguration unveiled and, therefore with it, the fulfillment of 9:1. The rule of God has arrived in power! What is more, they are full participants in the New Humanity which Jesus embodied. For even as Jesus descended from the mountain of metamorphosis and rejoined the community of disciples in the narrative world of Mark, the resurrected New Human Being in actuality has united himself with them. But, as in the story, he has found them sublimating. They prefer theological argumentation because they have circumscribed the extent and scope of their powers.

Jesus' healing of the epileptic therefore underlines the authority of the New Human Being but simultaneously also the ineffectiveness of the disciples' participation in God's rule. The case, however, is formidable. When he is brought to Jesus, the boy suffers an epileptic seizure: "And seeing him the spirit immediately convulsed him, and falling to the ground [the boy] was rolling (about) foaming." The spirit

demonstrates its awesome power before Jesus in order to display the
superiority it has exercised in the boy's life to this very moment.
Indeed, it has dominated him from birth, and its effects have jeopard-
ized his life. "It casts him into fire and into water so that it might
destroy him."

The father's expectations have been disappointed by the
powerlessness of the disciples. Perhaps Jesus himself will be unable to
exorcise the evil spirit. Perhaps his son's condition is hopeless. On the
verge of despair he pleads, "If you can do anything, help us, being
moved with compassion toward us!" In his response Jesus seizes upon
the condition with which the father introduced his entreaty: "If you
can![121] All things (are) possible to the one who believes!" No limits
are set, no qualifications are made. But instead of attributing unlimited
power to God, as might be expected,[122] Jesus' astonishing reply postu-
lates unlimited possibilities to those who have faith. His career as the
New Human Being has demonstrated it. His faith has enabled him to
calm a storm, to defeat a legion of demons, to raise the dead, to feed
the multitudes, and to walk on the sea. The source of these possibilities has been revealed in his unveiling as God's offspring in the
transfiguration.

The father, struggling to embrace the new hope that Jesus offers,
makes himself vulnerable to the unlimited possibilities of faith with
the desperate outcry, "I believe! Keep on helping my unbelief!" Faith
and despair are battling within him. Openly he concedes that he
cannot believe, while at the same time a shred of faith prevails. In the
background the disciples pose a stark contrast, for they have capitu-
lated and turned to theological dialogue with the scribes.

The exchange between Jesus and the father, perhaps especially the
latter's passionate affirmation of faith, has attracted the attention of
the crowd. As they begin to converge about the two, Jesus quickly
exorcises the spirit. "Mute and deaf spirit," he charges, "I command
you, come out of him and never again enter into him."[123] Forced to

121. See Moule, *An Idiom Book of New Testament Greek*, 110.

122. Grundmann, *Markus*, 254.

123. The omission of the word "unclean" in 9:25 in P[45], W, the Lake minuscules, and
the Sinaitic Syriac is worth noting and may be original. The narrator consistently refers
to this being as a "spirit," originally "a mute spirit" (9:17). This spirit appears to be
different from the "unclean spirits" or "demons." It does not cry out Jesus' identity, as
the others did. Unlike the others, it may not be generated by institutional realities or
systemic structures.

abandon its victim but desperate to prevail, the exiting spirit precipitates a final devastating seizure that seems intended to end the boy's life: "And crying out and convulsing him terribly he came out. And he became like dead so that many were saying that he died." For a brief moment Jesus appears to have been defeated. But, reaching out and taking hold of the boy's hand, as he did earlier to the synagogue ruler's daughter (5:41), he once again demonstrates the sovereignty of the New Human Being. In an act of resurrection he raises him up. To emphasize the Easter character of this event, the narrator utilizes both resurrection verbs: *egeirein*[124] ("to raise up, awaken") and *anhistēmi* ("to arise").[125] The boy has been liberated from the power of epilepsy and the physical devastation it has effected in his life. The past no longer determines his future. Restored and healthy, he has become a new creation.

Nothing is said of the reaction of the crowd or the response of the father or his healed son. Instead, the ending of the story refocuses on the ineffective disciples. After they have left the scene and only in the privacy of a "house church" where they can be together as a family, do they risk inquiry: "(Why) were we unable to cast it out?" Jesus' answer, "This kind is able to come out by nothing except prayer!" is startling, because prayer appears to have played no role in the restoration of the epileptic boy. No entreaty was offered up to God. No call for divine help was invoked. Nevertheless Jesus' surprising introduction of prayer at the conclusion of the episode hints at an interdependence of effort which his earlier words to the epileptic's father seem to have precluded. "All things (are) possible to the one who believes!" but in order that this is not interpreted simply as a humanistic effort, Jesus climaxes the event with an accent on prayer. Presumably it is directed toward the addressees of the Gospel in order to reorient them to a new collaboration with God that is reinforced by communion in prayer.[126]

Yet more than this is required in order to resolve the crisis of

---

124. Found in this sense in 1:31; 2:9–12; 5:41; 6:14; and 16:6. See Schweizer, *Good News*, 189.

125. Found in this sense in 5:40; 8:31; 9:31; 10:34; and 12:23.

126. Some manuscripts include fasting alongside prayer, but this is undoubtedly a later interpolation when prayer alone no longer seemed adequate for the empowerment of the disciples. See Schweizer, *Good News*, 189.

discipleship that has become acute among his followers. More teaching is necessary to correct their misunderstandings and to prepare them for what is yet to come. Ironically, Jesus' career in Galilee ends with a withdrawal from ministry to the people at large and a concentrated effort of renewed instruction to the disciples. Leaving the vicinity of Caesarea of Philip, where apparently they have been since Simon Peter's confession (8:27), he leads his followers on a peripatetic journey through Galilee. The imperfect tense of the verb *paraporeuomai* in 9:30 denotes continuous travel. No stops or pauses are made in any of the villages and towns. During this period of time he is committed to being alone with them: "He was not wanting that anyone should know. For he was teaching his disciples."

Above all, the disciples need to understand the destiny that awaits Jesus imminently in Jerusalem. He repeats the passion prediction he made earlier in response to Peter's confession in order to prepare them for his self-appointed destiny: "The Human Being is going to be delivered up into (the) hands of human beings, and they will kill him and being killed he will arise after three days." It is noteworthy that Jesus does not identify those who will put him to death, as he did earlier in 8:31. Perhaps it is the context that determines the use of "human beings" instead of "elders, chief priests, and scribes." Here, immediately after the liberation of a human being from the power of an evil spirit, the narrator stresses the irony of Jesus' forthcoming passion: "The Human Being is going to be delivered up into (the) hands of human beings, and they will kill him." Earlier in the context of Peter's confession of Jesus as the Messiah in the villages of Caesarea of Philip it was appropriate to identify the ruling elite who would be threatened by the appearance of a messiah and would be motivated to put him to death. In reaction Peter had vigorously rejected the notion of a suffering messiah. Now, on this second occasion, there is still no sign of understanding. Incomprehension continues. If the rule of God is coming in power, and the transfiguration has disclosed a glorious destiny for Jesus, how can he be subjected to suffering and death? A "paradigm shift"[127] for the reconstruction of the world is unfolding

---

127. A "paradigm" is a configuration of interconnections that builds world or a system of truth for those who commit themselves to it. For "paradigm shift," see Thomas S. Kuhn, *The Structure of Scientific Revolutions*, 2d ed. (Chicago: University of Chicago Press, 1963).

before them, one that appears to have no antecedents for them, one that does not correspond to their experience, their traditions, and their beliefs. For the present at least they are unable to grasp it; it eludes their understanding, and, what is more, they are afraid to question Jesus about it.

Jesus returns to Capernaum once more for a final visit (9:33). His work has come full circle. Here in this commercial center of Galilee he launched his ministry of teaching, liberation, and healing in order to fulfill his commission to establish God's rule. His disciples, who have followed him in response to his proclamation of the imminence of God's rule, have witnessed his extraordinary activity and struggled to determine who he is. Although they have been unsuccessful in identifying him, they have persisted in their hierarchical orientation. Dispossessed by the upper class, they remain captive to the prevailing mentality of their society. The socioeconomic pyramid, with its descending levels of power and privilege, is evidently considered to be natural.

Now, however, in the privacy of a house—could it be that of Simon Peter?—Jesus forces them into a showdown on the structure and character of God's rule. "What did you argue (about) along the way?" he inquires. They are too embarrassed to answer, for, as the narrator remarks in 9:34, "They had discussed with each other on the way who the greatest."[128] Unfortunately the narrator has not placed a verb or copula between the interrogative pronoun "who" and the adjective "greatest." Nevertheless it is tempting to think that the interpolation of two manuscript witnesses, the Bezae and the Koridethi, although it must be rejected on the basis of the form-critical principle that the more difficult reading is preferable, at least conveys the intention of the narrator: "who (of them should become) the greatest." For the question must arise out of their eschatological expectation of God's imminent rule in power, which, as Jesus told them, is approaching fulfillment. Past achievements could hardly account for their discussion. They have just experienced a major failure in their efforts to heal

---

128. Vv. 34 and 35 pose a number of textual problems that are difficult to resolve. The omission of the phrase "on the way" in v. 34 is attested by A, D, and a few other uncials, the old Latin tradition, and the Sinaitic Syriac. However, the frequent use of the word "way"—with its metaphorical allusion to the early self-identification of the Christian movement—as well as the evangelist's tendency toward repetition would support its inclusion in the text.

the epileptic boy. It is all the more ironic therefore that, while Jesus emphasizes his impending suffering and death, they persist in the grand illusion of a new pyramid in which they will enjoy elite positions of power and privilege. In spite of their questionable capabilities they are preoccupied with the identification of who will be the most distinguished among them.

Whether Jesus' immediate response in 9:35 should be deleted, as the Codex Bezae and the old Latin manuscript K attest, is difficult to determine. The apparent lack of connection between vv. 34 and 35 might account for the omission. Furthermore, almost identical words are spoken by Jesus to the disciples in 10:44. Yet the necessity of their repetition would serve to accentuate the disciples' identity. Moreover, the saying of 9:35 is a direct response to the preceding discussion if it is assumed that it was focused on the question of who would occupy privileged positions in the new order: If any wish to be first, let them be last of all and minister of all.

For reinforcement Jesus offers a model that elucidates his teaching and simultaneously subverts common practice. In full view of all his disciples he places a child before those who might be most inclined toward an elitist mentality, namely, the twelve, and by an embrace expresses his identification with it. For kings and lords, the rich and the powerful, might be received with an embrace and be employed as emissaries. According to Jesus, however, God's representatives are precisely those who have no status at all, who, like children, are lowly, weak, and defenseless. "Whoever receives one of these children in my name receives me; and whoever receives me, does not receive me but the one who sent me." The kind of humanness with which God identifies, which God chooses as the bearer of the divine presence in relation to all human activity, is encountered both in children and in Jesus, the New Human Being, who places himself in solidarity with them. For what they have in common as they live and work in a hierarchically constituted society is their vulnerability and defenselessness, their lowliness and powerlessness. The disciples therefore, as they participate in God's rule, are to be oriented toward those on the lower levels of the social pyramid who are as weak and defenseless as children. In their positions of leadership they are to consider themselves to be last of all and the minister of all, and, as they fulfill that self-understanding, they will bear God's presence to those whom they serve and simultaneously experience it among them.

A new point of departure for Jesus' teaching "in the house" in Capernaum is evoked by an emotional outburst from John, the son of Zebedee: "Teacher, we saw someone casting out demons in your name who is not following us, and we tried to stop him because he was not following us." Such exclusivism is characteristic of social movements which, in spite of their rejection of the moral order that exists, continue to structure reality in terms of binary oppositions, such as light and darkness, good and evil, and clean and unclean. John's narrow perspective prevents him from legitimating anyone engaged in liberation activity who is not directly linked to their fellowship, even if that activity is being conducted in the name of the founder of the New Humanity.

Jesus rejects such a limited view of the community that he is constituting. The new Israel or the New Humanity is a social reality of the one and the many into which all human beings are called. Its radical reconstruction of the world will subvert all dualisms and abolish all binary oppositions. There is therefore no more justification for exclusivism than there is for any kind of elitism. The fellowship of Jesus reaches beyond the small circle of those who surround him, beyond all lines drawn by human beings to establish their identity and status, security and self-worth. All who labor for human redemption belong to this universal company: "For there is no one who will do a mighty work in my name and quickly be able to speak evil of me. For who is not against us is for us."

In fact, there are those on the outside who may not be engaged in mighty works of liberation and healing. For one reason or another their resources are minimal. The most that they can do is to give the disciples a drink of water. Yet even they are not to be excluded, for their act, as insignificant as it may seem, contributes to human well-being. They too will have their reward.

Although there is no manuscript evidence that would uphold the deletion of the words "because you are of Christ" in 9:41, the phrase is nevertheless suspect. The more difficult reading would appear to be the very awkward construction: *en onomati hoti Christou este* ("in [my] name because you are of Christ"). Yet the use of the phrase "because you are of Christ" makes little sense in Mark's story world. Throughout the Gospel, Jesus identifies himself with the New Human

Being who is "lord," who has authority on earth, who must die and be resurrected. As a corporate identity as well as an individual identity the designation includes the community of Jesus' followers. To acknowledge that the disciples are "of Christ" or "of the Messiah" after Peter's messianic confession has been censured seems inconsistent and even contradictory. It is more Pauline in character, for it conveys the apostle's use of the corporate Christ as the body of the one and the many.[129]

If the pronoun *mou* ("my") is adopted, which stands before the causal conjunction *hoti* ("because") in the Sinaiticus, the Constantinopolitan tradition, and other manuscripts, and if the phrase "because you are of Christ" is omitted, the difficulties are resolved. The text would simply read, "For whoever will give you a cup of water to drink in my name." Such a solution, of course, seems too simple, yet the resulting reading corresponds to that of 9:39 and its employment of the phrase "in my name." The structural parallel between "whoever will do a mighty work in my name" and "whoever will give you a drink of water in my name" is attractive, because in both instances the emphasis is on the performance of acts in Jesus' name, not on the persons who are the recipients of these acts.[130]

It is in this vein that Jesus also continues. For those who can do nothing more than give a cup of water are the subjects of his concern. They are "the little ones" whose economic resources, social status, and political power are minimal and therefore belong to the underside of agrarian society. As "little ones," they are not to be confused with the "little child" of 9:36. These are the disinherited who, deprived of being, have virtually no identity and little or no sense of self-worth. Jesus reinforces his earlier identification with them by pronouncing a sentence on those who are found guilty of causing these insignificant ones to stumble. They will meet a fate that is as terrible as drowning in the sea with a giant millstone, the kind that can only be worked by donkey power, hung around the neck.[131]

129. See 1 Cor. 12:12, 27. Taylor (*St. Mark*, 408) also suggests that the idea is Pauline.

130. Taylor (*St. Mark*, 408) offers T. W. Manson's resolution of this textual problem, which is an attractive possibility, but it does not take into account the parallel structure with the focus on the doers of good works.

131. See J. Duncan M. Derrett, "MYLOS ONIKOS (Mk 9:42 par.)," *ZNW* 76 (1985): 284. Derrett's interesting probing of this text concludes that it is "another instance of Jesus' 'black humour.' "

At the same time, the disciples are to be aware of their own stumbling. There are obstacles and impediments that can limit or prevent their participation in God's rule, but they are not external entities, such as cultural snares, economic enticements, social temptations, or political seductions. They are, rather, parts of oneself, components of one's psyche, which express themselves physically through parts of the human anatomy, that can cause personal tragedy and existential ruin.

> And if your hand offends you, cut it off; it is good (that) you enter into life deformed than to go off into Gehenna into inextinguishable fire having two hands. And if your foot offends you, cut if off; it is good (that) you enter into life lame than having two feet to be cast into Gehenna. And if your eye offends you, cast it out; it is better (that) you enter into the rule of God one-eyed than having two eyes to be cast into Gehenna "where their worm does not die and the fire is not extinguished."

Whatever part of oneself causes stumbling, whatever member of the human anatomy perpetrates injustice—the hand, the foot, the eye—its loss is preferable to being thrown into hell. Jesus' summons is existential, not eschatological. "To enter into life" and "to enter into God's rule" are parallel phrases essentially synonymous in meaning. To enter into one is to enter into the other. If it is possible to enter into God's rule in the present, as Jesus himself has done, participation in life here and now must be a simultaneous realization. According to 10:17, that is precisely what the rich man craves. Jesus is challenging his disciples to outrageous action in order to avert self-destruction and living death in the present as well as in the future.

The elimination of offending appendages is an existential anticipation of the future. "For," as Jesus warns, "everyone will be salted with fire." That, it would seem, is his understanding of human destiny, if the singular "everyone" refers to human beings in general and not merely Christians in particular.[132] Jesus' mixed metaphor of "being salted with fire" combines two potent agents of purification: salt which cleanses and fire which refines. Purging, radical purging, awaits all human beings. History, as Jesus subsequently teaches in the "little apocalypse" of Mark 13, will culminate in an unprecedented affliction,

---

132. Against Belo, *A Materialist Reading*, 168. Belo believes 9:50 refers to purification by persecution—because the Christians in Rome whom Mark is addressing are suffering persecution—and therefore considers that "everyone" refers to Christians.

which will be so severe that "unless the Lord shortened the days, no flesh would be saved" (13:20). This eschatological reality can be obviated in the future by the same radical action that averts living death in the present. What is necessary is a decisiveness that does not flinch in the face of painful self-surgery.

Jesus abruptly readapts the metaphor of salt to articulate an exhortation that arises out of a rhetorical question on the use of the condiment and seasoning: "Salt (is) good; but if salt becomes saltless, with what will you season it?" Salt seasons food, but, he amusingly inquires, what will season salt if it becomes insipid? The presupposition here, it appears, is that the disciples are compared to salt as a flavoring. If they should become insipid or unsavory, who will serve as their substitute in society? And who will season them? Since there is no substitute for salt, the only answer is, Have salt in/among yourselves. In order to continue to be salt, to function as flavoring in the world, the disciples must have salt in themselves and among themselves. The preposition *en* is usually translated "in" but may also be rendered as "among."[133] Perhaps the narrator intends both meanings, since, in the light of the context, salt is both a cleansing agent and a seasoning. To have salt within oneself means to let it have its effect as a cleansing agent. How to "have salt among yourselves" Jesus does not say, but his concluding admonition provides a clue: "and keep the peace among each other." This closing charge brings his teaching "in the house" full circle to the original point of departure: the disciples' dispute of who will be greatest among them. Jesus, in contrast to their misconception, is building a community in which relationships are horizontally structured, as, for example, at table fellowship over a meal. The vulnerability, candidness, affirmation, encouragement, and love which a family expresses at dinner are the qualities that nourish, strengthen, and stabilize while they also foster integrity and peace. The wholeness and the vitality of the one and the many—the individual and the community to which she or he belongs—that originate from such

---

133. So also Michael Lattke, "Salz der Freundschaft in Mk 9:50c," *ZNW* 75 (1984): 54. Lattke offers an excellent survey of recent interpretations of this text and bases his own translation of *en* on similar instances in Mark. But he does not interpret the saying as a *part* of the *whole* of the Gospel. In the lexicons he finds such meanings as "sharing of salt as a token of friendship" and "to be old friends" to be related to hospitality and table fellowship. See pp. 55–58.

family dynamics will perpetuate a discipleship that is continually refined and savory in the world.

ENTERING JUDEA AND CONSTRUCTING THE WAY
INTO JERUSALEM
(10:1–52) _____

Jesus concludes his ministry in Galilee with the special instruction of 9:31–50 addressed to his followers as a response to their continued misunderstanding of the nature of discipleship. Leaving Capernaum with his company of followers he journeys into the regions of Judea and Transjordan. The latter territory, "the other side of the Jordan," would be reached and traversed first, but it appears to be characteristic of the narrator to place the final destination before the intermediate district or locality that is only a place of transit.[134] As they pass into Judea, crowds, who evidently have heard about Jesus, attach themselves to him and, according to his custom, "he was teaching them." He had begun his ministry in Capernaum in the same way.

Here, however, Jesus is unable to move from teaching to healing in order to give concrete expression to the reality of God's rule. Instead, he is challenged by Pharisees who appear to be guarding the boundaries of Judea and are eager to test his orthodoxy. They ask him "if it is right for a man to divorce his wife." Why this particular issue is raised is not immediately evident. Perhaps more than any other it will reveal the fundamental difference between Jesus and these guardians of the law. His response, in fact, not only elucidates his hermeneutical approach to the Old Testament but also discloses how his eschatological perspective determines his basic understanding of human existence.

More immediately Jesus replies with a counterquestion that tests their knowledge of the Torah and simultaneously uncovers their hermeneutical predisposition for a resolution of the matter: "What did Moses command you?" The Pharisaic point of departure, a quotation of Deut. 24:1, is revealing, because by eliminating the specific cases that accompany it in its original context, it tends to make divorce the rule rather than the exception: "Moses permitted to write a document of divorce and to divorce." Such a predilection for Deut. 24:1 as a

134. See also 7:31b; 11:1.

general principle exposes the ideological bias of these Pharisees: separation, an orientation that is already conveyed by the name they have chosen for their self-identification. The appellation "Pharisee" is probably derived from the Aramaic *perishayya,* which means "the separated one." Very likely the addressees of Mark's story world do not know that. But from the previous narrative they have already learned that the Pharisees maintain a pollution system that separates the world into the two realms of the clean and the unclean. Women particularly are disadvantaged by it, because their monthly cycle of menstruation is perceived to be a defilement due to the the loss of life through the menstrual blood.[135] The very formulation of the Pharisees' question indicates a bias toward the male: Is it right for a man to divorce his wife? This is not simply an interrogation about divorce in general, for there is no accompanying query about the legal right of the wife to divorce her husband or to consent or object to a divorce. A husband may divorce his wife voluntarily simply by means of a certificate of divorce. But conversely a wife does not have the same legal authority. She is juridically restricted in the initiation of a divorce action. She may sue for divorce, but the act itself is granted only to the husband.[136]

Jesus opposes the Pharisaic justification of male-initiated divorce by attributing to Moses an anthropological motive for this statute: "For your hard heart he wrote you this commandment." No such intention is articulated in the Torah, but it may be deduced from the contrast between the divine legislation enacted before the Fall and the Mosaic code purportedly handed down to Israel at the time of entrance in the promised land. Jesus refutes the Deuteronomic injunction with a fragmentary quotation of Gen. 1:27, derived from a context in which the man and the woman are created simultaneously, and continues with the ordinance that is spoken when the Lord God presents the woman to the man in Gen. 2:24: "But from the beginning of creation 'he made them male and female.' 'On account of this a human being will leave behind his (her) father and mother, and the two will become one flesh.' " Jesus' omission of the phrase, "and will cleave to his wife"

135. Lev. 17:14; 15:19–31; 12:1–8.

136. G. F. Moore, *Judaism in the Age of the Tannaim* (Cambridge: Harvard University Press, 1954), 2:125; and Strack-Billerbeck, 2:23–24 and 1:313–20. Also Mishna, *Yebamoth* 13:4–5.

indicates that both the woman and the man may initiate the movement that culminates in marriage. It is not just the male who leaves and cleaves but also the female. And in their wedlock they become "one flesh," a reality that Jesus emphasizes by repetition in 10:8b.

Marriage expresses the fundamental movement intended by God at creation: union. "What therefore God yoked together," Jesus declares, "let a human being not separate." The original will of the Creator has precedence over any subsequent concessions made to the weaknesses of human beings as a result of the Fall, especially if the reality of God's rule is to be reconstituted. Union was and, now more than ever, is the natural order of things. Separation and divorce are realities that originate from a pollution system that promotes inequality, oppression, and exploitation.

The reaction of the Pharisees is not noted; it must not detract from the impact that Jesus' teaching is intended to have on the Gospel's addressees. The implications of his words are conveyed to the disciples in the privacy of "the house." Here, as elsewhere in the narrative world of Mark, it serves as the symbol of the household of the New Humanity that Jesus is constituting and stands in contrast to the hierarchical institution of the synagogue and its ideology of separation. In response to their inquiry about his teaching on the issue of divorce Jesus declares, "Whoever divorces his wife and marries another, commits adultery against her; and if she divorcing her husband marries another, she commits adultery." While the second half of this teaching is often considered to be indicative of a Hellenistic milieu and even a modification of Jewish tradition based on Roman law,[137] it is more to the point to recognize Jesus' acknowledgment of the equality of the sexes in the initiation of divorce as well as in the establishment of marriage. A woman, like a man, can institute divorce proceedings against her spouse even as she also can leave her parents and cleave to a husband. But divorce for those already participating in the New Household of God, whether undertaken by one or the other, contradicts the fundamental direction of the divinely appointed movement of the new creation.

Appropriately "the house," which symbolizes the reality of the new family of humankind, continues as the setting for the brief episode

137. Grundmann, *Markus*, 272–73.

that follows: "They tried to bring children to him so that he might touch them." Who "they" are is not indicated. There is no antecedent for the pronoun that is intimated by the third person plural suffix of the verb *(prosepheron)*. Apparently their identity is unimportant. The focus is, rather, on the disciples, who frustrate their efforts and once again display their chronic condition of density. Earlier, in 9:36–37, they had witnessed Jesus embracing a child and identifying himself with its vulnerability and powerlessness: "Whoever receives one of these children in my name receives me; and whoever receives me, does not receive me but the one who sent me." Obviously the disciples have not grasped the significance of this teaching. With indignation Jesus rebukes them: Let the children come to me! Do not prevent them, for of such is God's rule.

Participation in this reality, however, is not to be restricted to children. In order to avoid that misunderstanding Jesus adds, "Whoever does not receive the rule of God **like a child** will by no means enter into it!" In their innocence and openness children manifest the qualities of authentic humanness that are characteristic of God's rule. Because of lack of experience, there is no cynicism or negativity; in spite of bad experiences the past does not immediately determine the future. To receive God's rule like a child depends on the qualities of vulnerability and trust, transparence and defenselessness, integrity and wholeness, expectation and humility. To enter into it, therefore, means to be released from any and every force in society that fates human existence. The past no longer determines the future. Consequently also defensiveness, cynicism, or negativity does not control the disposition to life, relationships with others, or the decisions that are made from day to day. This kind of humanness is divine and is willed by the Creator for all human beings. Jesus demonstrates his identification with those who embody it by taking them in his arms and in benediction putting his hands on them.

Jesus subsequently continues "into (the) way." By using the preposition *eis* ("into"), the narrator expresses a sense of direction. There is only one way, and its course is predetermined. Jesus knows the way, because he entered upon it through submission to John's baptism of repentance. Its end is like its beginning: death followed by resurrection.

As he proceeds, he is confronted by a kneeling individual who has run up to him and who, as the story progresses, appears to be a wealthy adult Jewish male. His running expresses earnest desperation; his kneeling, humility and subservience. Here is someone who seems to have the vulnerability and transparence of a child. His confidence is reflected in his form of address: "Good Teacher." The question he asks is philosophically acute but theologically erratic: "What shall I do so that I inherit eternal life?" Generally an inheritance is not earned by works; rather, it is awarded on the basis of genealogical lineage. It is ironic that this individual should be raising this question, for the eternal life that he craves is available to him on the basis of his integrity as a Jew, a member of God's elect people Israel. That, in fact, is what Jesus intimates in his response, "You know the commandments."

First, however, Jesus challenges the man's attribution of goodness to him: "Why do you call me good? No one (is) good except God alone." Jesus' objection to this predication discloses a vital aspect of the Gospel's Christology that has all too often been forgotten and consequently has resulted in the idolatry of Jesus. In spite of his union with God as a result of his re-creation by the Spirit at his baptism, in spite of his privileged status as God's surrogate and therefore also co-bearer of the divine epithet "Lord," Jesus remains a human being, but a New Human Being and, in view of his resurrection from the dead, the deified New Human Being. Although at this moment in the narrative world of the Gospel he embodies the eschatological reality of the New Humanity in whom the image and the likeness of God are restored, any goodness that is manifested in his life and activity is derived from the Creator. God is its only source, and Jesus and those who express it are simply serving as its communicators.

As for the inheritance of "eternal life," it is received naturally on the basis of the integrity of Jewish identity arising out of obedience to the commandments of the covenant that God established with Israel. Unfortunately, however, the meaning of "eternal life" has all too often been distorted by limiting it to a quantitative reality, that is, life beyond the grave, life that never ends. But Jesus' subsequent assessment of the reluctance of the rich to exchange their wealth for "eternal life" conveys another meaning: "How hard it is for those having possessions to enter into God's rule." Evidently "eternal life" is to be construed as the kind of life that the millennial reality of God's rule actualizes, specifically a dynamic state of personal and social existence that is not controlled by the fear of death and therefore is free from the infection of alienation and narcissism, their concrete expressions of greed, injustice, exploitation, oppression, dispossession, and the living death which they generate.

In this respect it is noteworthy that the commandments of the covenant that Jesus proceeds to cite as requisite for "eternal life" are not those of the first Table of the Law which stipulate human obligations to God, the originator of the covenant. This particular hunger can be satisfied only by the observance of the injunctions of the second Table. "Eternal life" is gained by the fulfillment of justice in human relationships: You shall not kill; you shall not commit adultery; you shall not steal; you shall not testify falsely; and—if it is genuinely Markan—you shall not defraud.[138]

It is an extraordinary irony that "eternal life" should result from obedience to these commandments, for it is their very fulfillment that imposes the heavy burdens of necessity, limitation, and even death. This may be more obvious of the fourth commandment, the first of the second Table but the last one that Jesus quotes. To honor one's father and mother in first-century Palestine—and elsewhere—required caring for them in their old age. Evidently some of Jesus' contemporaries, as 7:8–13 indicates, resorted to korban in order to escape this necessity. But the other commandments impose their own limitations on human beings, depending of course on how they are defined. Not killing, not committing adultery, and not stealing or testifying falsely can be observed as merely negative prohibitions that essentially involve an avoidance of these proscribed activities. In fact, this may be the way in which the rich man understands them, for he claims to have observed them from his youth, yet obviously without experiencing the benefits of the covenant from which they are derived.

But his wealth has also not satisfied his hunger for authentic life, in spite of the realms of possibility that it opens for him. As a potentiality of possibility, money can buy cultural enrichment and personal growth through travel, education, and books. Money can purchase freedom

---

138. Some significant manuscript witnesses: B, W, the majority of the remaining witnesses, the Sinaitic Syriac, and Clement of Alexandria omit this last injunction. It is not found in the Matthean and Lukan parallels—all of it strong evidence of its secondary character as a scribal insertion.

from a life of subsistence and its burdens of poverty and its inhuman consequences. But wealth has also not succeeded in opening the door to real life in the present.

Sensing the rich man's sincerity and desperation, Jesus reaches out to him in love and proposes a radical course of action that will move him beyond his impasse: "You lack one thing! Go, sell all that you have and give to (the) destitute and you will have treasure in heaven, and come follow me." Selling all his possessions and giving the money to the destitute, while canceling whatever possibility he has enjoyed through his wealth, will begin to open life for those who do not have it. And following Jesus into this kind of vicarious self-cancelation will lead directly into re-creation by God's Spirit, a horizontally structured participation in God's rule and therefore also the present experience of authentic life which can never end because it issues directly from the Creator.

Jesus' proposal, however, is too severe and costly. It dismays the rich man, because "he was having many possessions." Over the years, apparently, he had grown accustomed to the benefits that his wealth conferred, and perhaps so dependent on them that it was unthinkable to him now to surrender his wealth and embrace the nothingness which seemed to lie beyond it. Better the limited possibility that wealth afforded and the minute quantities of life that it imparted than seemingly none at all. Petrified and invulnerable, afraid to expose himself to the uncertainties and insecurities of the future, he went off grieving. The vulnerability of a child and the benediction that Jesus had pronounced on it hold no attraction for him, and therefore he is unable to enter into God's rule and also simultaneously to inherit eternal life.

By refusing to follow Jesus in this radical way, the rich man also intimates that his observance of the law is essentially negative and superficial. For him the commandments do not extend beyond their literal prohibitions. The possessions he has accumulated in the agrarian society of the first century can have been gained only through the injustice of economic exploitation and perhaps social and political oppression. The wealth he enjoys had been expropriated, either directly or indirectly, from others below him in the socioeconomic pyramid of Roman Palestine. As long as he does not fulfill the justice which the law of the covenant demands in human relationships, he dooms himself to inauthentic existence. His hunger for real life will never be satisfied.

As the rich man departs, Jesus turns to his disciples with the observation, "How hard it is for those having possessions to enter into God's rule!" His words stun the disciples into silence. For emphasis he repeats his declaration but with the affectionate address, "Children." Perhaps he wishes to affirm their own childlikeness and entry into God's rule, while at the same time underlining the great hindrance posed by property, possessions, and wealth. Indeed, the startling metaphor that he adds intensifies the difficulty into a virtual impossibility: "It is easier for a camel to go through the eye of a needle than a wealthy person to enter into God's rule." Outraged, the disciples object with a question that conveys a note of despair: "And who is able to be saved?" Since all people, the poor as well as the rich, use their means, whether great or small, to ensure some degree of security for themselves, how is it possible to become so free, so open to the future, as to live in and with insecurity in the face of the contingencies of human existence? Jesus, looking at his disciples intently, as if to burn the only resolution of this dilemma into their minds, answers simply, "With human beings impossible, but not with God. For all things (are) possible with God." That is, not human effort which is subject to the weaknesses of the flesh, but the unlimited possibilities of the Creator will accomplish the salvation of human beings by drawing them into the Creator's own freedom and sovereignty, a reality conveyed by the transfiguration of the New Human Being.

Peter, reminded in this context of his own vulnerability in responding to Jesus' call, invokes an evaluation of the discipleship that he and his companions have expressed: "Look, we left all things and have followed you!" In contrast to the rich man, they have given up their possessions; indeed, in their repentance they have renounced all things in order to follow Jesus into the reality of God's rule. What is the outcome of the nothingness they have embraced?

By countering the losses of their sacrifice with the gains of their entry into God's rule, Jesus affirms the validity of their discipleship: "Amen I say to you, there is no one who left home or brothers or sisters or mother or father or children or fields because of me and because of the good news (who) does not receive a hundred times more homes and brothers and sisters and mothers and children and fields now in this right time *(kairos)*—along with persecutions—and in the coming age eternal life." The former values of home, family, and possessions into which they were socialized are being replaced by those which belong to the reality of God's rule which Jesus is establishing. Moreover, in addition to the quantity and quality benefits which this *kairos* (the right time) brings, they are simultaneously inheriting everlasting life in the age to come. Yet while they incarnate the values of God's rule and experience its "hundredfold" benefits, they will suffer persecution and, as a result, continue to be last in the old order that is passing away. But eventually the reconstitution of all things will be fully actualized, and those who are first now will be last, and those who are last now will be first.

This reversal will begin to be manifested in the architectonic center of Judaism. For Jesus, as the narrator observes (10:32), is now constructing the way into another experience of nothingness: "Now they were **on the way** going up into Jerusalem, and Jesus was going before them." It is at this point in the story of the good news that a marked shift occurs in the role that Jesus has been fulfilling as the divine surrogate or agent in concretizing God's rule. Since his entry upon the way and its concomitant experiences of death and resurrection, Jesus as the embodiment of the New Humanity has manifested the unlimited possibilities of participation in God's rule and its reordering of power. He has exorcised demons, cleansed lepers, set free the crippled, stilled a storm, raised the dead, fed multitudes, opened the eyes of the blind, and walked on the Sea of Galilee, and his deification as God's son has been disclosed in his transfiguration.

Now, however, he assumes the role of John the Baptizer. As he and his followers continue on the way that John inaugurated, he, Jesus, becomes "the messenger" who goes before them in order to continue the construction of the way. "They were on the way going up into Jerusalem, and **Jesus was going before them**." Like John, he will lead them into the experiences of death and resurrection. Both the death and the resurrection will be his own, but his disciples will be drawn into them in vicarious participation. For eventually the construction of the way and the role of the divine agent in concretizing God's rule will be handed over to them. If and when they enter into a reordering of power, the responsibility of making God's future present for their fellow human beings will fall on them.

There must be a sense of expectation among the disciples as they ascend to Jerusalem following Jesus "on the way," for the narrator observes that they were "astounded . . . and afraid." What has evoked these emotions is not explained. How much they have grasped from the earlier passion predictions is not indicated. Clearly, however, there is an anticipation of decisive change. The very consistency of the character and course of Jesus' ministry in Galilee would evoke it. If he challenged the ruling elite in the province, how much more those in the capital city. If his ministry in Galilee had been devoted to liberation and restoration, how much more at the center of power where the oppressive institutions that control Jewish life and society are maintained. To the disciples a great confrontation that would result in decisive change would seem both logical and necessary. But also, of course, there would be far-reaching consequences for Jesus as well as for them. Accordingly, their feelings of astonishment and apprehension correspond to their expectations of what will happen in Jerusalem.

For Jesus, however, this is an anabasis that will culminate in death and resurrection. He has already delineated the destiny of the New Human Being to his followers: "It is necessary for the Human Being to suffer many things." The necessity is not determined by masochism but rather by a disposition of vulnerability, and openness to all of life and with it both good and evil.

As the New Human Being, Jesus has already displayed the divine possibilities of being "seated on the right hand of Power" resulting from his re-creaction by the Spirit and his attendant entry into a horizontal relationship with the Creator. But now the possibilities of this position must be turned over to others. For the goal of the New Human Being is nothing less than the liberation of all human beings from all forces of domination, and it cannot be achieved by occupying that position alone and perpetuating the power and privilege which it bestows. That in fact would negate the integrity of the New Human Being. For in its very nature the reality of the New Human Being is dialectical, simultaneously embracing the possibilities of being seated on the right hand of power as God's offspring *and* the limitations that are inherent in flesh-and-blood existence.

By assuming the role of forerunner—as John did for him!—Jesus also accepts the limitations of his mortality and the necessity of his death that belongs to it. Not only is it necessary for the New Human Being to suffer many things because of a healthy, joyful, life-affirming vulnerability, it is also necessary for the New Human Being to die so that others may enter into a reordering of power in order to recover their autonomy and freedom. Indeed, if the New Human Being is ever to become a corporate reality, Jesus must live and act dialectically, using both the possibilities of his life and the necessity of his death under God's rule on behalf of others.

This, as he specifies for the first time, must occur in Jerusalem. It is the navel of the earth, the architectonic center of Judaism, but as such it is also a paradoxical reality. For while, on the one hand, it is God's earthly residence, and therefore the one place in the world where heaven and earth are united, it is also, on the other hand, "the heart of darkness" insofar as its institutions are the source of the evils of classism, sexism, and racism in Judaism. At this *axis mundi* Jesus will embrace the necessity of his death and use it to negate the old order of oppression and dispossession that has dominated God's people. Subsequently the New Human Being must also arise again in Jerusalem in order to establish a New Humanity that cannot be abolished by the power of the old order.

The inevitability of his death and resurrection in Jerusalem, however, is conveyed only to the twelve. They are the representatives of the new Israel, and it will be their responsibilities to transmit this paradox to the others when they are ready for it, not the least by embodying the example he is also setting for them. But these twelve males appear to have at best a limited grasp of what Jesus has communicated to them. Two of them, ignoring his announcement of his impending death, petition for elite participation in his forthcoming glory which they glimpsed in his transfiguration. Moreover, they have approached him with a childish mentality of wanting an unqualified approval of their wish even before they express it: "Teacher, we want that whatever we request of you, you will do for us."

James and John, sons of Zebedee, the owner of a successful fishing enterprise, desire to be co-enthroned with Jesus: "Give us that we may be seated in your glory, one on your right hand and one on your left hand." It seems appropriate that these two should make this request, for in following Jesus they may have sacrificed more than any of the other disciples. Not only have they left their family, they have also given up a lucrative fishing business.

Jesus reproves them for the ignorance which their petition displays: "You don't know what you are requesting!" And without pausing, he proceeds to challenge them with two symbolic expressions of his forthcoming passion: "Are you able to drink the cup which I drink or to be baptized with the baptism with which I am baptized?" In anticipation of his institution of the Eucharist, Jesus appropriates the symbol of the cup in order to convey the reality of the death he will experience. Later, in the field of Gethsemane he will take up this symbol again and pray to escape the horror of desolation which the cup contains: "Abba, . . . all things (are) possible for you. Remove this cup from me!" To reinforce this destiny, Jesus also looks back to the beginning of his career and utilizes the experience of his baptism as another symbol of his forthcoming death. Indeed, it was this earlier embrace of his own death, by submitting to John's baptism of repentance, that set him on his course. For the end is already implicit in the beginning, and the beginning predestines the end.

Without hesitation the two brothers insist, "We are able!" Their bold but naive self-confidence leads them into an immediate identification with Jesus. If he can drink the cup, so can they. His distinctive kind of baptism therefore must also be available to them. If, then, they have the capacity to drink the same cup and be baptized with the same baptism, what should prevent them from being co-enthroned with him?

Jesus not only acknowledges their capacity but assures them that they will indeed follow him in drinking the same cup and being baptized with the same baptism. For him, they are not elitist realities reserved for himself. Being baptized with the same baptism is, in fact, a distinguishing feature of true discipleship. Without it there can be no participation in God's rule. Furthermore, drinking the same cup involves them in his life, the life that he will offer up for them and their liberation; and it will draw them into the reality of the New Human Being and its concrete fulfillment in their own lives.

However, whether participation in both leads directly to co-enthronement with Jesus depends on God's appointment. It is not mine to give you, he says, "but it is for those for whom it has been prepared." Being seated with him in his glory, both on the right hand and on the left, is not denied to the disciples. But there are no privileged positions in God's rule, no ranks of status, no levels of authority. If anyone wishes to be first, Jesus had taught his followers earlier, she or he will be last of all and minister of all (9:35). Now, in this context of the Zebedee brothers' pursuit of elitist positions for themselves, and the indignation of the other disciples, Jesus proceeds to reinforce this teaching by contrasting the pyramidal verticality of the kingdoms of this world and the kind of human relationships that maintain the horizontality of God's rule which he is building. "You know," he says, "that those supposing to rule the nations lord it over them and the great ones tyrannize them. But it is not so among you! Rather whoever wants to be great among you will be your minister; and whoever wants to be first among you will be a slave of all."

This is how equality and justice are actualized and, concomitantly, how authentic community and communion are constituted and maintained. Moreover, this is the life style of the New Human Being! "For the Human Being did not come to be ministered to but to minister and give his life as a ransom for many." By adding the phrase "to give his life as a ransom for many" Jesus appropriates for himself as the New Human Being the role of sacrificial victim which Isa. 53:10–12 assigned to the Servant of the Lord. Previously he simply announced his forthcoming passion and resurrection. Now, for the first time, in this context of his teaching on the egalitarian structure of the community he is establishing, he attributes a vicarious significance to his death. Later, in Jerusalem, at the celebration of the Passover, he will again identify himself as the sacrificial victim whose blood of the covenant is going to be poured out on behalf of many. Jesus' sacrifice is not simply a substitutionary martyrdom which results in God being moved to spare the guilty. The offering of his life or self (*psychē*) is an eschatological ransom which delivers the creation from its bondage to sin and death by reconstituting the relationship between God and human beings. The "many" for whom this price of release will be paid are not limited to an exclusive number of people. Jesus' use of the word corresponds to contemporaneous Palestinian Jewish usage and actually means "all."[139] When he makes himself an offering for sin, he will bear the iniquities and transgressions of all human beings.

139. Joachim Jeremias, *polloi*, *TDNT*, 6:536, 543–45.

Special insight is required to "see" this drama unfold during the crucifixion, and this appears to be the point of the following episode which occurs on the threshold of the passion. Accompanied by his disciples and a considerable crowd of people, Jesus passes through Jericho on his way up to Jerusalem. He is temporarily halted by a blind beggar, Bartimaeus, the only individual identified by name in the healing stories of the Gospel, who, according to the narrator's word-play, is seated **at the edge of the way.** Being blind, he has had to resort to begging and consequently has become an "expendable" at the bottom of the socioeconomic pyramid of Roman Palestine. Hearing that Jesus is passing by, he begins to cry out, "Son of David, Jesus, show me mercy!" His use of "Son of David" to identify Jesus corresponds to Peter's earlier confession of Jesus as "the Messiah," a confession that Jesus rebuked and replaced with the New Human Being who must suffer. Now, in this context, many of those who are accompanying Jesus, both disciples and members of the crowd, issue the rebuke. The disciples may recall Jesus' censure; the crowd, on the other hand, may sense the anomaly of a blind individual begging Jesus for mercy by addressing him as "Son of David." For, according to 2 Sam. 5:8, "the blind . . . are hated by David's soul."

Can Bartimaeus really believe that a son of David would be moved to show him mercy? Perhaps he has sufficient insight into the character of Jesus to be so persistent. Perhaps he is willing to take the risk of defying historical continuity. He evidently believes that Jesus can help him and therefore refuses to be silenced, but his blindness appears to extend into his understanding of who Jesus is. Like the blind individual of Bethsaida who foreshadowed the blindness of Peter and the inadequacy of his christological identification of Jesus, he must have his eyes opened.

Jesus stops and summons him to be brought to him. Encouraged by the crowd, Bartimaeus leaps up and comes to Jesus as though his call has already opened his eyes. Two alternative actions are offered by the manuscript tradition of 10:50 in conjunction with his leaping. According to the majority of the scribal transmissions of the text, he threw away his outer garment, a cloak, indicating perhaps a desire to be unhindered in his approach of Jesus. On the other hand, a few versions (Minuscule 565 and the Sinaitic Syriac) recount that he put on his cloak before coming to Jesus, perhaps in order to appear before him fully dressed. Of the two possibilities, the act of throwing away the outer garment may be the more original because of its metaphorical character of stripping away the old in order to make oneself more presentable for a new beginning.

Jesus forces Bartimaeus to make his petition more explicit. "What do you want me to do for you?" he inquires. Certainly that should have been obvious. Yet perhaps Jesus intends to evoke from him an acknowledgment of his inability to see. It may also be the intention of the narrator to elicit such a response from the addressees of the Gospel. Simply and without exasperation Bartimaeus replies, "Rabbouni, that I shall gain sight." The "Son of David" title has been abandoned, and a new form of address, one, in fact, that occurs only here in the Gospel, has been used in its place.

What this epithet means is difficult to determine. Elsewhere in the New Testament it is found only in John 20:17, where it is translated as "teacher." As a result, it is often mistakenly regarded as a virtual synonym of "Rabbi," although no rabbi is ever addressed as "Rabbouni" in the writings of Rabbinic Judaism. The Aramaic translations of the Old Testament employ this form for "lord" in all its meanings; but, afterward in early Jewish literature, it is reserved by the Jews for God alone.[140] If, as Gustav Dalman asserts, "Rabbon(i)"—the "i" is simply the suffix that means "my"—and "Rabban" were in use as collateral forms, "Rabban" may have been developed as a style of address applied to great teachers, after "Rabbon" or "Ribbon" became restricted in its use to God alone.[141] Indeed, as Dalman points out, "it is a remarkable fact that in early Jewish literature, apart from the Targums, it is scarcely ever used except as referring to God."[142]

What is its significance here? In substituting "Rabbouni" for "Son of David," Bartimaeus may be expressing the kind of differential homage that is paid to Abraham and other great figures who are addressed in this manner in the Targums, the Aramaic translations of the Old Testament. On the other hand, in appropriating this form of address reserved for God alone in early Jewish literature, he, like the Greek woman of 7:28 in her singular use of "Lord," may be identify-

140. Gustav Dalman, *The Words of Jesus* (Edinburgh: T. & T. Clark, 1902), 35.
141. Ibid.
142. Ibid., 325.

ing Jesus more directly as a co-bearer of this title and therefore also a bearer of divine authority."

Jesus, in contrast to his earlier healing procedure, does not anoint or touch his eyes. He simply sends him away with the acknowledgment, "Your faith has saved you."[143] Evidently salvation involves seeing, not only physical sight but also genuine perception. Bartimaeus not only gained sight immediately[144] but he was following him **on the way**." The implications of this conclusion may be twofold. To follow Jesus on the way into Jersualem requires open eyes, that is, eyes of penetrating perception into the events that will unfold as the story moves to its culmination in his death and resurrection. Furthermore, although Jesus is the Messiah, as the opening verse of the Gospel conveys, the content of this title cannot be defined by previous tradition or limited to the typology of the Son of David. The reader must be conscious of this throughout the remainder of the narrative: from the moment Jesus is welcomed into Jerusalem with the cry, "Blessed is the coming rule of our father David" to Pilate's placement of the superscription on the cross, "The King of the Jews."

ENTRY INTO JERUSALEM, NEGATION OF THE TEMPLE INSTITUTION, AND CONFRONTATION WITH THE RULING ELITE (11:1—12:44)

After ascending the steep road from Jericho, Jesus arrives in the outskirts of Jerusalem at Bethphage and Bethany. His immediate destination is the Mount of Olives. This is indicated by the narrator's use of the preposition *pros* with the accusative case, denoting direction "toward." Two disciples are sent to procure a colt for him, most likely a young donkey, but specifically one on which no human being ever has sat. The peculiar emphasis on the pristine quality of the animal, which

---

143. These are the same words Jesus spoke to the hemorrhaging woman of 5:34. She risked the transgression of the law in a desperate effort to be cured. Bartimaeus has had his eyes opened as a result of a faith that dared to hope in spite of an inappropriate or inadequate Davidic typology.

144. Also implied in the use of this verb is that the LXX version of Isa. 42:18, which uses the same verb, has been fulfilled.

is intensified by the employment of a double negative (*oudeis oupō*),[145] suggests a symbolic union between the colt and Jesus. Only a donkey on which no human being has ever sat can carry the New Human Being into Jerusalem.

The disciples are to take the animal that is tied up in the opposite village in a quarter where its streets converge; and if anyone should attempt to prevent them, the reply, "The Lord has need of it" will remove any objections. As earlier, in 5:19, the sense of "the Lord" is deliberately ambiguous. It is the divine epithet of the Creator (1:3), but it is also a title by which Jesus has been addressed (7:28), and Jesus himself has related it to the New Human Being (2:28). Moreover, since he "comes in the name of the Lord," he can identify his need with that of the Lord.

The colt is brought to Jesus and prepared for its special task by the disciples, who saddle it with their own clothing. As he rides into the city, he is welcomed by the people, who honor him with the only red-carpet treatment they can offer: their cloaks spread out into the way and reeds cut from the fields. Joining together in a "Hosanna" or a "Save Us" chorus, they sing the introit liturgy of the temple derived from Psalm 118 and acclaim him as "the one who comes in the name of the Lord." According to their conviction, he will save them by inaugurating "the coming rule of our father David."

Like Solomon of old, Jesus is riding a donkey to his enthronement, but while the former used David's animal (1 Kings 1:33, 38) in order to express the reality of dynastic rule, Jesus sits astride a colt on which no one has ever ridden. His will be a radically different kind of coronation. A plaited crown of thorns will be thrust upon his head, and his throne will be the cross on which he will be crucified as "The King of the Jews." In the culmination of this extraordinary event, he will be the Messiah supremely, for by his death he will effect what no king before him ever succeeded in accomplishing: the conquest of evil and death.

After entering Jerusalem, Jesus proceeds directly to the temple. His purpose is not religious; he does not worship or have sacrifices offered up on his behalf. He goes into the sacred precinct in order to look

---

145. This is indicated by the narrator's use of the preposition *pros* with the accusative case.

about at all things. After an inspection of its activities, he leaves the city and returns to Bethany for the night accompanied by the twelve. The events of the following day clarify the critical nature of his visit and perhaps even intimate it to be a fulfillment of Mal. 3:1b–2, "And the Lord whom you seek will suddenly come to his temple; the messenger of the covenant in whom you delight, behold, he is coming, says the Lord of hosts. But who can endure the day of his coming, and who can stand when he appears?" Bearing both identities—the Lord and the messenger of the covenant—Jesus continues to embody the paradox of Mark 1:2–3[146] and to prepare for the day of the Lord's coming and the judgment which it brings.

On the following morning Jesus returns to Jerusalem. Along the way he sees a fig tree full of leaves and approaches it in order to pluck its fruit and satisfy his hunger. But he finds no figs, only leaves. Of course, he should not have expected any fruit, for, as the narrator observes, it was not the season for figs. Certainly Jesus, who has lived in Palestine all his life, is aware of this. A tree that participates in the orderly cycles of nature can only produce its fruit in season. Jesus' expectation is unreasonable, yet without hesitation he proceeds to curse the tree: "From now on may no one ever eat fruit from you!" To let his disappointment overwhelm him to the extent of pronouncing such a malicious judgment must have made him appear spiteful and irrational to his disciples. They "were listening," the narrator observes.

As on the previous day, they enter Jerusalem and make their way to the temple. Inside the sacred precinct Jesus unexpectedly launches an attack on the business enterprises that are being conducted for the pilgrims who have arrived from many different parts and places of the Greco-Roman world to celebrate the Passover. He drives out those who are selling *and* buying—which would include the pilgrims. He overturns the tables of the bankers who are selling the Jewish half-shekel for the payment of the temple tax. He unseats those engaged in the sale of doves for sacrificial offerings. Surprisingly, no effort is made by the temple police, the business people, or the pilgrims to stop him. To what extent his disciples may have assisted him in this violent undertaking is not indicated. His precipitous action may have caught everyone by surprise, while its radical nature may have stunned into

146. See above, pp. 73–74.

disbelief and immobility. For, although disturbances and riots had broken out in the sacred precinct on prevous occasions, none appear to have been aimed at the abolition of the temple institution itself.

This is not an act of reformation intended to eliminate business activities from the observance of the cult or to separate trade and commerce from the worship of God. Jesus is not "cleansing the temple." As "the one who comes in the name of the Lord," he is closing it down: "He was not allowing that anyone carry about a vessel through the temple." Ending the payment of the temple tax and the sale of doves and terminating all activity in the sacred precinct signify the end of the cult and its hierocracy and the tributary mode of distribution which both maintain. No Jew before him—not even the Essenes, who rejected the temple and withdrew to the Judean wilderness of Qumran—had conceived of such a final act of invalidation. His condemnation is based on the incompatibility between the divine will expressed in the Scriptures and the actualities of the institution: "Has it not been written, 'My house shall be called a house of prayer for all nations'? But you have made it a den of bandits!"

It is this episode which makes the seemingly senseless act of cursing the fig tree intelligible, while at the same time its far-reaching significance is obviated by it. The two incidents are interdependent and have a direct bearing on each other in terms of both comparison and contrast. Scrutinizing all things in the temple on the previous day corresponds to Jesus looking for fruit to satisfy his hunger. Like the fig tree, the temple is intended to serve the needs of human beings. But while a fig tree can produce fruit only in its season, the temple as an institution that mediates divine-human relationships cannot be, indeed must not be, regulated by the cycles of nature. It must bear fruit in season and out of season in order to satisfy the human hunger for transcendence. When, like the fig tree, it shows only leaves, it has lost its integrity, it is no longer fulfilling its purpose and therefore stands under divine judgment.[147] The cursing of the fig tree symbolizes the condemnation of the temple institution which, as the central systemic structure of Judaism, has been regulating the religious, political, economic, and social life of the Jewish people.

147. The prophets Jeremiah and Uriah had set the precedent for pronouncing condemnation on the institution of the temple when it did not fulfill its divinely intended purpose of serving all of the people of Israel. See Jeremiah 26.

For centuries the temple had functioned as the control center of the tributary mode of production that appropriated the agricultural surplus of the peasant cultivators and shepherds of the rural countryside and redistributed it among its priests, Levites, and lay officials. In time it became the hub of all commercial enterprise and activity—at least in the province of Judea—although it was always subject to the imperial power that dominated the country and drew off much of its profits in the form of taxes and tribute. Additionally the temple received a vast income from the temple tax which the law required every Jew to pay annually, gifts from the wealthy individuals, revenues from its landholdings, and profits from the sale of sacrificial animals and money exchange. In effect, it served as the central bank of worldwide Judaism, and all of its assets and dispersements were controlled and administered by the priestly aristocracy.[148]

Obviously the negation of this central systemic structure of Judaism, which Jesus symbolically enacts, marks the termination of its power and privilege but especially its oppression and dispossession of the Jewish masses.

Furthermore, the cancellation of the temple also abolishes the dehumanizing and tyrannical pollution system which it maintained—to the advantage of the ruling elite—by its inherent separation of the sacred and the secular. Its abrogation removes the foundation of a symbolic world divided into the opposed realms of "the clean" and "the unclean" and their corresponding moral definitions of good and evil. Since the temple is no longer validated, it cannot serve as the basis for differentiating the holy and the profane, and therefore with the removal of this barrier the two realms are reunited and the control of the priesthood is dissolved. Consequently it is no surprise that the sacred aristocracy, specifically the chief priests and the scribes, whose guardianship of the temple has been self-serving, begin to pursue the same objectives sought earlier by the Pharisees and the Herodians in Galilee (3:6): they were seeking how they might destroy him.

The effect of the curse pronounced on the fig tree is revealed on the following morning as Jesus and his disciples return to Jerusalem: "They saw the fig tree withered from (the) roots." However, it is not

---

148. See Neill Q. Hamilton, "Temple Cleansing and Temple Bank," *JBL* 83 (1964): 365–72; and Belo, *A Materialist Reading*, 63–67.

possible to discern this kind of process of desiccation. The roots remain invisible, and therefore it is impossible to determine whether the tree withered from the roots upward or from the branches downward. Obviously this detail is oriented toward the temple which the fig tree symbolizes and conveys the finality of its rejection. There is no hope for renewal or revitalization, for the roots are dead; and it is only a matter of time before the rest of the tree reveals this terminal condition. That is, the desiccation of the temple, dead at its roots, even though it continues to show life in its continued operation, will eventually be manifested as obviously as it has been in the withering of the fig tree.[149]

As they survey the dead tree, it is Peter who recalls the curse of the previous day: "Rabbi, look, the fig tree which you cursed is withered." Since the fate of the temple is symbolized by the fig tree, the question of its replacement in the life of Israel becomes critical, even if, unlike the fig tree, its demise is not yet evident. What will serve as God's residence on earth in the future? What will take the place of this architectonic center? How will the world be ordered without an *axis mundi* to separate the sacred from the secular? Does not the reunion of the two realms reconstitute primordial chaos? Will human beings be able to survive in such conditions?

Jesus shows that he is quite aware of the problems that the cancellation of the temple raises. The comprehensive answer he offers is simply, "Have the faith of God!" Although his exhortation is generally translated into English as "Have faith in God!" the preposition "in" does not occur in the Greek text. A genitive construction is employed which is usually identified as an "objective genitive." That is, the word in the genitive case, "God," is considered to be the object of the word it modifies, in this case "faith." But there is no other instance of an objective genitive in Mark's Gospel. Moreover, such a translation would seem to be out of place in view of Jesus' entry into a reordering of power and the resulting horizontal relationship which he enjoys with the Creator. As the New Human Being, he displays what "the confidence of God" is like by stilling the storm and walking on the Sea of Galilee. It is the capacity to exercise divine sovereignty over chaos

---

149. At the opening of his apocalyptic discourse in Mark 13, Jesus will openly predict the temple's destruction.

and the creative capability of ordering a world that is no longer determined by fixed boundaries between the sacred and the profane. Such an emulation of God's confidence enables an individual to say to **this mountain**—specifically the *axis mundi* of Mt. Zion on which the temple stands—"Be raised and cast into the sea!" And, as Jesus affirms, it shall be so! That, of course, eliminates the one place on earth where heaven and earth are united, that absolute point of reference which, like the North Star, serves as a compass and guarantees a divine security in the passage through life. Yet it is in this chaos and the freedom that arises from it—as terrifying as it may be—that human beings can begin to recover the sovereignty that the Creator willed for them by making them in the divine image and likeness. What is more, they can enter into a collaboration with the Creator in order to make all things new. The possibilities are unlimited. "On account of this I say to you, 'All such things as you pray and request, believe that you received, and it will be to you." Jesus employs the past tense, "believe that you **received**," in order to pinpoint the moment of entry into a reordering of power as the beginning of a new consciousness that in faith is open to all possibilities. At the same time, however, the exercise of such a faith includes closing the past for others in order to enable them to move into an unlimited future and thereby guaranteeing the same passage for oneself. "And when you stand praying," Jesus charges, "forgive if you have anything against anyone so that your Father in heaven also forgives you your offenses."

When Jesus returns to the temple, he is confronted by the chief priests, the scribes, and the elders. The implications of his actions in the temple on the previous day have not been lost on them. Since these are the three groups that constitute the Great Council of the Sanhedrin, this may be an unofficial judicial inquiry. An interrogation may produce evidence that can be used against him and result in bringing him to trial on substantive charges before the court. At the very least, this is an opportunity that may enable them to find a way to destroy him. "By what authority," they demand to know, "do you do these things?" And then rephrasing the question, they ask, "Or who gave you this authority that you do these things?"

Showing no sign of intimidation, Jesus shrewdly reduces the vertical distance between them and places them on an equal footing with himself by making a counterchallenge. As a result, he also frees himself from the necessity of answering their question and any possible self-incrimination that might be drawn from it. At the same time, his interrogation establishes a context for a possible reply. "I will question you one thing," he asserts, "and, should you answer me, I will also say to you by what authority I do these things. The baptism of John, was it from heaven or from human beings?" Because of the interdependent relationship between John and Jesus their response to his question will expose the extent of their openness to the reply he will make to their original demand and indicate what possibility of understanding exists between them. If they can acknowledge the divine origin of John's baptism, they should have little difficulty in affirming the heavenly source of the authority that Jesus has exercised throughout his ministry and more particularly now in his abolition of the temple institution.

But they refuse to commit themselves to any reply. For, on the one hand, they are unwilling to acknowledge the divine origin of John's baptism and, on the other hand, because they fear the crowd they are afraid to reveal what they think. Honest self-disclosure might cause them to be rejected by the Jewish masses. Consequently, since it is evident that there is no possibility of establishing a common ground of understanding between them, Jesus also refuses to answer their question.

Instead, he tells them the parable of the wicked tenants. A landowner plants a vineyard, leases it to peasants, and withdraws to his own place of residence. Whether he is a foreigner is not indicated; in any case, he is an absentee landlord. Even though the vineyard will not be productive for at least five years, labor is necessary to tend the vines and carry on the continuous process of cultivation and weeding. The expenses during this period of time will be defrayed by growing grain and vegetables between the rows of vines.[150] Although Jesus does not specify a time period in his parable, his audience would infer a period of tenancy before the first payment was due. When the season of the fruit finally arrives, the landlord sends a slave to collect the rent. He is beaten and sent back to his master empty-handed. Numerous other slaves are sent, but those who survive the treatment of the peasants are

---

150. See Klyne Snodgrass, *The Parable of the Wicked Tenants: An Inquiry Into Parable Interpretation* (Tübingen: J. C. B. Mohr [Paul Siebeck], 1983), 34.

forced to return to the owner of the vineyard without any payment:
some were beaten, one was struck on the head, and others were killed.
The treatment that these slaves received may be informed by prophetic
history, and to that extent, at least, the story is allegorical. Perhaps the
slave who is struck on the head intimates the fate of John the Baptizer.[151]

Eventually the owner decides to send his "beloved son," a phrase
that the addressees of the Gospel will immediately recognize on the
basis of its earlier use in 1:11 and 9:7 and naturally identify with Jesus.
By such adaptation of the original parable the narrator extends the
allegorical character of the story for this particular context, but without sacrificing its parabolic impact. The sending of the son suggests a
recourse to legal action: "They will respect my son." Only someone
who was involved in the ownership of the land could represent the
landlord and serve as a legal claimant.[152] The tenants, however, kill the
son to forestall any legal action, dispose of the corpse, and take
possession of the vineyard. The lapse of time between their entry into a
contract with the owner and the murder of his son may cover the
period of time that the law requires for the acquisition of the land.[153]

Jesus concludes the story with a question, and without waiting for a
reply he offers his own answer. "What will the lord of the vineyard do?
He will come and destroy the tenant farmers and give the vineyard to
others." Those who kill the heir are dispossessed by the owner. But this
self-evident punishment must be understood in the light of the story's
unusual beginning in which Jesus links the prophetic allegory of the
vineyard in Isa. 5:1–7 to what may have been a common Galilean
episode of class conflict. To his elite audience the introduction of the
story—"A human being planted a vineyard and placed a wall around
(it); and dug a wine vat and built a tower"—would evoke the memory
of Isaiah's Song of the Vineyard. For them the implied identification of
the absentee landlord with God, the vineyard owner of Isaiah's allegory, would be entirely natural. Being absentee landlords themselves,

---

151. Clearly Mark has adapted Jesus' parable to this particular literary context of
Jesus' encounter with the ruling elite in Jerusalem who have confronted him with an
unofficial judicial interrogation.

152. Snodgrass, *The Parable of the Wicked Tenants*, 37–38.

153. See Mishna, *Baba Bathra* 3:1, 3. Also Snodgrass, *The Parable of the Wicked
Tenants*, 38–39.

they would have no difficulty in thinking of God in the same way and therefore would easily be drawn into the story.

But while they associate the landlord of the vineyard with God, they are forced to identify themselves with the tenants to whom the vineyard has been entrusted. Metaphorically, for a brief moment, they are obliged to see themselves as caretakers of God's vineyard, Israel, who are not fulfilling the covenant to which they had bound themselves. Yet more ironically perhaps, by being inclined—as landowners generally would be—to assent to the retribution that the owner of the vineyard inflicts on the tenants, they are compelled to pronounce judgment on themselves. As they have dispossessed, so they will be dispossessed!

Jesus does not identify those to whom the vineyard will be given. They are often considered to be the gentiles.[154] But while this is true for Matthew's version of the parable (Matt. 21:43), the "others" of 12:9 may refer to the disenfranchised lower classes to whom and for whom Jesus has directed his ministry. The scriptural text that he appends to the parable conveys a similar reversal. Drawn from Ps. 118:22–23, the introit liturgy of the temple from which the crowd derived its "Hosanna" chorus to accompany Jesus' triumphal entry into Jerusalem, it offers a change of metaphor. In place of the vineyard, a building is inferred; instead of tenant farmers, builders. "The stone which the builders rejected, this became (the) keystone! From (the) Lord this happened, and it is marvelous in our eyes." Although this image of the rejected keystone is usually interpreted christologically by being identified with Jesus,[155] by analogy in view of the change in metaphor, it more appropriately refers to the "others" who receive the vineyard at the conclusion of the parable. The crowd who accompanied Jesus into Jerusalem singing the Hosanna chorus of Psalm 118 is the stone rejected by the builders but who, by divine reversal, will be made into the keystone of the living temple that God is building.

Although these members of the Sanhedrin are among the "outsiders" of 4:11 to whom "all things happen in parables," they do understand the story that Jesus has addressed to them. This is no riddle they are unable to decipher. Determined by their position at the top of the socioeconomic pyramid and victimized by its perspective,

154. E.g., Schweizer, *Good News*, 241; and Belo, *A Materialist Reading*, 187.
155. So Belo, *A Materialist Reading*, 186.

they nevertheless experience a moment of perspicacity. They see themselves reflected in the conduct of the tenant farmer: they have not fulfilled the contract into which they entered with the owner of the vineyard, and therefore they stand condemned. But in this moment of seeing, they refuse to see; in this moment of hearing, they refuse to understand. Consequently they prevent themselves from repenting and experiencing forgiveness. Instead, they become more determined to destroy Jesus, but for the time being they are unable to act, because they fear the crowd. Ironically, they will actualize the conclusion of the parable by delivering the "beloved son" up to the Romans for execution, and, as a result, he and the household he is building (3:20, 31–35) will become the keystone to the New Humanity that God is constituting.

Another encounter with the ruling elite takes place that underlines their determination to do away with Jesus. By leading him into a controversial issue in which he might stumble into self-incrimination, they may be able to find some ground for legal action against him. The Pharisees and the Herodians, who had already plotted against him in Galilee (3:6), are the first to be sent by the Sanhedrin in order that "they might catch him by a word." Their duplicity is evident in their flattering preface: "Teacher, we know that you are true and are concerned about no one's (favor); for you do not look at the appearance of human beings, but in accordance with the truth you teach the way of God." It seems that even his enemies recognize his integrity. But they acknowledge it only in order to draw him out on a very delicate matter, indeed, a volatile political issue: "Is it right to give tax to Caesar or not? Should we give or not give?"

Aware of their hypocrisy, Jesus confronts them with their obvious intention: "Why do you test me?" For he knows that the Herodians represent Roman interests and that at least some of the Pharisees are allied with them. When he asks from them a denarius, the Roman coin used to pay taxes, they immediately produce one. Made of silver, probably minted under Tiberius and bearing his divinized image with the accompanying inscription, "Tiberius, Caesar, Augustus, the son of the divine Augustus," it is an offense to Jewish sensibility.[156] Yet they

---

156. Grundmann, *Markus*, 327. His entire discussion of this episode is very perceptive, 325–28.

have one readily available and are compelled to identify its image as that of Caesar. Their acknowledgment serves as Jesus' point of departure: "The things of Caesar give back to Caesar and the things of God to God." It is an answer they cannot debate or denounce, for it articulates a point of view not unlike their own but with a significant difference. They render to Caesar the things that belong to Caesar and to God the things that belong to God, but without integrity. For they do not differentiate clearly the boundary lines between the two realms of jurisdiction. Jesus does not merely assert, "Give to Caesar the things of Caesar," but "Give **back** to Caesar . . . ." Since the coin bears Caesar's image and inscription, it represents his political power and economic interests but absolutized by his blasphemy of self-deification. By having the denarius in their possession, they have subjected themselves to its ultimate claims.[157] However, by returning to Caesar that which belongs to him, namely, the coin and all that it falsely represents, they are free to give God the things that belong to God. Indeed, one can only render to God all the things that rightfully belong to God as the Sovereign Creator by returning what belongs to Caesar in order to be liberated from his claims. The consequences that would follow such actions are not discussed. Overwhelmed with astonishment at his reply, the Pharisees and the Herodians are unable or unwilling to pursue the matter further.

The next encounter involves Jesus with a group of Sadducees, an aristocratic party consisting of upper-class priests and lay "elders." There is no indication of any ulterior motive as they approach him with an illustration of the absurdity of the resurrection of the dead. They may be included in the round of challenges directed toward Jesus to show how far his perspective is removed from that of all or at least most of the ruling elite in the architectonic center of Jerusalem. In their ideological orientation they are not only antimillennialists but also practical realists, for they challenge the credibility of the eschatological reality of levirate marriage. Since the law decrees that a man is obligated to marry the wife of his deceased childless brother in order to raise up offspring for him, what ultimately happens when seven brothers end up marrying the same woman? Whose wife will she be at the resurrection of the dead? The question itself does not pose a legal

157. Ibid., 327.

problem for the Sadducees, but, as far as they are concerned, it exposes the incredibility of the resurrection.

Whether their scriptural canon is limited to the Torah of Moses is uncertain. Nevertheless, Jesus counterchallenges their use of Moses to negate the reality of the resurrection by invoking an earlier witness of Moses drawn from the context of Israel's liberation from Egyptian enslavement. The exodus which dominates the cultic and ethical legislation of the Torah apparently remains at the periphery of their ideology and the self-understanding which is informed by it. If, in fact, the exodus were at the center of their world view, they would not be who they are and could not collaborate with Roman imperialism or any other exploitative power in dispossessing and dehumanizing the people whose ancestors God had delivered from bondage.

Jesus first corrects their false understanding of the nature of the resurrection. The new creation does not stand in material continuity with the present order of things but is realized by a transformation of the old creation. Earthly life, therefore, does not mirror the realities of the new heaven and the new earth which the resurrection will inaugurate. Levirate marriage or any unusual circumstances arising from it cannot be used to undermine or illuminate it. "For when they arise from the dead," he asserts, "neither do they marry nor are they married, but they are as the angels in the heavens."

Second, even though the teaching of the resurrection is not explicit in the Torah of Moses, its presuppositions are present and should be evident to any Jew who is able to penetrate into the meaning of the text: "Do you not read in the book of Moses . . . ?" As already indicated, Jesus focuses specifically on the event that initiated the exodus and brought Israel into a covenantal relationship with Yahweh. At the burning bush, where Moses was commissioned to undertake the liberation of the Hebrews, Yahweh introduced himself as "the God of Abraham, the God of Isaac, and the God of Jacob." Why should Yahweh link himself with those who are already dead? What kind of effective power would that convey at this critical moment? For Moses it would have no meaning at all unless it intimated that for this God who is confronting him even the ultimate reality of death cannot cancel an earlier covenant that was enacted or the lives of those who entered into it. The patriarchs—and matriarchs!—with whom Yahweh identifies must still be alive, if they continue to serve as Yahweh's representatives even in the present. God is not God of the dead, Jesus declares, but of the living! In this way he not only exposes the superficiality of the Sadducees' hermeneutics; but more significantly, he confronts them with their basically un-Jewish orientation, and with greater vehemence he does not hesitate to repeat his earlier charge, "You are greatly deceived!"

A lawyer, "one of the scribes," overhears this theological debate and, because he is impressed with Jesus' response to the Sadducees, approaches him with a question of his own. "Which commandment," he asks, "is first of all?" There is no explicit indication of a devious motive or hostile intention, yet in view of Jesus' encounter with the Sadducees, the scribe wants to determine the character of his Jewishness.

Without hesitation Jesus responds to the question by quoting the central confession of Judaism, the great Shema of Deut. 6:4: "Hear, Israel, (the) Lord our God is one Lord, and you shall love (the) Lord your God out of your whole heart and out of your whole soul and out of your whole understanding and out of your whole strength."

Heart, soul, mind, and strength: these are the anthropological realities that are to be directed totally to God in love. In the Israelite understanding of the human being the heart is the central organ of the body that makes it possible for the limbs to move.[158] It is where vital decisions are made, and the arms and legs are set in motion. Without a heart the human being has no will. The heart can be stubborn and refuse to move the body in order to fulfill a plan or complete an action. The heart can be weak, sickened by fear, overwhelmed by troubles and therefore cause paralysis. The heart can also be joyful, because fear has been dispelled and troubles have been eliminated. When, according to Jeremiah's vision of a new covenant, the law of God is inscribed upon human hearts, human beings will be set free to act in accordance with God's will naturally. To love God out of a whole heart means to be completely unhindered to fulfill the Creator's will for authentic human existence.

To love God out of a whole soul means to be single-minded in orienting oneself toward the breath of the Creator which constituted the human being as a living self. "As the heart longs for flowing

158. Wolff, *Anthropology of the Old Testament*, 40–45.

streams, so my soul longs for you, O God. My soul thirsts for God, for the living God," sings the psalmist (Ps. 42:1–2). It is the breath of the Creator that renews the soul and imparts new possibility, freedom, and life to those who are overburdened by necessity, limitation, and death. To love God out of a whole soul is to fulfill that possibility, freedom, and life.

To love God out of a whole mind is Jesus' addition to this summary of the first Table of the Law. What he is referring to is not so much the mind itself but its reasoning capabilities and the totality of understanding which it has gained through its intellectual powers. To love God out of a whole mind, therefore, does not mean to concentrate all the powers of the intellect on knowing God. God is known by the soul or self. God is known in the heart, not by the mind or its capabilities. To love God out of a whole mind is to direct the flow of human affection to the Creator with all the understanding that has been acquired and to use the gift of intelligence to enlarge that understanding.

Finally, strength! To love God out of the totality of strength means to combine all of the physical capabilities and powers that a human being possesses in expressing devotion to the Creator, the source of all power. The commandment that is "first of all" is a summons to fulfill all of the aspects of human being in love to God.

Jesus demonstrates his Jewishness to the lawyer with a very orthodox response to his question, but before the lawyer can reply he adds a commandment that does not belong to the Shema but is drawn from Lev. 19:18: "You shall love your fellow human being as yourself." Evidently the commandment that is first of all cannot stand alone. It must be accompanied by a second which has equal weight, for Jesus adds, "No other commandment is greater than these." Indeed, the two cannot be separated from each other. For to love God out of a whole heart is to be free and courageous in fulfilling the will of God in our relationships with our fellow human beings and with ourself. To love God out of our whole soul is to open ourselves to actualizing the possibility and freedom of God in all levels of human society. To love God out of a whole mind is to employ all the powers of the intellect in devotion to the Creator by discovering new and superior ways of building social and economic institutions that eliminate poverty, ignorance, and disease.

The lawyer expresses his approval of Jesus' response: "Quite right,

Teacher!" and proceeds to validate his answer with further quotations from the Old Testament. The monotheism of the Shema is supported by a citation from Deut. 4:35: "There is one and there is no other except him." Second, the slightly abbreviated twofold summary of the law is joined to a text from 1 Sam. 15:22 which indicates that he has grasped the interdependence of the two commandments: "And to love the fellow human being as oneself is greater than all whole burnt offerings and sacrifices."

After Jesus commends the scribe for his wise answer, "You are not far from the rule of God," the narrator concludes the episode with the observation, "And no one dared to question him further." The strategy of placing this incident after the two previous confrontations is to have Jesus' orthodoxy acknowledged by "one of the scribes," an officially recognized interpreter of Moses' Torah. Jesus, in spite of his conflict with the ruling elite, is a true Jew. Indeed, he is more genuinely Jewish than the Sadducees. He not only believes in the oneness of God, he knows the power of God and demonstrates an understanding of God's will.

At the same time, however, it is to be made plain that his interpretation of the Scriptures is not only authoritative, it is superior to that of Judaism's official interpreters, the scribes. Now that no one dares to question him further, he takes the offensive. Curiously he returns to the temple which he has condemned. But since the effect of his cancellation is not yet evident, it may still serve as a place of teaching, perhaps especially if it involves posing a challenge to the scribal interpretation of the son of David Christology, which may have been pervasive in Judaism at this time.[159] At the architectonic center of Judaism, in Jerusalem in the temple, Jesus raises the question, "How (is it) the scribes say that the Messiah is Son of David?" His query not only challenges scribal exegesis, it also raises the christological riddle of the Gospel. Simon Peter confessed Jesus to be the Messiah. Blind Bartimaeus addressed him as "son of David." If the Messiah is the son of David, then he is the bearer of the royal prerogatives and qualities of his father. David and his messianic descendant are essentially equal, even if the latter is an eschatological figure who will be divinely endowed with powers that David himself did not possess.[160]

159. Perhaps the scribal identification of the Messiah with the son of David is best expressed in *Psalm of Solomon* 17, which may have originated in the previous century.
160. See *Psalm of Solomon* 17.

But, as Jesus observes on the basis of Ps. 110:1, "David himself [to whom the psalm is attributed] said by the holy Spirit, '(The) Lord said to my lord, "Sit at my right hand until I put your enemies under your feet." ' " Although Psalm 110 appears to be a royal psalm expressing Yahweh's invitation to an anointed king to ascend the throne, "Sit at my right hand," there is no hint that he is David's son. He must, in fact, be more than David's son, for, as Jesus observes, "David himself calls him lord, so in what way is he his son?" Since in Israelite-Jewish culture a son could never become the lord of his father—with the interesting exception of Joseph and Jacob[161]—David must be referring to someone other than any of his descendants in spite of the dynasty which Yahweh had promised to him in 2 Sam. 7:8–16. But who this might be is never made explicit.

No further implications are drawn from this conclusion. No attempt is made to determine the identity of David's lord. The matter is left as an enigma for Jesus' hearers in the temple to resolve for themselves. Yet at this point the ambiguity of Jesus' messiahship—and the so-called messianic secret, if there is any in the story world of Mark—should be dissolved for the disciples, or at least for the addressees of the Gospel. David's lord is none other than the New Human Being whom Jesus embodies and manifests. As such, he is the lord who has need of a donkey on whom no one ever sat in order to ride to his unusual coronation in Jerusalem. He is the New Human Being who is "lord of the sabbath." He is the one who exercises divine authority over the demons and unclean spirits and therefore is addressed as "Lord" by the Syrophoenician woman. He is the co-bearer of the divine epithet because he is "seated on the right hand of power." If there is any messianic secret that is to be disclosed to the disciples inside as well as outside the narrative world of the Gospel, it is the identity of Jesus the Messiah, Jesus Christ, as the New Human Being who, because he is David's lord, cannot be David's son.

Because the large crowd in the temple is listening to him gladly, Jesus continues his teaching. In spite of his earlier affirmation of a particular scribe, he presses his attack on these official lawyers of

161. The youth of 14:51–52 and 16:5 who mirrors Jesus' destiny parallels the career of Joseph in Genesis 37—41. Sold into slavery by his brothers, Joseph is forced to flee from Potiphar's wife, leaving behind his garment. "Buried" in prison for two years, he emerges at the beginning of the third year, interprets Pharaoh's dream, and is co-enthroned with Pharaoh, arrayed in a white garment of royalty.

Jerusalem. Not only is their interpretation of the Scriptures defective but their life style is hypocritical. They emphasize their elite position in society by walking about in long robes, publicly acknowledged by greetings in the marketplaces, seats of honor in the synagogues, and reclining couches of prestige at banquets. Yet their deeds do not correspond to their teaching or the honor they insist on as the interpreters of God's law to the people. They are basically schizophrenic, for on the one hand they devour the houses of widows, while at the same time for pretense they offer up long prayers. They "will receive greater condemnation," is the sentence Jesus pronounces on them.

In a final scene in the temple a stark contrast between the piety of the rich and the piety of the poor manifests itself as Jesus sits opposite the contribution box observing the crowd passing by and throwing in their charity donations. Many rich people deposit large sums of money. A poor widow drops in two lepta, the smallest copper coins in circulation; and she provides the context for the pronouncement he makes to his disciples: "Amen I say to you, this poor widow cast more than all those casting into the contribution box. For all cast out of their abundance, but this one out of her poverty cast everything which she had, her whole life." While the elite scribes devour widows' houses and perhaps give to charity out of the wealth they have expropriated from others, the poor—as represented by the widow—express the kind of devotion to God and their fellow human beings that Jesus had articulated earlier in his response to the questioning scribe. As destitute as they may be, they demonstrate in deed that they love God out of their whole heart, soul, mind, and strength, even, like the widow, to the extent of giving all they have.

TEACHING ON LAST THINGS
(13:1–37) _____

After contrasting the charity of the destitute widow with that of the rich, Jesus leaves the temple. He will never return. He has already condemned it, and what he has just experienced only confirms his earlier judgment. As an institution it no longer fulfills its divine purpose. Those who function in it are not changed by it; they exploit the power and the privilege which they have for self-aggrandizement. When upon exiting his followers marvel at the great stones and the impressive buildings of the temple, Jesus predicts their destruction. "You see these great buildings? Not a stone will be left on a stone," he declares, "which will not be torn down!" The time will come when the sentence he has passed upon the temple will become evident in its catastrophic destruction.

This prophecy serves as the point of departure for Jesus' discourse on "the last things." The scene changes to the Mount of Olives "opposite the temple," where Jesus is seated with four of his disciples: Peter, James, John, and Andrew. They are the original four whom he called at the outset of his ministry alongside Lake Galilee, and they will become the recipients of his final teaching. Tell us when these things will be, they ask, and what is the sign when all these things are going to be consummated? Although the two questions are not synonymous, they are related to each other. While the first is oriented toward Jesus' prophecy regarding the temple, the second focuses on the nature of the end. The juxtaposition of the two questions suggests that, for the disciples, the ruination of the temple is linked to the consummation of history. Very likely they are serving as the spokespersons of a particular eschatological orientation that unites these two events. When the temple is destroyed, history will reach its divinely appointed goal. Evidently for the addressees of the Gospel the former has already occurred. Jesus' prediction has been fulfilled, and the temple lies in ruins. Since other cataclysmic events in history and nature are taking place, the second question has become critical: "And what is the sign when all these things are going to be consummated?"

Jesus begins his discourse with a warning: "Keep on being aware lest anyone deceives you!" Such a stern response to his disciples' questions intimates prevalent views that must be subverted from the outset and, simultaneously with them, those who are inculcating them as self-legitimated representatives of Jesus: "Many will come in my name saying 'I am,' and they will deceive many." The disciples are to be on guard against those who correlate historical catastrophes of war— such as the great war of the Jews against Rome—and the natural disasters of earthquakes and famines with the grand culmination of God's apocalyptic intervention. All of these realities—wars, earthquakes, famines—as tragic, painful, and embittering as they may be, are necessary. They must happen, but they do not foreshadow the end. They are only the beginning of the contractions of a long process that

will climax in the birth of a new age. Jesus' metaphorical pronouncement, "These things (are) the beginning of the birth pains!" hints at a
pregnancy, mysteriously concealed in the creation and, after a long
period of gestation, arriving at the time of birth. The initial labor pains
have already begun. But these phenomena—the destruction of the
temple, wars, earthquakes, and famines—are not signs of the end. The
convulsions and contractions of Mother History must continue until
the good news of God's rule reaches all people on earth: "And unto all
nations first it is necessary (that) the gospel be proclaimed."

The disciples will be involved in that enterprise and consequently
will experience persecution and death. "So keep on being aware of
yourselves," Jesus admonishes them. While they are to be on guard
against being deceived by others, they must also be alert to the
tribulations they will encounter as they fulfill their mission. "They will
deliver you up to sanhedrins and to synagogues (where) you will be
beaten," he predicts, "and you will stand before governors and kings
because of me for a witness to them." The ordeals of suffering and
death will not only be inflicted by political and religious institutions.
They will also arise in the home and the family: "And brother will
deliver up brother unto death and father child, and children will rise
up against parents and put them to death. And you will be hated by all
on account of my name." Faithful discipleship will be costly, almost
unbearable. No alleviation can be expected. Their sufferings belong to
the labor pains which Mother History must endure in order to give
birth to the new creation. Only those who endure to the end with her
will be saved. But they will be inspired and fortified by God's Spirit:
"And when delivering you up, they lead (you) away, don't be anxious
beforehand what you'll speak. . . . For you are not the ones speaking,
but the holy Spirit."

After having identified the destruction of the temple, wars, earthquakes, and famines with "the beginning of the birth pains," and
conveyed to his disciples a glimpse of their own future in fulfilling their
mission, Jesus returns to the matter that gave rise to his discourse on
eschatology. While the destruction of the temple is not explicitly
mentioned again, the forces that will bring it about are covertly
identified: "When you see the abomination of desolation standing
where it should not—let the reader understand!" Once again the
narrator enters the story but here for the first time to call the reader to

attention.[162] But what is the reader to understand? Jesus' use of Daniel's reference to the desolating sacrilege of the temple (Dan. 9:27; 11:31; 12:11), the detestable altar dedicated to Zeus that Antiochus IV had set up in order to enforce his program of Hellenizing Judaism, is to be identified with an analogous desecration linked to the forthcoming ruination of the Jewish center of the world. For the disciples within the story this would be a future occurrence, but the reader of the story would identify the abomination of desolation with the standards of the Roman legions which were erected and worshiped in the temple area after the destruction of the temple.[163] Is the exhortation to the reader, "Let the reader understand!" intended to reinforce the separation between this tragic holocaust and the consummation of history? That would seem redundant, because Jesus already has disconnected the desolation of the temple from the signs immediately preceding the end. More likely the narrator is calling the reader disciple to reflect on this great tragedy and the circumstances that accompanied it and to understand them paradigmatically. What the abomination of desolation will be in the future and where it will arise the reader of course cannot know. But in accordance with its character and its previous appearances it will be identifiable as an anti-God reality that will attempt to usurp God's central place in society and in the lives of those who participate in it. When such desolating forces of sacrilege manifest themselves, the conditions they engender will be as bitter and painful as those which accompanied the destruction of Jerusalem: "Then let the ones in Judea flee into the mountains. Let the one on the roof not descend nor even enter to take anything from his house. And let the one out in the field not return home to take his cloak." Decisive action, which involves abandonment of homes, fields, and even clothing for the sake of speedy flight, will be the only effective response. The disciples must be free and unencumbered. They should pray that seasonal conditions, such as winter and the lack of food, and that religious observances such as the sabbath, do not put

---

162. The narrator's calling the reader to attention would indicate reader rather than hearer addressees. Certainly some of the addressees of Mark's Gospel were readers, but, given the poverty and the lack of education of the peasants and the artisans in the rural countryside, it is difficult to believe that most of them were literate.

163. See Josephus, *The Jewish War* 6.328, 402.

additional restrictions on their freedom of movement. Pregnant women and mothers nursing children will be at a great disadvantage. Like the nightmare of the Jerusalem holocaust, the horror will increase; and it will exceed that of any previous event or period in history: "For those days will be an affliction which has not happened to such an extent from the beginning of creation which God created until now and never will be." For the disciples in the story, the "now" would refer to their time in Jerusalem; but for the readers whom the narrator is addressing, the "now" must refer to their time after the destruction of Jerusalem. And even greater affliction lies in the future, and it will be so severe and horrendous that no one would survive at all unless that time were shortened. When the birth pains have reached their greatest intensity, then for the sake of the elect God will finally intervene and reconstitute all things.

Under such frightful circumstances the disciples must be especially wary of false messiahs and prophets. More than ever they will be in danger of being deceived. For when their suffering seems almost intolerable, they will be more vulnerable to seductive rumors of the Messiah's rendezvous: "Look here (is) the Messiah!" "Look, there!" "Don't believe it," Jesus warns, "but false messiahs and false prophets will rise"—as in the turmoil of those years before the destruction of Jerusalem!—"and do signs and wonders in order to mislead, if possible, the elect." In view of such overwhelming seduction Jesus admonishes his followers once more, "But you keep on being aware! I've told you all things beforehand." These predictions, reinforced for the addressees of the Gospel by the fulfillment of his prophecy of the ruination of the temple, should equip the disciples with a measure of defense in order to endure to the end.

Finally, when the birth pains are at their worst, the old age will pass away. The heavenly luminaries will collapse, all light will be extinguished, and the world will be plunged into primordial darkness. "But in those days after that affliction," Jesus declares, "the sun will be darkened, and the moon will not give its radiance and the stars will be falling from heaven." Since Jewish apocalypticism considers stars to be angels or heavenly beings who are representative of the empires, kingdoms, and polities in the divine council, these cosmic events will culminate in the shaking of "the powers in the heavens" and signal the passing away of the institutional structures they had erected for the exploitation of the masses of humankind.[164] All those realities which transcended individual human life, the so-called powers and principalities, established by the forces of imperialism that by oppression and dispossession have diminished human existence, will be transformed.[165] Only after the powers in the heavens have been shaken, only after hierarchical structures have been horizontalized, can and will the New Humanity be born as a corporate, social reality. "And **then** they will see the Human Being coming on the clouds with much power and glory. And **then** he will send the angels, and he will gather together his chosen from the four winds from (the) end of the earth to (the) end of heaven." History at last will have arrived at its divinely appointed goal. Human destiny will be fulfilled, and those who have recovered the divine image and likeness in which they were created will participate fully in God's power and glory.

In response to the disciples' second question, "What is the sign when all these things are going to be consummated?" Jesus has offered only the vaguest answer: "When you see the abomination of desolation standing where it should not." The burden lies on them! They must judge when and where that will take place, but even more critically they must determine what it is. Without a specific sign to ascertain the season of time, they are left vulnerable and insecure. Yet that is as it should be, for it is their very vulnerability and insecurity that will foster watchfulness.

Therefore, in conclusion Jesus returns to their earlier question, "When will these things be?" and gives them an answer that will reinforce the watchfulness required for eschatological living. "So from the fig tree learn the parable!" The disciples inside and outside the story world of Mark's Gospel have already had to learn a parable from the fig tree about the condemnation of the temple. The fig tree will also serve as a metaphor for the future. As its budding marks the advent of summer—in contrast to the nondeciduous trees of Palestine—so also "when you see these things happening, you know that he is near, at the very door." The growing intensity of Mother History's contractions and

164. See Psalm 82; Dan. 8:10–25; 10:13; 12:1; *1 Enoch* 1:5; 6:2–8; 12:3–6; 14:3–6; 15:4—16:2; *Jub.* 4:15; 5:1; *T. Reub.* 5:6–7; *T. Naph.* 3:5; *2 Enoch* 7:18; Jude 6; 2 Pet. 2:4; Rev. 12:3–4.

165. Walter Wink, *Naming the Powers: The Language of Power in the New Testament* (Philadelphia: Fortress Press, 1984), 13–35.

the accompanying temptation to be lured into illusory resolutions of the
great suffering that prevails should make them aware that the birth of the
new creation is near. What they can be sure of is that "this generation will
by no means pass away until all these things happen." Actualization is
certain. "This generation," however, does not merely refer to Jesus' contemporaries but to the generation of humankind; it will not cease to exist
until the goal has been reached. Indeed, nothing, not even the passing of
heaven and earth, can prevent the fulfillment of Jesus' words. They are the
guarantee, "Amen I say to you," of the New Human Being.

But the precise time is incalculable: "About that day or hour no one
knows, neither the angels in heaven nor the son, only the Father." For
an ending that will be sudden and unexpected, continuous vigilance is
the only recourse: "Keep on being aware! Keep on being awake!" To
underline the urgency of such a style of life, Jesus brings his discourse
to a close with another metaphor: "For you don't know when the right
time (kairos) is: like a departing human being leaving his house and
giving his slaves authority, to each his work, and to the doorkeeper he
commanded that he watch." Similarly, Jesus endows his disciples with
authority and places the rule of God under their jurisdiction. Such a
trust requires faithfulness. Each has her or his own work. But what is
needed above all is watchfulness: "Therefore keep on watching—for
you don't know when the lord of the house comes, either at evening or
at midnight or at cockcrow or in the morning—lest coming suddenly he
finds you sleeping." The uncertainty of the time and suddenness of the
arrival demand a never-ending alertness; and to impress this on the
reader disciples as well, the narrator has Jesus end his discourse repeating
his earlier charge: "What I say to you, I say to all, 'Keep on watching!' "

THE ANOINTING OF THE MESSIAH AND THE
BEGINNING OF THE PASSION[166]
(14:1–52) _____

It is a curiosity that up to this point in the Gospel the narrator has
avoided all time references—deliberately, it would seem. No dates

166. Trocmé (The Formation of the Gospel According to Mark, 215–59) concludes
that Mark's Gospel passed through two editions, the first included chaps. 1—13, written around A.D. 50. Chapters 14—16, which "convey certain theological ideas that are
scarcely compatible with the conviction of Mark 1—13," were added later to produce
the second edition (p. 240) by "an anonymous ecclesiastic of the Roman community"
(p. 246) and was attributed to Mark. How much incompatibility there is between chaps.
1—13 and 14—16 evidently depends on how the Gospel is read.

have been used to establish a temporal framework for Jesus' ministry or any of its activities. Geographical settings have dominated the plot line of the story. The narrator has recounted the movement of Jesus from place to place: Nazareth to the Jordan River; into the wilderness; back to Galilee; at the edge of the lake; Capernaum; and various other regions of the Galilean province, such as towns, villages, fields, the other side of the lake, and eventually Judea and Jerusalem. The phrases "on that day" (4:35), "after some time" (2:1), and "in those days" (8:1) offer no chronological orientation, and the time references, "forty days" (1:13) and "after six days" (9:2), are symbolically determined by the events to which they are linked.

Instead, an eschatological framework sets the context for Jesus' career. It is the *kairos,* the right time or season of God's rule into which he entered at his baptism and which he has been constituting for his fellow Jews through his deeds and words. *Kairos* (time as event) rather than *chronos* (measured time) determines the ministry of Jesus; consequently there is no need to measure time by a calendar or a clock.

It is striking therefore that Jesus' entry into his passion is fixed by a time reference, not by a date but by a Jewish festival: "Now it was the Passover and the feast of Unleavened Bread after two days." Or, in other words, the time is two days before the Passover and the succeeding festival of Unleavened Bread which the former inaugurates. In this context, according to the narrator, the ruling elite, specifically the chief priests and the chief interpreters of the law, confer with one another how they might apprehend Jesus and put him to death. All their earlier efforts to trick him into self-incrimination have failed. Since no legal recourse is open to them, they evidently have resolved to do away with him by treachery. The means, it would seem, are justified by the end. Thus, it is within the time frame of the Passover that Jesus will enter into his passion, and it is in the light of this celebration of liberation that his death and resurrection are interpreted.

While the days are lived in Jerusalem, the nights are spent in Bethany. According to 11:11, Jesus and his followers retreated to this nearby village in the evening. Now, on one of these two days before the Passover he is dining in the house of someone called Simon the Leper, who apparently has been cured of his disease, perhaps by Jesus himself,[167] and is once again a full participant in Jewish society. Whether

167. Could he be the leper of 1:40–45?

he is the one who offers Jesus hospitality of room and board is not indicated. During the meal an unnamed woman unexpectedly enters in order to anoint Jesus with a very expensive perfume. By breaking into this communion which would be limited to men, she is transgressing a social prohibition.[168] Yet any self-consciousness or embarrassment she might feel is neutralized by the one objective she pursues. She has brought with her a box made of alabaster containing pure nard ointment, a costly perfume made from the root of a fragrant East Indian plant and worth more than three hundred denarii, the wages that a day laborer would earn in a year. She breaks the alabaster box and pours the ointment over Jesus' head. Surprisingly, what agitates the men reclining at the table with Jesus is not her presumption of entering their dinner party or her arrogance in assuming the prerogative of an Old Testament prophet in order to perform the ceremony of anointing Jesus as king. They do not appear to grasp the significance of her act. They are outraged by what she has done, but their focus is on the waste that has been perpetrated: the ointment could have been sold for a year's wages and the money given to the poor.

Jesus, who is no less concerned about the plight of the poor, rises to her defense. Leave her alone, he charges. Why cause her trouble? She carried out a good work on me. The destitute you have with you at all times, and whenever you want you are able to do good to them. But me you do not always have. Jesus is not acknowledging that poverty is a permanent, ineradicable, social condition, as is all too often assumed. The verb he has employed is in the present tense: The destitute you **have**—not "will have"—with you at all times. The disciples can continuously do charity for the poor. But Jesus is proceeding to his imminent death, and there will be no further opportunity to express to him directly their love and affection.

Moreover, the woman's act holds special significance for him: "She undertook to anoint my body unto entombment." Her lavish anointment, however, is not merely an anticipation of his burial. While it is true that the three women who bring aromatic oils to Jesus' tomb on Easter morning are unable to fulfill their purpose of completing the

---

168. E.g., the excuse of the third individual in the parable of the Great Banquet in Luke 14:20. See Kenneth E. Bailey, *Poet and Peasant: A Literary-Cultural Approach to the Parables in Luke* and *Through Peasant Eyes: More Lucan Parables, Their Culture and Style*, 2 vols. in 1 (Grand Rapids: Wm. B. Eerdmans, 1984), 98–99.

burial process because he has been resurrected, she has performed a ritual that was exclusively restricted to the male sex. Old Testament prophets anointed kings in order to signify their divine election to ascend the throne and exercise sovereignty over Israel. This unnamed woman has assumed the role of prophet but in order to anoint Jesus as the Messiah in death.[169] He is the Christ who will rule from the cross. He is the king who negates himself and returns the sovereignty to his people. Or, as he identified himself earlier, he is the New Human Being who came not to be ministered to but to minister and give his life a ransom for many. He is the monarch who dies on behalf of his subjects' sins.

Up to this point in the narrative none of Jesus' disciples appear to understand his unusual messiahship. None of them grasp who or what he really is, except this unnamed woman who bursts into a men's banquet, performs her ministry, and then disappears. Although she is not named, Jesus asserts that what she has done will be remembered as long as the gospel is proclaimed. For what she has undertaken conveys one of the central features of the good news: the immense irony of Jesus enthroned on the cross as "The King of the Jews" who, in contrast to all other messiahs and regents, does not perpetuate himself or his rule.

A woman has played a decisive role in Jesus' career in relation to the culminating event of the Gospel. In a radical break with the past she has acted on behalf of God to anoint Jesus as Messiah. Up to this moment he has refused the title or at least the traditional content that it carries. He does not want to be a typical king in the traditions of Israel's history, either in terms of popular expectations or royal ide-

169. See Elizabeth Schüssler Fiorenza, *In Memory of Her: A Feminist Theological Reconstruction of Christian Origins* (New York: Crossroad, 1983), xiv, but she does not follow through on the impact this has on Jesus, which is reflected in his confession before the Sanhedrin in 14:62. She is certainly right in her claim that the women are true disciples in the Gospel. But she is wrong, like others, in concluding that Mark depoliticizes the Gospel and shifts the blame for Jesus' death from the Romans to the Jewish establishment. They have an equal share. See also Werner H. Kelber, "Conclusion: From Passion Narrative to Gospel," in *The Passion in Mark: Studies on Mark 14—16*, ed. Werner H. Kelber (Philadelphia: Fortress Press, 1976), 173. Kelber recognizes the frame of women disciples for the passion and resurrection narrative but does not distinguish this unnamed woman as anything more than a disciple "following Jesus as the Crucified One." She is, in fact, the only one in the Gospel who understands the distinctive character of Jesus' messiahship.

ology.[170] He has no intention of seating himself or letting himself be seated at the apex of a new social, economic, and political pyramid. However, from this point in time, as will become evident, he will embrace the epithet because of the unnamed woman's anointing of him as Messiah in death. To the extent that this aspect of the gospel has been comprehended, this woman and what she did have also been remembered and proclaimed.[171] But where the good news has been misconstrued and its Christology misinterpreted, she has been neglected and forgotten.

A startling contrast subsequently emerges. Immediately after this unnamed woman has fulfilled her ministry of anointing Jesus as the Messiah, Judas Iscariot, "one of the twelve," meets with the ruling elite in order to betray Jesus. The narrator provides no explicit motive for his treason. But the juxtaposition of these two episodes may hint at offense by the anointment and possibly also its waste of more than three hundred denarii. Judas seems to have comprehended the significance of the preceding incident, and his willingness to deliver Jesus up to the governing class indicates a rejection of Jesus' distinctive messiahship. Whether or not this is the case, Judas' betrayal of Jesus poses an ironic contrast to the unnamed woman's anointing of Jesus as the Messiah in death. Through Judas' treachery the chief priests have finally found a way to carry out their thwarted intentions to destroy Jesus: "Now those hearing were glad and promised to him silver. And he was seeking how he might conveniently deliver him up."

When the morning of the great feast arrives, Jesus dispatches two of his followers—as he did prior to his triumphal entry into Jerusalem—to make the necessary preparations for their celebration of the Passover. The time is designated as the first day of the festival of Unleavened Bread; but in actuality, according to Jewish reckoning, this is the day before the Passover and its immediately succeeding week-long festival of Unleavened Bread. More precisely, it is the Day of Preparation when the Passover lambs will be slaughtered. The narrator seems to be calculating the time according to gentile rather than Jewish

170. Again, Horsley, "Popular Messianic Movements Around the Time of Jesus," 472–95.

171. This is what Schüssler Fiorenza (*In Memory of Her*, xiii–xiv) does not appear to have realized.

custom: the day begins at sunrise instead of sunset.[172] Therefore, although the Passover meal has not yet been eaten, yet because it will be eaten before the day is over—according to Hellenistic reckoning—it is the first day of the festival of Unleavened Bread.[173]

As previously, two disciples are sent ahead to carry out a particular task. In both instances Jesus knows in advance what they will encounter. Like an Old Testament prophet, he displays an amazing capacity of foreknowledge. Earlier, on three different occasions he predicted his forthcoming suffering, death, and resurrection; and shortly, during the Passover meal, he will announce his betrayal by one of the twelve. Although this capability is sometimes ascribed to Jesus on the basis of an identification with the Hellenistic "divine man" *(theios anēr)*, it seems more valid, in accordance with the narrative world of this Gospel, to attribute such powers to Jesus' identity as the New Human Being.[174] His entry into a reordering of power, which establishes his horizontal, interdependent relationship with the Creator, enlarges his capacity for perspicacity and enables him to know God's will and how it must be fulfilled in history for the victory of God's rule. Now, on this occasion, he again demonstrates this extraordinary capability. "Go into the city," he charges the two, "and a human being will meet you carrying a pot of water. Follow him, and, wherever he enters, say to the housemaster, 'The teacher says, "Where is my guest room where I may eat the Passover with my disciples?"' And he will show you a big room upstairs furnished (and) ready; and there prepare for us." Since every resident of Jerusalem is obligated to accommodate pilgrims and provide a room for their celebration of the feast, the two will encounter no difficulties in making the necessary arrangements.[175]

That evening the Passover meal is eaten in Jerusalem but, surprisingly, only with the twelve. Those "around him with the twelve" of

---

172. Burkill, *Mysterious Revelation*, 259–60.

173. Grundmann, *Markus*, 381.

174. It is possible, of course, that features of the "divine man" have been woven into the Gospel's Christology of the New Human Being, although Theodore J. Weeden ("The Cross as Power in Weakness," in *The Passion in Mark*, ed. Kelber, 127–29) argues that "Divine man Christology is repudiated as false and replaced by a son of Man Christology." See also Theodore J. Weeden, *Mark—Traditions in Conflict* (Philadelphia: Fortress Press, 1971), 52–69.

175. Strack-Billerbeck, 4:41–76.

4:10 are excluded. Contrary to the expectation raised by Jewish tradition and by Jesus himself, "where I may eat the Passover with my disciples" women and children are not present. Such irregularity hints at some theological strategy. The twelve, of course, are representative of the entire community, but why are only the representatives and not all the members of the community partakers of the meal? On this evening, in the architectonic center of Judaism—Jerusalem—these twelve, for better and for worse, are the embodiment of the new Israel that Jesus had constituted "on the mountain" in 3:13–19. Because they symbolize the community of the New Humanity, they can serve more universally as the representatives of both present and future generations of the new people of God. Their participation in this Passover which Jesus transforms into the meal of a new exodus, "the Lord's Supper," is representative of all who, in their celebration of liberation, let themselves be drawn into a dialectical identification with the actualities of both the new creation and the old creation and their corresponding realities of human wholeness and brokenness.

But before Jesus draws the twelve into this paradox, he reveals, with the assurance of an oath, that one of them will betray him: "Amen I say to you, one of you will deliver me up, one eating with me." His foreknowledge can be established with an oath because it is supported by Scripture: "Even my bosom friend in whom I trusted, who ate of my bread, has lifted his heel against me" (Ps. 41:9). Since the same verse is quoted by the Qumran Teacher of Righteousness in 4QH 5:22–24, it may have become an essential feature of the righteous individual who suffers injustice even at the hands of his friends.[176] While an unnamed woman anointed him as Messiah in death, Judas, one of the twelve, will serve as an agent of his suffering and death.

Jesus' prediction with its conviction of certainty appalls his table companions, and one after another they attempt to assure him with questioning uncertainty: "Surely not I?" In response he insists that it is one of them, "one of the twelve," and underlines the intimacy of the communion which the betrayer enjoys by adding, "the one dipping with me into the bowl." Ironically, even this contingency is anticipated in Scripture, and Jesus must submit to its necessity if God's rule is to

---

176. Grundmann, *Markus*, 385; also Vernon K. Robbins, "Last Meal: Preparation, Betrayal and Absence," in *The Passion in Mark*, ed. Kelber, 30.

be victorious: "The Human Being goes as it has been written about him but woe to that human being through whom the Human Being is delivered up. Better for him if that human being were not born." No Old Testament text refers specifically to the destiny of "the Son of Man." But since Jesus has already linked the eschatological reality of the New Human Being to the suffering Servant of Isaiah 53 who, according to Mark 10:45, will "give his life a ransom for many," he may be alluding to the prophetic portrayal of the one who is unjustly condemned, executed, and buried.[177] For Jesus, the way of the New Human Being is a necessity articulated by the Word of God, and he willingly subjects himself to it. For Judas, however, it is a matter of choice. He has not been predestined to betrayal; no necessity has been imposed on him.[178] His is a decision made in his own freedom. But its gravity is awesome, because it involves him in nothing less than the destruction of the First Final Human Being and the attendant eschatological realization of the beginning of a New Humanity in which he himself has intimately participated. The woes that history has endured to give birth to this "last Adam" will inflict such torment of conscience on him that he will wish he had never been born.

When Judas leaves the communion is not indicated. Perhaps he slips away before the institution of the Eucharist, perhaps while Jesus and his disciples are making their way to the field of Gethsemane. He will reappear later in the darkness of the night at the head of a mob armed with swords and clubs in order to seize Jesus and deliver him to the Sanhedrin for a second trial.

During the meal, "while they are eating," Jesus takes bread, pronounces a blessing, breaks it, and gives it to his disciples: "Take. This is my body." Previously at the feeding of the five thousand and the four thousand, he had followed the same ritual. Now, however, in this climactic moment of his ministry in the architectonic center of Judaism, at a Passover celebration with the twelve who personify the new Israel, he identifies the bread which he breaks and distributes with his own body.[179] Its wholeness, like the loaf, will be broken in order to give life to those who partake of it. This is the wholeness that Jesus

177. See Isa. 53:3–12.

178. Against Robbins, "Last Meal," 32. It is Jesus' death, not Judas' betrayal, that fulfills the sovereign purpose of God.

179. T. Burkill, *Mysterious Revelation*, 273.

embodies as the New Human Being—God's beloved son, and it is communicated in and under the materiality of bread. By eating it they will have a share in his forthcoming sacrificial death and the liberation of the new exodus which it will inaugurate from within this center of the world. By eating it they become part of him and are drawn into his life, freedom, health, and wholeness. Their communion with him guarantees their participation in the New Humanity which originated from the Creator and will be sustained by the Creator into all eternity. In this new body that is constituted they are joined in death and in life, in life and in death, to the New Human Being who did not come to be ministered to but to minister and give his life a ransom for many. As a result, the members of this New Humanity continue his ministry of liberation and restoration. Finally they also take up their cross and follow their pioneer in being broken for others. In these concrete ways the reality of the Christ event continues to be manifested in history by those who offer up themselves as living sacrifices for the reconciliation of the broken, alienated, and enslaved humanity of the old creation.

After the distribution of the bread, Jesus takes a cup of wine and, following the same ritual, offers a prayer of thanks and gives it to his disciples. While they are drinking from it, he announces, "This is my blood of the covenant which is being poured out on behalf of many." Even as he identified the bread with his own body, he now identifies the content of the cup with his blood. Since "the life of every creature is in the blood," the pouring out of blood results in death (Lev. 17:11, 14). Jesus, by shedding his blood, will fulfill the sacrifice of the suffering Servant who, according to Isa. 53:12, "poured out his life unto death." At this Passover, therefore, he is "like a lamb that is led to the slaughter, and like a sheep that before its shearers is mute, . . . when he makes himself an offering for sin" (Isa. 53:7, 10). Moreover, by designating his blood as the "blood of the covenant," he implies the establishment of a new covenant, perhaps the very one that Jeremiah anticipated:

> Behold, the days are coming, says Yahweh, when I will make a new
> covenant with the house of Israel and the house of Judah, not like the
> covenant which I made with their fathers when I took them by the hand
> to bring them out of the land of Egypt, my covenant which they broke,
> though I was their husband, says Yahweh, But this is the covenant
> which I will make with the house of Israel after those days, says
> Yahweh: I will put my law within them, and I will write it upon their

hearts; and I will be their God, and they shall be my people. And no longer shall each human being teach his/her neighbor or each his/her siblings, saying "Know Yahweh!" for they shall all know me, from the least of them to the greatest, says Yahweh; for I will forgive their iniquity, and I will remember their sin no more. (Jer. 31:31–34)

The original covenant that Moses enacted at Sinai, after the exodus, and sealed with "the blood of the covenant" drawn from sacrificial animals and thrown upon the people to unite them in community with God will be replaced by the covenant that Jesus will establish with his own blood. While he is the Passover victim who offers up his life as a ransom for many, his blood, which is poured out unto death, efficaciously seals the new covenant. The cup, therefore, from which the disciples drink, unites the Passover celebration of the exodus and the Sinai covenant and thereby links together redemptive deliverance and new community with God through one vicarious sacrifice. As in 10:45, the "many" for whom both liberation and the new covenant will be established, according to Palestinian Jewish usage, is inclusive and means "all," gentiles as well as Jews.

Jesus concludes his sacramental identification of the cup with an eschatological affirmation that looks forward to the resumption of this table fellowship after the reality of God's rule has effectively been established: "Amen I say to you, I will absolutely not drink of the fruit of the vine until that day when I drink it new in God's rule." Since the cup conveys the realities of redemptive deliverance and the enactment of a new covenant, Jesus cannot and will not partake of wine again until these actualities have been actualized. First he must drink what the cup symbolizes, suffering and sacrifice, which, as he acknowledges in his Gethsemane prayer, he dreads to consume. A significant feature of the Golgotha scene that must not be ignored is Jesus' rejection of wine mixed with myrrh when it is offered to him as an anesthetic to alleviate the pain of crucifixion (15:23).

Since he has expressed this promise not to drink wine again until he drinks it new in God's rule, fulfillment must be assumed, although the ending of the Gospel leaves the matter inconclusive. Jesus' oath of 14:25 anticipates the establishment of God's rule in power (9:1), not the parousia of the New Human Being.[180] Whether the disciples ever

180. Against Robbins, "Last Meal," 37–39. Robbins contends that Jesus will drink the cup again with his disciples at the messianic banquet when "the Son of Man" comes. Mark 14:25 does not look forward to the parousia but to the establishment of the rule of God in power at Jesus' resurrection.

followed Jesus to Galilee and entered into a new table fellowship with him there is the strategic question that the narrator places before the addressees of the Gospel.[181] If they did, they would have shared the cup with him again, but in celebration of the realization of redemption and with it a new covenant.

After concluding the Passover meal with the singing of a hymn, Jesus and his disciples leave the city and make their way to the Mount of Olives. It is here that he began his triumphant entry into Jerusalem; it is here that his passion will soon commence. Evidently the mountain has a particular significance.[182] Its character becomes more apparent through Jesus' prediction of his disciples' offense: "You all will be scandalized, for it is written, 'I shall smite the shepherd, and the sheep will be scattered.' " The prophecy that Jesus quotes is derived from Zech. 13:7 which foretells a specific circumstance of the Day of the Lord that will prove to be especially offensive to the disciples. God will be actively involved in this eschatological event and will strike down the anointed leader. The suffering and the sacrifice into which Jesus will enter here on the Mount of Olives are to be interpreted in the light of this particular feature of the prophetic vision of the Day of the Lord.

But, as Jesus has announced before, there will be a resurrection which will culminate this eschatological event of judgment and will simultaneously inaugurate a new exodus. For he also promises, "Nevertheless, after I'm raised I'll go before you into Galilee." As he went before the disciples to lead them up to Jerusalem for a vicarious participation in his death (10:32), so he will also serve as their forerunner in conducting them out of Jerusalem and back into Galilee—perhaps even beyond. The judgment that will be enacted will cancel Jerusalem as the architectonic center of the world. No longer will the boundaries of Israel be sanctified by the holiness of Jerusalem and its temple.[183] Consequently the traditional structures of the sacred and the secular will be dissolved. The new exodus will reverse the movement that dominated the Old Testament Scriptures. No longer will there be any geographic location on earth to which human beings

181. See below, pp. 249–50.

182. Is the Mount of Olives the site of Jesus' quotation of Zech. 13:7 because of its occurrence in the same eschatological context of the Day of the Lord in Zech. 14:4?

183. For the ten degrees of holiness that surround the Holy of Holies in concentric circles, see Belo, *A Materialist Reading*, 79.

can withdraw in order to experience communion with God and to escape the chaos and darkness of the secular world. Heaven and earth will be united wherever the New Humanity is actively engaged in justice and reconciliation and concomitantly expanding the reality of God's rule.

Peter, however, objects to Jesus' all-inclusive prediction of his disciples' lack of constancy. "Even if all will be scandalized, yet not I!" he insists. In response to this arrogant self-assurance Jesus employs the Amen formula, with which he disclosed his betrayal by one of the twelve, in order to confront Peter with the collapse of his own discipleship: "Amen I say to you, today, in this very night, before a cock crows twice, you will deny me three times." The period of denial is delineated very concretely by moving from the general time of "today" to the specific hours of the night in which Peter's repudiation will take place. His threefold disavowal will occur before the second cockcrow or between the hours of midnight and three in the morning.[184] But he stubbornly refuses to admit the possibility of Jesus' warning, even though it has been uttered with the oath-like certainty of an Amen declaration. With great bravado he asserts that he will remain steadfast in his loyalty even in the face of death: "If it is necessary for me to die with you, I will by no means deny you!" His avowal is echoed by all of the disciples.

On the Mount of Olives they arrive at a field called Gethsemane, a place of no unusual significance but remembered because of its link with Jesus' passion. Commanding his disciples to sit while he prays, Jesus takes Peter, James, and John with him to serve as his companions in prayer. They had accompanied him into the home of the synagogue ruler and witnessed the resurrection of his daughter (5:37–43). They were with him on the Mount of Transfiguration and had experienced his unveiling as God's beloved son. Before their entry into Jerusalem, James and John had maintained their capability of drinking the cup that he will drink; and after the Passover meal, when they had reached the Mount of Olives, Peter had avowed his constancy by declaring his willingness to die with him. The three appear to be the disciples best suited to support him with their encouragement and strength of resolve.

184. Grundmann, *Markus*, 396. See the discussion in Jeremias, *Jerusalem in the Time of Jesus*, 47–48 n. 44.

Overcome by profound distress and stunned by the enormity of the prospect confronting him, Jesus withdraws from them also: "My soul is sorrowful to death! Remain here and keep watching." Removing himself a short distance, he falls to the ground and begins to agonize in prayer. This is the only context in the Gospel in which the narrator reports the actual words of Jesus' prayer: "Abba, Father, all things (are) possible for you. Remove this cup from me! Yet not what I want but what you (want)." The extraordinary address he employs, "Abba," which is inadequately translated as "father," is the Aramaic colloquial form of *ab* ("father"), meaning "Papa" or "Daddy," and reveals the intimacy of his relationship with the Creator. It is the only time it is used in the Gospel. After acknowledging what he had previously insisted to the father of the epileptic in 9:23, "All things (are) possible" for you, he commands God to take away the cup. Is it a necessity after all? Must he really drink its content? Can he not be spared this terrible ordeal? What he dreads is not the terror of death. That continues to be a fundamental misunderstanding of the cup.[185] Jesus already embraced his mortality at his baptism. Nor is he overwhelmed by the anticipation of the pain of crucifixion. He will refuse to accept the anesthetic of wine mixed with myrrh that will be offered to him before the nails are pounded through his hands into the wood of the cross.[186] What he fears is the horror of being abandoned by God. For, as he announced in his quotation of Zech. 13:7 to his disciples after their arrival at the Mount of Olives, God will take an active part in this eschatological event of Jesus' sacrifice: "I shall smite the shepherd." This is the judgment that he must suffer in his self-sacrifice as the New Human Being who has twice been validated as God's beloved son and who came to "give his life a ransom for many."

As bitter as the cup will be and as much as Jesus shrinks from the horror of drinking it, he is also ready to submit to its necessity, if this is the only way in which the new exodus can be inaugurated and the new covenant established. "Yet not what I want but what you (want)," he amends his petition.

---

185. E.g., Werner H. Kelber, "The Hour of the Son of Man and the Temptation of the Disciples," in *The Passion in Mark*, ed. Kelber. In contrast, Grundmann, *Markus*, 400–401.

186. Paul Winter, *On the Trial of Jesus*, 2d ed. (Berlin: Walter de Gruyter, 1974), 95: "No nails were used for affixing the feet."

When he returns to the three men whom he had taken with him, he finds them asleep. James and John, who insisted on being able to drink his cup, and Peter, who was ready to die with him, prove to be incapable of offering him any of the strength and resolve they claimed to have. Instead, Jesus is compelled to warn them of the dangers they confront as his followers: "Keep on watching and praying so that you don't come into being tested. The spirit (is) eager, but the flesh weak." He leaves them a second time, desperate to determine the course he should take, and prays the same prayer. Unable to find a resolution, he turns to the three again for reinforcement only to discover that they are unable to stay awake. Their eyes are heavy with sleep, and because they have no comprehension of what is overwhelming him, they do not know what to say.[187]

Finally a third struggle in prayer results in clarity of purpose and resolution. Reinforced now with the strength and courage necessary to undertake this ordeal, Jesus returns to challenge the three. With a note of sarcasm he confronts them with their self-indulgence in sleep: "Are you going to sleep and rest forever?" "It's settled!" he declares, expressing the conviction of his resolution. "The hour came!" Hesitation and procrastination are no longer possible. The eschatological drama of the Day of the Lord has begun, and "the New Human Being is being delivered up into the hands of sinners." "Rouse yourselves!" he commands. "Let's go! Look, the one delivering me up has approached." All of the so-called "Suffering Son of Man" prediction will now begin to be fulfilled. Now at last the disciples must understand.[188]

Judas arrives with a sword- and club-bearing crowd from the ruling elite, "the chief priests and scribes and elders," and identifies Jesus with a betraying kiss. No resistance is offered by him as he is ap-

187. Kelber ("The Hour of the Son of Man and the Temptation of the Disciples," 43–46) has analyzed this very clearly, but because he does not understand the cup, he places a one-sided emphasis on 14:33–42 in the failure of the disciples in perceiving what is taking place. The content of Jesus' prayer, in the light of 14:27, is also significant for the structure of this episode.

188. Ibid., 55. Kelber correctly assesses 14:41 as "the high point of the conflict between Jesus and the disciples over the issue of a suffering Son of Man." But this is not the culmination of "the suffering Son of Man" Christology. Although the title is not linked again to the keynote of suffering, the reality itself will reach its culmination dialectically on the cross in fulfillment of 14:62. It is not over the issue of a suffering messiahship that Jesus and his disciples parted in conflict (p. 57). In cowardice and continued incomprehension they abandon Jesus.

prehended and bound for delivery to the Sanhedrin. One of his followers, however, reacts to this violent seizure by drawing his sword and severing the ear of the high priest's slave. But the effort is futile. Jesus, having resolved his course of action through agonizing struggle in prayer, refuses to be drawn into this cycle of action and reaction. Yet as he submits to his illegal arrest, he excoriates his captors, who have seized him clandestinely under the cover of night: "As against a bandit you come out with swords and clubs to seize me. Daily I was with you in the temple teaching, and you did not take hold of me." But this too is an essential feature of the drama that the Old Testament foresees as indispensable in the accomplishment of God's purpose in history, and Jesus subordinates himself to its necessity. With confidence he acknowledges that the course he has chosen, even in its initiation in his unlawful seizure, is in fulfillment of the Scriptures.

At this critical moment, however, Jesus is abandoned by all of his followers: "Leaving him they all fled." To whom the word "all" refers is unclear.[189] There is no immediate antecedent for it, and the reader must return to 14:27, 29, 31 for its previous uses. The twelve had shared the Passover meal with Jesus, and after Judas' withdrawal the remaining eleven may have accompanied Jesus to the Mount of Olives and its field of Gethsemane. Yet when Jesus uses the word "all" in 14:27, he seems to be addressing the entire community of his followers and not merely its remaining eleven representatives. When "all" insist that they will remain loyal to him, more than eleven appear to be involved. This is substantiated by the narrator's return to the inclusive designation of "disciples" in 14:32 and the note of 15:41 that "many ... women" accompanied him up to Jerusalem. Therefore, it is not only the eleven who take flight. All of the disciples, both men and women, desert him, and Jesus is left alone with his captors.[190]

But no! One of his followers is determined to remain faithful to him and the promise made a little earlier with the other disciples (14:31). It is a *neaniskos,* in Greek a youth of approximately sixteen years. He has mistakenly been identified as the evangelist Mark, who has anonymously injected an autobiographical incident into the narrative in

189. In puzzlement, Rudolf Bultmann (*History of the Synoptic Tradition,* trans. from the 3d ed. by John Marsh [New York: Harper & Row, 1963], 269) asks who the "all" refers to in 14:50.

190. Kelber, "The Hour of the Son of Man and the Temptation of the Disciples," 57.

order to lend greater authority to his witness. But there is no evidence that Mark was a disciple of Jesus before the crucifixion. The young man is an unnamed follower who belongs to the larger circle, "the ones around him with the twelve." In contrast to the others he endeavors to be loyal to Jesus: "And a certain youth tried to follow him wearing a linen cloth over (his) naked (body)."[191] The Greek noun *sindōn*, which is employed here, is not a garment or an item of clothing. It is simply a coarse linen sheet or shroud; and there is no evidence that it was ever used as a form of dress, particularly at night. It is the kind of material that is used to prepare a dead body for burial, and its significance will emerge more clearly when Joseph of Arimathea purchases a *sindōn* for the entombment of Jesus' corpse.[192] More immediately, it is the action that is meaningful: "And they take hold of him. But he, leaving behind the linen cloth, fled naked."

All of the disciples except one have fled. Only a stouthearted youth persists in following Jesus into his passion. But when violent hands are laid on him, he too takes flight, abandoning his linen shroud and streaking into the night naked. What purpose does this strange happening serve? What narrative strategy does it fulfill? Is there any connection between this young disciple and the *neaniskos* of 16:5 whom the women discover in the empty tomb "seated on the right hand and wearing a white robe"? In one context a streaking youth leaves behind a coarse linen sheet, in another context a youth is seen wearing a white garment.

From time to time it has been suggested that this brief episode of a young man fleeing naked connotes an aspect of Amos's prophecy of the Day of the Lord:[193]

"Flight shall perish from the swift, and the strong shall not retain his strength, nor shall the mighty save his life; he who handles the bow shall not stand, and he who is swift of foot shall not save himself, nor shall he who rides the horse save his life; and *the one who is stout of heart among the mighty shall flee away naked on that day*," says Yahweh. (Amos 2:14–16)

191. The main verb is in the imperfect tense and could be interpreted as a conative imperfect.

192. These are the only occurrences of the word in Mark's Gospel. See below, pp. 239–40.

193. See E. Hoskyns and F. N. Davey, *The Riddle of the New Testament* (London: Faber & Faber, 1931), 66–67; and Grundmann, *Markus*, 407.

A little earlier, when Jesus and his disciples had reached the Mount of Olives, he had cited a singular feature of the Day of the Lord from Zechariah's prophetic portrayal, which, because of its forthcoming fulfillment, would scandalize them: "I shall smite the shepherd, and the sheep will be scattered." Now at the moment of his arrest and the beginning of his passion, the narrator, by recounting this incident, signals the beginning of the Day of the Lord. For, as Amos predicted, "and the one who is stout of heart among the mighty shall flee away naked on that day."

But there are a number of other significant implications. Since the coarse linen sheet was worn over the youth's naked body, and since Joseph of Arimathea buys a coarse linen sheet for the burial of Jesus' body, some kind of identification between the coarse linen sheet and the human body of flesh and blood seems to be implied by the narrator. The shroud symbolizes Jesus' corpse! Consequently the young man who abandons the linen cloth, as he runs away naked, serves as a mirror of Jesus' destiny. Although his arrest marks the beginning of the Day of the Lord and his suffering and death as the Passover victim, he will escape. At the same time, however, he will leave behind his corpse.

This young disciple, however, not only reflects Jesus'destiny; he also shares in it. Indeed, he is the personification of the disciples' vicarious participation in the actuality of the New Human Being who must "suffer many things, be rejected . . . and killed and after three days to rise up." He has followed Jesus the forerunner, who is constructing "the way up into Jerusalem," and at this moment he symbolically represents the disciples' involvement in Jesus' death. For his abandonment of the linen cloth and his naked flight into the night express his entry into the reality of death that occurs in baptism, a rite of passage that Jesus himself entered at the Jordan River under the ministry of his forerunner John and is now entering again.[194]

194. This little piece of narrative repertoire along with its complement in 16:5 may well reflect the early Christian understanding and practice of baptism as proposed by Robin Scroggs and Kent I. Groff, "Baptism in Mark: Dying and Rising with Christ," *JBL* 92 (1973): 531–48. Old clothes, representing the old creation inaugurated by Adam and Eve and subject to the infection of sin with its concrete expression of injustice, oppression, and exploitation, may have been taken off. After immersion, the symbolic experience of dying with Christ, new clothing, perhaps even a white robe, was put on to signify participation in Jesus' resurrection and its inauguration of a new creation. See Gal. 3:27; Rom. 6:3–14; Col. 3:12–14; Eph. 4:22–24; 6:11–17; Rev. 7:9; and 22:14, which express various aspects of this understanding of baptism.

THE TRIALS
(14:53—15:20) _____

Jesus is led away to the high priest, who has convened a special session of the Sanhedrin at his residence instead of at the usual place of venue, the council chamber. Here is another irregularity underscoring the treachery of the governing class. Jesus' trial, like his nocturnal arrest, must be conducted secretly in order to find a way to eliminate him as a threat to their maintenance of world.[195]

Peter, who apparently has remembered his avowal of loyalty, follows the procession into the courtyard of the high priest to await the outcome with the retainers and servants while "warming himself toward the light." The phrase of 14:54 is startling, because the natural expectation is that Peter is warming himself at the fire, as, in fact, it is translated in most English versions. But the word *pyr* ("fire"), which occurs in 9:48–49, is not used here. Instead, the narrator has chosen the noun *phōs* ("light"). Peter is deriving warmth from some kind of light, and the most reasonable assumption seems to be that its source is Jesus, who is inside the high priest's palace being interrogated before the Sanhedrin.[196] In this dark moment of the night—and the Day of the Lord that is unfolding—the light emanating from Jesus is so strong that he, Peter, is able to draw warmth from it for himself. It should renew and strengthen the avowal he had made a short while before on the Mount of Olives.

The judicial process begins with an interrogation of witnesses in search of testimony that would constitute valid grounds for an indict-

_____

195. For an analysis of the historical problems of the trial before the Sanhedrin, see Burkill, *Mysterious Revelation*, 280–318. Since the intention of this study is to comprehend the narrative of Mark's Gospel and to actualize its "prefigured meaning," no effort has been made to determine the historical reliability of these traditions, in this context the so-called five infringements of rabbinic law in the arrest, trial, and condemnation of Jesus. It must not be forgotten that Mark's Gospel reflects the orientation of the lower classes; and the narration of Jesus' passion, like that of John's martyrdom, is done according to the bitter and resentful perspective of those who continued to be exploited and oppressed by their rulers and whose champions advocating structural, social, and economic changes are destroyed by them. See also Winter, *On the Trial of Jesus*, for an examination of the historical problems; and Ernst Bammel, ed., *The Trial of Jesus: Cambridge Studies in Honour of C. F. D. Moule*, Studies in Biblical Theology, Second Series, 13 (London: SCM Press, 1970). John R. Donahue ("Temple, Trial and Royal Christology," in *The Passion in Mark*, ed. Kelber, 62) also maintains that "the Marcan narrative must be bypassed as a primary source of historical reconstruction."

196. A parallel is the narrator's reference to "one loaf" in 8:14, which hints at a pre-Johannine interpretation of Jesus as "the bread of life." In this context the intimation appears to be that Jesus is "the light."

ment. Many come forward to testify against Jesus, but their evidence cannot be corroborated. No two or three witnesses, required by Jewish law to establish a legitimate charge, can be found to agree. "For many were testifying falsely against him . . . saying, 'We heard him saying, "I will tear down this sanctuary made by hands, and after three days I will build another not made by hands." ' And not even so was their testimony consistent."[197]

When it becomes obvious that an indictment cannot be secured on the basis of the testimonies that have been offered, the high priest himself enters into the proceedings in order to examine Jesus: Aren't you answering anything at all which these are testifying against you? But Jesus remains silent, refusing to defend himself. Moving the interrogation in a new direction, the high priest confronts Jesus with the question of his identity: "Are you the Messiah, the son of the Blessed One?" This query, like the entire judicial process of Jesus' trials, belongs to the narrative world of Mark's Gospel. It should not be assumed that these proceedings have been derived from a court transcription of the trial or from a tradition of eyewitness testimony. Historically speaking, it is very improbable that Jesus identified himself as the Messiah. The question, "Are you the Messiah, the son of the Blessed One?" is intelligible only from within the narrator's development of "The Beginning of the Good News of Jesus Christ." The repertoire of traditions, adapted and synthesized by the author,[198] builds its own story world in which the gradual disclosure of Jesus' identity as the Christ reaches its culmination in Jesus' self-disclosure at his trial before the Sanhedrin. His response to the high priest's question is the only self-confession he makes in the Gospel, and it reveals the full scope of the dialectical Christology that the author strategically

197. Donahue ("Temple, Trial and Royal Christology," 68–70) synthesizes all of the temple references and correctly concludes that "the community is the other temple which Jesus will build."

198. It is very doubtful that there was a pre-Markan passion narrative. All of the details of the story cohere perfectly and are intimately linked to the entire story world of this literary composition. See also Eta Linnemann, *Studien zur Passionsgeschichte*, FRLANT 102 (Göttingen: Vandenhoeck & Ruprecht, 1970). Linnemann on the basis of a form and redaction critical analysis concludes that Mark collected and assembled individual traditions.

constructs as a prefiguration of meaning to be actualized by the reader.[199]

Why should Jesus reply to a query about his identity that has been worded in terms of a title that had evoked censure from him earlier when it had been conferred on him by his disciples (8:29–30)? He may not have rejected the title of "Christ" or "Messiah," but the content it carried, as Peter's counterrebuke intimates, was objectionable to him. In its place he substituted the christological reality of the New Human Being, the titular identity that has dominated the Gospel, but with the new features of suffering, death, and resurrection: "And he began to teach them that it is necessary for the Human Being to suffer many things . . . to be rejected . . . and to be killed . . . and after three days to rise up." If he has already refused to respond to the false testimonies of the witnesses before the Sanhedrin, particularly the charge of tearing down the sanctuary and replacing it with one made without hands, how can he answer the high priest's question about his identity without misinterpretation?

Yet astonishingly and unexpectedly he replies unambiguously, "I am." Apparently he is now prepared to embrace the title as well as any consequences that may arise from it. But why the change? What motivates him to acknowledge this identity at this critical moment in his trial when it has involved so much misunderstanding? This public admission of his messiahship before the ruling elite of the Jewish nation must originate from the unnamed woman's prophetic act of anointing him as the Messiah in death, the Messiah who negates himself. As the anointed king, now enabled to ascend the throne of the cross, he is free to declare his messiahship publicly, regardless of the misunderstanding which may be evoked, because the distinctive character of his kingship will soon be manifested.[200]

But the "I am" of Jesus' response to the high priest's question is

199. Donahue ("Temple, Trial and Royal Christology") correctly states that "Son of Man is the prism through which the titles Messiah and Son of the Blessed (God) are to be viewed" but proceeds to do the opposite and make the Messiah the prism through which "the Son of Man" is viewed. The parallels derived from David's career are closer to the royal Christology that Matthew develops in his passion narrative. See Herman C. Waetjen, *The Origin and Destiny of Humanness: An Interpretation of the Gospel According to Matthew*, 2d ed. (San Rafael, Calif.: Crystal Press, 1978), 202–3.

200. So also Kelber, "The Hour of the Son of Man and the Temptation of the Disciples," 46; and Norman Perrin, "The High Priest's Question and Jesus' Answer," in *The Passion in Mark*, ed. Kelber, 93.

more than an admission. Identical to the word with which he identified himself to his disciples as he walked on the Sea of Galilee, it is another disclosure by the narrator of the nature of Jesus' relationship with the Yahweh of the Old Testament. His appropriation of the revelatory "I am," enunciated by Yahweh in the Septuagint's translation of Exod. 3:14, is based on his call into being as God's beloved son at his baptism and its reaffirmation on the Mount of Transfiguration. It is corroborated by his divine act of trampling "the waves of the sea" and manifesting a Yahweh-like sovereignty over chaos (Job 9:8). The "I am" of Jesus therefore not only affirms his identity as the Messiah but also confirms the distinctive christological content of the title which the narrator conveys in the high priest's apposition, "the son of the Blessed One." As the Christ he is nothing less than God's offspring and surrogate and therefore also, as he intimated in 12:35–37, David's lord.[201]

It must be added, however, that the construction of this pleonastic christological ambiguity is possible only in Greek and is based on the Septuagint's translation of the Hebrew *ehyeh* ("I will be") in Exod. 3:14b as *egō eimi* ("I am"). Because the translation of the "I am" back into Hebrew or Aramaic would not necessarily convey the same meaning in this context, further evidence emerges that this scene in the trial of Jesus, as well as the trial itself, is a narrative construction that must be attributed to the christological strategy of the author.

But there is more! Jesus continues his confessional declaration with an amplification that parallels his earlier response to Peter's christological identification: "And you will see the Human Being seated on the right hand of Power and coming with the clouds of heaven." The Messiah, the Son of the Blessed One, is to be identified with the New Human Being! Not in terms of suffering and death, but viceregency! Now that Jesus has entered into his passion, he returns to the status of the New Human Being that dominated the first half of the narrative world of the Gospel. He is God's viceregent, co-bearer of the divine epithet "Lord" who acts on God's behalf in closing the past and opening the future (2:10) and who has authority to determine when

201. Unfortunately Perrin ("The High Priest's Question and Jesus' Answer," 81–83) ignores the "I am" of 6:50 and the pericope of 12:35–37 and therefore claims that this is the moment the messianic secret is being formally disclosed. Perhaps it is, but in a more complex manner.

and how the sabbath is to be observed (2:28). At the same time he is also the New Human Being of the future who will come riding God's chariot, the clouds, in order to become God's viceregent. In his amplification Jesus unites Ps. 110:1 and Dan. 7:13, but in an unnatural or illogical order. To make this more apparent, it is necessary to complete his confession in accordance with the expectation of Dan. 7:13. The "one like a human being" rides the divine chariot of the clouds in order to be presented to "the Ancient of Days" for the receiving of "dominion, glory, and kingdom" (Dan. 7:14). In other words, to become God's viceregent on earth! The unabbreviated combination of Ps. 110:1 and Dan. 7:13–14 reveals more clearly the logical contradiction of Jesus' confession: And you will see the New Human Being seated on the right hand of Power and coming with the clouds of heaven *in order to* receive dominion, glory, and kingdom. How can Jesus claim both to be seated and to be coming to be seated as God's viceregent? Logically speaking, he should have placed Dan. 7:13 before Ps. 110:1. Initially the New Human Being comes in God's chariot and subsequently is co-enthroned with God.

However, such a logical arrangement of these two Old Testament texts does not correspond to the dialectical Christology that has been developed by the narrator in the story world of the Gospel. As contradictory as it may seem, Jesus is God's viceregent, yet at the same time he is only in the process of becoming co-enthroned with God.[202] As a result of his re-creation by the Spirit at his baptism, he entered into a reordering of power which seated him at the right hand of God. In his identity as the New Human Being, who is simultaneously the Creator's offspring and viceregent, he exercises the Creator's authority and power while he himself already participates in it and labors to make it present for his Jewish contemporaries, especially the poor and the dispossessed. Nevertheless, there are countless others beyond his ministry who remain to be drawn into this eschatological reality. Until they are incorporated into this reordering of power, until they are co-enthroned with the Creator, Jesus himself cannot be "seated on the

202. Again, see Perrin, "The High Priest's Question and Jesus' Answer," 89–95, and idem, *A Modern Pilgrimage in New Testament Christology* (Philadelphia: Fortress Press, 1974), 10–22. In spite of his orientation to Jewish apocalypticism in his scholarship, Perrin does not consider the dialectical eschatology and Christology of this verse or the dialectical relationship of the millennial reality of the One and the Many in Dan. 7:13, 27.

right hand of Power." He is still only coming to enthronement. For the "one like a human being" of Dan. 7:13 is the corporate reality of the New Humanity (Dan. 7:27).[203] It is the community of the One and the Many that is destined to recover what the Creator has willed for all human beings. No longer will the world be divided by pollution systems into the realms of the sacred and the secular, the clean and the unclean. No longer will binary oppositions separate human beings into the privileged and the unprivileged, the powerful and the impotent, the rich and the poor, men and women, and whites and people of color. Until that goal is attained, however, Jesus is still riding God's chariot waiting for his disciples to continue to complete the work he inaugurates, so that they and all of humanity with him can finally be "seated on the right hand of Power."

Upon hearing this christological declaration, the high priest tears open his garments in order to expose his breast and thereby signify that a blasphemy has been committed.[204] But what precisely that blasphemy is he does not indicate. God has not been cursed. Yahweh's name has not been spoken. Can it be that Jesus' use of the "I am," which is intelligible only within the Hellenistic framework of the story world of this Gospel, is the basis of the charge? Or is the blasphemy Jesus' audacious claim to have entered into a reordering of power and to be horizontally related to the Creator in his embodiment of the eschatological reality of the New Human Being? In view of the elite self-understanding of the high priest, fostered by his hierarchical position at the apex of a supposedly divinely ordained pyramid of power and concomitantly his status as the one mediator between God and Israel—only he appears before the mercy seat of the Holy of Holies once a year!—Jesus' blasphemy would appear to be his self-identification as the New Human Being who is co-enthroned with God and therefore whose divine authority calls that of the high priest and the Sanhedrin into question.[205]

Such a radical paradigm shift would also be heresy to the elite chief priests, scribes, and elders who compose the Great Council of the Sanhedrin, and they do not hesitate to join the high priest in condemn-

203. Compare Barnabas Lindars, *Jesus Son of Man*, 101–14, esp. 110–12.
204. Grundmann, *Markus*, 415.
205. Ibid.

ing Jesus to death. Moreover, their animosity toward him erupts into physical violence as they terminate their judicial hearing, and they inflict bodily abuse and humiliation on him: "And some began to spit at him and to cover his face and to beat him and to say to him 'Prophesy!' " Not unexpectedly even the retainers, who are in the employ of these aristocratic elites, and into whose charge Jesus is placed, receive him "with blows" and thereby express their identification with them.

Peter, who in the meantime has been warming himself in the courtyard awaiting the outcome of the trial,[206] is recognized by a maidservant: "You too were with the Nazarene Jesus!" But he feigns ignorance: "I don't know or understand what you are saying" and escapes into the forecourt of the high priest's palace. His quick withdrawal may have confirmed her suspicion; and when she subsequently encounters him again, she identifies him to the bystanders: "This is one of them." Fear prevails, and Peter denies his discipleship a second time. His Galilean dialect, however, betrays his origin, and the bystander who recognizes it insists that he must be a follower of Jesus. To save himself by disassociation he resorts to cursing and swearing. Generally the former of the two verbs, "to curse," is transitive and requires a direct object. Whom or what is Peter cursing? Jesus, himself, or the bystanders? While no indication is given, it may be implied.[207] While the first two denials disputed his attachment to the circle of Jesus' followers, the third, "I don't know this human being whom you speak of!" effectively dissolves his relationship with Jesus. For by employing the traditional ban formula in Judaism, "I don't know you!" supported by curses and oaths, he renounces Jesus and relegates him to the nonexistent.[208] At this moment he also effectively cuts himself off from the light.

Jesus' prediction of 14:30 has been fulfilled, and the second crowing of the rooster, immediately after the third denial, reminds Peter of the warning he had received. In the dark brooding that is precipitated, he is forced to confront his illusions about himself: his ostentatious

---

206. For a redaction critical treatment of this episode of Peter's denial, see Kim E. Dewey, "Peter's Curse and Cursed Peter," in *The Passion in Mark*, ed. Kelber, 96–114.

207. See the discussion of Helmut Merkel, "Peter's Curse," in *The Trial of Jesus*, ed. Bammel, 66–71. Merkel argues, along with others, that Peter curses Jesus.

208. Ibid., 69. See also Matt. 7:23 and 25:12; and Strack-Billerbeck, 1:469.

boldness, his blustering courage, and his affected fearlessness. As a result of his pretense even the light emanating from Jesus, which had warmed him in the high priest's courtyard, was unable to infuse him with inner resilience and strength of constancy. In deep remorse he weeps inconsolably.

Although Jesus has been condemned to death on a conviction of blasphemy, the particular mode of punishment prescribed for it by Lev. 24:16 is not carried out. Jesus is not executed by stoning.[209] Whether or not the Jewish judiciary could exercise capital powers and impose the death penalty continues to be hotly debated. In the narrative world of Mark's Gospel, however, the Sanhedrin appears to be "a political institution with . . . legislative, executive and judicial powers."[210] Historically speaking, according to Paul Winter, "The Sanhedrin had full jurisdiction over Jews charged with offenses against Jewish religious law and had the authority openly to pronounce and carry out sentences of death in accordance with the provisions of Jewish legislation."[211] In this case, however, death by stoning, as prescribed by Lev. 24:16, does not occur. Instead, the Sanhedrin reassembles later in the night apparently to hold another judicial session. Jesus himself does not appear to be present, but, according to the narrator, the entire court reconvenes itself in order "to prepare a plan" or "to hold a consultation."[212] The object or purpose is not stated but is intimated by the outcome. Early in the morning Jesus is bound and delivered up to the tribunal of the Roman procurator, Pontius Pilate, indicted on a new charge. Originally the Sanhedrin had found him guilty of a religious crime, blasphemy. Now, however, the accusation against him is political; and it is implied in Pilate's opening question: "You are the king of the Jews?" Evidently the "plan" or "consultation" of the court led to a decisive change in the charge

209. Josef Blinzler, "The Jewish Punishment of Stoning in the New Testament Period," in *The Trial of Jesus*, ed. Bammel, 147–61; also Winter, *On the Trial of Jesus*, 97–104.

210. Burkill, *Mysterious Revelation*, 282.

211. Winter, *On the Trial of Jesus*, 109. Winter goes on to say, "Only after the fall of Jerusalem was the Sanhedrin deprived of its right to execute persons whom it had tried and sentenced to death." See also 127–28. Against Winter and Burkill, see David R. Catchpole, "The Problem of the Historicity of the Sanhedrin Trial," in *The Trial of Jesus*, ed. Bammel, 59–65.

212. The manuscript tradition of 15:1 offers both readings.

against Jesus. The political crime of revolt against the state has replaced the offense of religious heresy. The motive for this alteration is not cited or conjectured. Nevertheless, since the Sanhedrin declined to execute Jesus by stoning in accordance with Lev. 24:16 and chose instead to deliver him up to Pilate on the new charge of insurrection, which was punishable by crucifixion, it would seem that the Roman mode of execution was favored. But for what reason? If crucifixion was not a Jewish form of capital punishment, why in this case would it be preferable to stoning?[213] Clearly the intention of the ruling elite is not simply to destroy Jesus but to negate any possible effects of his ministry that might survive his death. Execution by stoning, although it is not without its own stigma, could conceivably elevate him to the heroic ranks of the great prophets of Israel and result in the invigoration and expansion of the movement he had inaugurated. Crucifixion, however, is not only an agonizing and ignominious death; its victims also stand under the damnation of the law: "For a hanged human being is accursed by God" (Deut. 21:23). Its application to Jesus is attested to by the apostle Paul in Gal. 3:13: "Christ redeemed us from the curse of the law, having become a curse for us—for it is written, 'Cursed is everyone who hangs on a tree.' "[214] While the narrator does not elucidate the motive of the Sanhedrin in revising the charge against Jesus, his conviction as a revolutionary would guarantee his execution by crucifixion, invoke upon him the curse of Deut. 21:23, and make him a pariah to the Jewish people for generations to come.

But more immediately it is necessary to secure a conviction, and that was by no means a foregone conclusion, even though Pilate's question, "You are the king of the Jews?" is phrased as though the charge had already been established and Jesus stood condemned. He, however, returns the question to the Roman governor without affirmation or denial. "You are saying it," he replies, indicating that it is Pilate's confession and not his own. To prevent a dismissal of the case, the chief priests introduce their own accusations against Jesus, but he

213. Winter, On the Trial of Jesus, 96: "Crucifixion was not a punitive measure that can be shown actually to have been used by the Jews during or after the lifetime of Jesus." Moreover, Winter points out that there was not a word for it in Hebrew or Aramaic; it was circumscribed with the phrase "to hang up alive" (p. 97).

214. Perhaps this is why, according to Paul, the crucified Christ is a stumbling block to the Jews (1 Cor. 1:23).

refuses to respond to them even when Pilate presses him for a reply: "Don't you answer anything at all? See how much they accuse you!" His quiet rejection of self-defense leaves the procurator astonished and wondering and eventually leads him to the realization that the chief priests had delivered him up out of ill will.

At this point the crowd intervenes and reminds Pilate of his annual Passover custom of releasing for them one prisoner of their choice. Even if this tradition has no historical basis, as is generally concluded,[215] it is a vital piece in the evangelist's repertoire and contributes to the development of the Passover interpretation of Jesus' passion within the narrative world of the Gospel. Although the Jewish people are free to choose for themselves whom they want Pilate to pardon— and others, such as the two bandits who were crucified with Jesus, are available!—their choice is actually limited to two individuals. This may appear to be self-contradictory,[216] but it is determined by the design of the author. For the tradition of 15:6–15 dominates the narration of Jesus' trial before Pilate and conveys a reenactment of a central feature of the very first Passover: divine and human preferences in the binary opposition between the Hebrews and the Egyptians. Here in contrast, the choice is between Jesus and Barabbas. But in what way are they opposites? Both of them appear to have been engaged in revolutionary activity. Jesus is on trial as an insurrectionist. Barabbas is identified as one "bound with the revolutionaries who [plural] in the revolt had committed murder." Of course, the lack of precision in this sketchy identification is puzzling.[217] Is Barabbas simply in jail with a number of rebels who had been arrested in a riot in which someone was killed, or is he, as one of the rebels, an accessory to both the revolt and the murder? The matter seems to be indeterminable. Yet this vagueness is not to be attributed to carelessness of expression. No need for greater precision is required. It is enough to identify Barabbas with the revolutionaries who had killed in a recent uprising, and as such he stands in contrast to Jesus. Together they constitute a binary opposition of two distinctive ways of establishing the eschatological reality of God's rule.

215. Winter, *On the Trial of Jesus*, 131–43.
216. Ibid., 134.
217. Ibid., 139.

In the narrative world's context of the Passover and its celebration and anticipation of Israel's liberation they stand before the tribunal of Pontius Pilate, the representative of imperialist Rome; and the people of Israel must choose between them. There is no apologetic motive here to exonerate the procurator or to place the administration of Roman justice in a more favorable light.[218] The narrator clearly regards Pilate to be ultimately responsible for Jesus' death. Instead of administering justice and setting Jesus free, he resorts to political expediency in order to placate the crowd. He chooses to let the people determine the outcome, although he realizes that the chief priests had brought Jesus before his tribunal out of ill will and is unable to determine what crime Jesus had committed (15:14). He pardons Barabbas and delivered up Jesus—after having him flogged—to be crucified (15:15).

More important, however, than the Roman miscarriage of justice is the choice between Jesus and Barabbas that confronts the Jewish people. They must decide who will die and who will be set free. Originally, at the first Passover, God chose to strike down the firstborn sons of the Egyptian oppressors and simultaneously to liberate the Hebrews from their enslavement in order to establish a new society of justice and equality. Now, however, at this Passover, a profoundly ironic reversal occurs.

Jesus, who repented under John's baptism and was re-created by God's Spirit to become the first, final Human Being, was ordained by God to pioneer a New Humanity that would be engaged in the building of God's rule. Paradoxically the fulfillment of this divine call into new being will necessitate divine rejection, for it involves nothing less than the project of eradicating the human infection of sin and its concrete manifestations of injustice, oppression, and exploitation. On the one hand, Jesus will atone for sin as the Passover sacrifice; he will give his life a ransom for many in order to achieve divine-human reconciliation. On the other hand, he will also abolish sin by serving as the scapegoat bearer and carrying it into the oblivion of divine judgment. Jesus, although chosen by God, will be struck down by God—as were the firstborn of the Egyptians.

---

218. Against Winter, *On the Trial of Jesus*, 70–89, see S. G. F. Brandon, *The Trial of Jesus of Nazareth* (New York: Stein & Day, 1968), 81–106.

Barabbas corresponds to the Hebrews of the first Passover. He is in prison "bound with the revolutionaries." Quite naturally the Jewish crowd, exploited by Roman imperialism and oppressed by their own ruling class, identify with him. Indeed, their inclination toward him would be unusually strong in this Passover context; and it would not require a great deal of manipulation by the chief priests (15:11) to influence them to choose him. Barabbas is the choice of the people, and at this Passover he experiences the liberation of Pilate's pardon. Ultimately, whether he becomes aware of it or not, he will also be included in the forgiveness of God which Jesus, the one rejected by the people and also to be rejected by God, will gain for him by his sacrifice.

The objective of weaving this tradition of 15:6–15 into the narrative world of "The Good News of Jesus Christ" is not to censure or condemn the Jewish crowd for their choice of Barabbas instead of Jesus. The strategy of this piece of repertoire is, rather, to confront the addressees of the Gospel with a similar choice which they must make in their own context. As they reach this point in the story, they too must choose between Jesus and Barabbas. Each of them represents a way into the future of the Passover anticipation of a new world.

For those in the historical context of the Gospel, the years immediately following the destruction of Jerusalem, the choice is existential. It will determine the future for both the individual who chooses and the society in which the choice is made. The Zealot revolt against Rome failed. The way that Barabbas embodied proved to be disastrous. Freedom was not realized, justice and equality were not achieved. Whom will Mark's audience choose? Which of the two represents the road to liberation? Within the narrative world of the Gospel, Jesus has been constructing a new way, but, as will become ever more evident, its price is formidable. For, as Jesus challenged his disciples while still in Galilee, if any wish to come after me, let them deny themselves and take up their cross and follow me. For those who want to save their life will lose it, but those who lose their life on account of me and the gospel will save it.

THE CRUCIFIXION, DEATH, AND BURIAL
(15:16–47) _____

After Jesus has been flogged, he is handed over to the soldiers, who take him into the courtyard of the praetorium where the entire cohort is called together. They will hold their own ceremony of enthronement before they carry out his execution.[219] It is his investiture before he mounts the throne of his cross. He is dressed up in a purple robe, a woven crown of thorns is placed on his head, and he is hailed as "king of the Jews." The soldiers bow before him in mock worship as they strike his thorn-crowned head with a reed and spit on him. When they have exhausted this theatrical game, they reclothe him with his own garments and lead him out of the city to be crucified.

Jesus, however, weakened by the scourging he has suffered, is unable to carry the crossbeam *(patibulum)* to the site outside the city where the vertical stake *(simplex)* stands planted in the ground. A passerby therefore is pressed into service by the soldiers to carry the heavy wooden bar. He is named Simon of Cyrene, and he is identified as one "coming from (the) field." He is a peasant who works on the land, and, like most other peasants of his time, he is subject to exorbitant rents and numerous taxes and consequently to marginal existence. Throughout his Galilean career, according to the narrative world of the Gospel, Jesus had concentrated his ministry in the rural countryside, actualizing the reality of God's rule among the peasants by his teaching, exorcisms, and healing. Now at the end of his life one of them carries his cross. He is distinguished as "the father of Alexander and Rufus." Apparently these two sons are known to the addressees of the Gospel, and through them they have a direct link to Jesus' passion.

The procession ends at a site appropriately named Golgotha, which, for the benefit of the addressees, is translated into Greek as "Skull Place." Here the crossbeam is laid on the ground, and Jesus, having been stripped of his clothing, is placed on top of it with his arms stretched out on each side of the wooden bar. Whether nails or ropes were used to fasten his hands to the wood is not indicated. Since the soldiers offered him the anesthetic of wine mixed with myrrh, it appears likely that nails were driven through his palms or wrists to

219. Winter (*On the Trial of Jesus*, 147–49) cites a remarkable parallel of a "sequence of theatrical street performances" by an Alexandrian mob to ridicule Agrippa I, recounted by Philo in *In Flaccum*. The "typical" features of this mockery suggest the dramatic pattern of a popular mimic play or burlesque performed by street actors or players. The author of Mark's Gospel may have appropriated it to reinforce the reality of Jesus' crucifixion as the ultimate absurdity, which calls everything into question that human beings have devised to construct their world: their systems of justice, their exercise of power, their self-understanding, their definitions of reality, and their structures of government. A parody or a parody of a parody.

secure him to the crossbeam.[220] His feet were either nailed or tied to the upright post with ropes, possibly also left dangling a short distance from the ground.[221] Crucifixion

> represented the acme of the torturer's art: atrocious physical sufferings, length of torment, ignominy, the effect of the crowd gathering to witness the long agony of the crucified. Nothing could be more horrible than the sight of this living body, breathing, seeing, hearing, still able to feel, and yet reduced to the state of a corpse by forced immobility and absolute helplessness. We cannot even say that the crucified person writhed in agony, for it was impossible for him to move. Stripped of his clothing, unable even to brush away the flies which fell upon his wounded flesh already lacerated by the preliminary scourging, exposed to the insults and curses of the people who can always find some sickening pleasure in the sight of the tortures of others, a feeling which is increased and not diminished by the sight of pain—the cross represented miserable humanity reduced to the last degree of impotence, suffering and degradation. The penalty of crucifixion combined all that the most ardent tormentor could desire: torture, the pillory, degradation, and certain death, distilled slowly drop by drop.[222]

Such profound suffering could be alleviated, at least to some extent, by the anesthetic of wine mixed with myrrh which is offered to Jesus. It would seem sensible to drink as much of it as possible. But he refuses it! "The Human Being must suffer many things" he had taught his disciples earlier, but surely this cannot be what he meant. Jesus is not an advocate of suffering for its own sake or even for the sake of self-redemption. Nor is his rejection of the painkiller motivated by a necessity to drink as deeply as possible from the cup of human misery in order to identify with those who suffer it. He simply does not want his senses dulled, even if the pain is excruciating. He is determined to remain conscious and in as full a possession of his faculties as he can under such dreadful circumstances in order to maintain the integrity of his identity as the New Human Being—the son of God. Although he is physically immobile on the cross, although in time and space he is subject to the limitations of crucifixion, he can still be autonomous and free. He is still able to exercise a significant measure of self-determina-

220. Grundmann, *Markus*, 432.

221. See Winter, *On the Trial of Jesus*, for more precise details.

222. Quoted in Olive Wyon's translation of Maurice Goguel, *The Life of Jesus* (London: George Allen & Unwin, 1933), 535–36. Also Winter, *On the Trial of Jesus*, 96.

tion.[223] Even attached to a cross he can express the kind of human being that the Creator wills for all humankind:

> What is the human being that you are mindful of her,
> And the son of the human being that you care for him?
> You have made them both little less than God.
> You have crowned them with glory and honor.
> You have given them sovereignty over all things. (Ps. 8:4–6)

By continuing to exercise his freedom and sovereignty Jesus can remain true to his identity and simultaneously fulfill his promise to the high priest and the Sanhedrin: "**You will see** the Human Being seated on the right hand of Power." Even in the agony of his crucifixion they —and, of course, also the addressees of the Gospel!—will witness the reality of Jesus' self-identification in his exercise of royal sovereignty.[224]

Ironically, the inscription indicating the charge against him, which he probably carried around his neck during the procession to Golgotha and which is now attached to the cross above his head, is profoundly true. In death, as well as in life, he is the Messiah, but the Messiah who embodies the New Human Being who has been generated by God. Or, as the Roman executioners have formulated this identity in their distinctively gentile manner, he is "The King of the Jews." Yet even as "The King of the Jews" he retains his horizontal relationship with his fellow human beings—as he did throughout his ministry—by being enthroned in nakedness with the two robbers who are crucified with him. Instead of being elevated as Messiah in royal splendor, with James and John, the sons of Zebedee, being seated on his right and left, Jesus is enthroned on a cross as the king of the Jews with two bandits who are suffering the same fate of crucifixion but who disassociate themselves from him with reproaches. Although they reject him, he, as the New Human Being, abolishes any vertical distance that might exist between them by dying with them in the same manner.

---

223. "A very passive figure" is a very inadequate way of describing Jesus during his passion. So Perrin, "The High Priest's Question and Jesus' Answer," 91, borrowing from H. Boers. However, throughout his passion, up to the moment of his death, Jesus is actively engaged in maintaining his freedom and integrity.

224. So also Perrin, "The High Priest's Question and Jesus' Answer," 91, but he views "the crucifixion—burial—resurrection as one continuous event," yet the matter is more dialectical than that, especially in Jesus' fulfillment of 14:62.

But it is this identification with them as well as with all the others who are present at this crucifixion, especially the members of the Sanhedrin who delivered him up to the Romans, that becomes the lightning rod that draws God's wrath upon him. For in his silent suffering Jesus maintains his solidarity with *all* of his fellow human beings, regardless of whether they are for him or against him. The reality of God's rule is not a world of binary oppositions, divided into the realms of the good and the evil, but rather a world of the One and the Many. Jesus, the New Human Being as the One, does not surrender his identification with the Many, although at this moment he has been completely abandoned.

All of his disciples have deserted him. Peter returned briefly; but when he thought his life was in jeopardy, he terminated his relationship with him with curses and oaths. Only the women who followed him from Galilee are present at this crucifixion, but they are looking on from a distance, probably because they cannot bear to witness his horrible suffering at close hand (15:40–41).

While the soldiers are absorbed in dividing Jesus' clothing among themselves by throwing dice, those who are passing by below his cross, who in fact may have been among the false witnesses at his trial, deride him with the testimony they gave against him: "Aha! the one tearing down the sanctuary and building (it) in three days, save yourself (by) descending from the cross!" The chief priests and the scribes mock his weakness with sarcastic ridicule which they exchange with one another in his hearing: "He saved others, he is unable to save himself. The Messiah, the king of Israel! Let him now descend from the cross so that we may see and believe!" Abandoned by everyone, except the women who have been following him, Jesus is alone and desolate.

Yet while Jesus submits to society's worst usage, he does not let his desperate and agonizing condition determine his actions. Being "seated on the right hand of Power" also implies at-one-ment with God and with fellow human beings. Jesus does not, therefore, react to his tormentors by retaliating in kind, by repaying their abuse and maltreatment with invectives or imprecations. In his freedom he chooses to remain outside the evil cycle of an eye for an eye and a tooth for a tooth. In his sovereignty he chooses to remain mute and to suffer silently.

Jesus' silence, however, should not be interpreted as a secret, internal rejection or even an indifference toward those who are responsible for his terrible predicament. That would simply be another form of action and reaction which would negate his identity as the New Human Being who is co-enthroned with God. He neither says nor does anything that would express his rejection of his enemies. In his silence he embraces them completely. In every respect he retains his integrity and remains outside the cycle of retaliation. Raised up on a cross and separated from humankind, he refuses to let himself be alienated.

Ironically, therefore, it is Jesus' integrity as the New Human Being that determines his fate. By maintaining his identification with his fellow human beings, even his enemies, he becomes the target of God's wrath. The enshrouding darkness, the darkness that occurs "over the entire earth," signifies within the narrative world of the Gospel the cosmic judgment that is taking place. At the sixth hour, or high noon, the brightest time of day, when the sun is at its zenith position in the sky, the darkest moment in human history is reaching its climax. This is the time that Jesus begins to experience what he dreaded most in the agonizing Gethsemane prayers: the cup of dereliction. The divine judgment of "the Day of the Lord," signaled by the naked youth streaking into the night at the moment of his arrest in Gethsemane, is culminated at the ninth hour by the awful cry of desolation. "My God, my God," Jesus shouts, "why did you abandon me?" Whether God's desertion is real or imagined makes little difference. Jesus is conscious of divine withdrawal. He is no longer being sustained by God's empowering Spirit, although he remains true to his identity as the New Human Being. His quotation of Zech. 13:7 on the Mount of Olives (14:27) has been fulfilled. God has smitten the shepherd, and the sheep have been scattered.

By remaining true to his identity as the New Human Being and refusing to disassociate himself from his fellow human beings, although rejected by them and separated from them by crucifixion, he becomes their representative before God. Burdened, however, with their evil through his identification with them, he is struck down and suffers the consequences of divine retribution intended for them. He assumes the role of the suffering Servant of Isaiah 53 who "was wounded for our transgression and bruised for our iniquities . . . and on him Yahweh laid the iniquity of us all." For Yahweh as God must also act in freedom and with integrity to punish injustice and wickedness. That is the supreme irony of the crucifixion. Jesus persists as the New Human Being, and God must act true to character. Both fulfill their authentic identity, and that puts them on a collision course.

Two results emerge from this divine-human interaction. On the one hand, atonement is effected, and God and human beings are reconciled to each other. For in his experience of divine abandonment Jesus also refuses to renounce or surrender his solidarity with God. Even in his desolation he still cries, "*My* God, *my* God." Rejected and smitten by both God and humankind, he nevertheless cleaves to both as he absorbs their enmity. Consequently he becomes the bridge that unites them, the bridge that spans the nothingness of death and links human beings once more to the source of life and possibility. On the other hand, in his complete isolation from God and human beings he becomes the embodiment of the scapegoat who bears the human infection of sin into the oblivion of nothingness.[225] Jesus not only uses his suffering to atone for sin and thus to satisfy God's justice. In accordance with the expectation of Jewish millennialism he also inaugurates the abolition of sin.[226] The end of the condition of sin and the alienation it fosters clears the ground of human existence in community for the establishment of God's rule once and for all. Without divine-human reconciliation and the eradication of sin, the incarnation of God's rule could never be actualized.

The narrator's rationale for presenting Jesus' cry of desolation in Aramaic is difficult to resolve. The use of what would be regarded as Jesus' own native speech lends greater authenticity to this climactic moment of the story and makes a powerful impact on the addressees. For it is not the original Hebrew version of Ps. 22:1 that Jesus appropriates to convey his experience of being smitten by God. He, the New Human Being, who is David's lord, expresses David's experience of abandonment in his own vernacular.

At the same time, the Aramaic version of Ps. 22:1 also serves as a

225. See Lev. 16:6–22, which presents the ritual of selecting two goats, one for Yahweh and one for Azazel. The former is sacrificed as a sin offering for Israel in order to reflect reconciliation; the other, bearing the sins of Israel, which the high priest has enunciated over its head, is sent into the wilderness to the demon Azazel.

226. See the expectation of this reality in Jer. 31:29 and Ezek. 18:2–4; also *1 Enoch* 5:6–9 and 2 Baruch 73—74.

point of departure for the misunderstanding of the bystanders who hear Jesus' cry of dereliction and misinterpret it as an invocation to Elijah.[227] One of them fills a sponge with wine vinegar, places it on a stalk, and offers it to Jesus evidently in order to provide a momentary refreshment and delay impending death. "Let's see if Elijah comes to take him down," he exhorts in defense of his action. The irony, however, is that Jesus himself at this moment is playing the role of Elijah, as John the Baptizer did at the beginning of the Gospel. Even as John embodied the voice of one shouting in the wilderness, Prepare the way of the Lord, Jesus, the scapegoat bearing the human reality of sin into the realm of nothingness, shouts the cry of dereliction and thereby signals the coming of God for judgment.[228] In this astonishing manner Jesus, who alongside the Baptizer personifies the second career of Elijah in fulfillment of Mal. 3:1 and 4:5–6, prepares the way for the Lord at the end of the story world of the Gospel. In accordance with the imperative of the quotation of Isa. 40:3 in 1:3, the paths have been made straight for God's coming, and the rule of God can now be constituted on a new foundation.

With that work completed, Jesus exercises his sovereignty as the New Human Being once more and with one final exhalation dismisses his life: "But Jesus, letting go a great cry, expired." He does not cling to life. He does not linger on in this crucified state of slow, agonizing death. Physical death does not intimidate him; he already embraced it at his baptism under John. He has fulfilled his mission. He has used his life and power as the New Human Being on behalf of others. At the end he does not merely suffer death; he freely enters into it.[229]

227. Schweizer (*Good News*, 352) rightly asks how Jesus' use of Ps. 22:1 in Aramaic could be misconstrued as a call to Elijah. But for a Greek-speaking gentile audience of Mark's story world that would probably be no problem at all; and it is vital to the author's story world construction to fulfill Jesus' role identity as an Elijah figure who, by shouting in the wilderness of nothingness as the embodiment of the scapegoat, prepares the way for God's coming for judgment.

228. The verb *boan* is used only twice in the Gospel, in 1:3 and here in 15:34 which harks back to 1:3.

229. Contrary to John R. Donahue ("From Passion Traditions to Passion Narrative," in *The Passion in Mark*, ed. Kelber, 12), Jesus' cry does not end the rule of darkness and inaugurate the new age. Judgment must still be completed by the rending of the sanctuary curtain. It is the Easter event that inaugurates the new age. Nor does Jesus' cry halt the conquest of evil, as Weeden asserts in "The Cross as Power in Weakness," 130. Nor does the cry of expiration "depict Jesus as being overpowered by the forces of evil," as Kelber claims in "Conclusion: From Passion Narrative to Gospel," 161.

In this way the narrator comes full circle. At the beginning of the Gospel, when Jesus repented and entered into his death in the Jordan River under the baptism under John, the heavens were torn apart and God's Spirit descended into Jesus in order to re-create him as the New Human Being and to call him as "beloved son" to enter into collaboration in constituting God's rule. Now, at the end of his life, at the moment of his physical death, the curtain of the sanctuary is torn apart, and God comes forth again. Jesus' earlier symbolic act of invalidating the temple institution is consummated by the divine exit from the Holy of Holies. Consequently the architectonic center of Judaism is canceled. The old order, which is represented by the temple, its sacrifices and its hierocracy, is abolished. Jerusalem is no longer the navel of the world where heaven and earth are united and where God's presence is uniquely experienced. Heaven and earth have been reconciled cosmically and universally. Accordingly, the binary opposition between the sacred and the secular, constituted by the temple as the *axis mundi* of Judaism, is dissolved. Both are reunited, and the entire creation once again becomes ambiguously sacred and profane. Henceforth no geographical, religious, social, sexual, or racial lines can be drawn to separate the clean from the unclean, good from evil, life from death. God's presence will be experienced everywhere and anywhere without the necessity of atoning sacrifices or a mediating priesthood. God's presence will be experienced wherever the eschatological reality of the New Humanity that Jesus incarnated throughout his ministry is encountered.

This is certified by the witness of the centurion who has been supervising the three crucifixions. When he observes how Jesus expired, he acknowledges, "Truly this human being was God's son!" Whether the phrase "this human being" is the narrator's wordplay on the title "the son of the human being" and is intended to evoke the memory of Jesus' confession before the Sanhedrin in 14:62 is uncertain but is nevertheless a valid possibility. At the outset of the Gospel the Heavenly Voice acknowledged Jesus to be "my beloved son." In this culminating moment at the conclusion of the passion, the title "son of God," which is based on the heavenly identification, is linked to a phrase that implies Jesus' self-understanding and is used to testify that even in this unclean and evil scene of crucifixion the reality of God has been glimpsed in the manner in which Jesus suffered and died. If the members of the Sanhedrin have not **seen** "the Human Being seated on the right hand of Power" as Jesus had promised in 14:62, it has been evident to the Roman executioner—and also, it is hoped, to the addressees of the Gospel.

However, what is evident to the disciples at this point is not indicated. Presumably the men have not returned from their flight. Peter is brooding somewhere in Jerusalem. Judas' fate will remain unknown. Only the women have been present at the crucifixion, but because they have looked on from a distance they may not be aware of what others who are closer to the cross—including the addressees of the Gospel—have seen and heard. Three of them are identified by the narrator: Mary Magdalene and Salome, who are named for the first time and of whom nothing is known, and Mary, the mother of James the Little and Joses. The last is none other than the mother of Jesus, who was introduced in 6:3, along with her other sons: James, Joses, Judah, and Simon, all brothers of Jesus. That she is not identified as Jesus' mother should not be surprising in the light of 3:31–35. Apparently, as her son's career ends, she is no longer an outsider; she has become a member of his new family. But because she now belongs to this community of the New Humanity which transcends blood relationships and racial ties, it is no longer important that she be identified as his mother. That gives her no special status in this new family. She, along with the other two, however, becomes a witness to the crucial events of Jesus' death, burial, and resurrection. In contrast to the connection of the old order which did not sanction feminine testimony, the truth and the reliability of these traditions are established within the community of the New Humanity by these women.

Jesus, although crucified as an insurrectionist as well as cursed by the law, is not buried as a criminal. As the sabbath approaches and the necessary preparations are made for its observance, his corpse is removed from the cross in order to avoid the desecration of this sacred time, in accordance with Deut. 21:23. Ironically, a member of the ruling elite, Joseph of Arimathea, takes the initiative to give Jesus an honorable burial. He is introduced as a "prominent council member," but he should not be identified with the Sanhedrin whose members unanimously condemned Jesus to death (14:64). He must be a counselor of Arimathea, a city with which his name is linked. Uncharacteristic of the upper class, however, he is also a millennialist "waiting for the rule of God" (15:43).[230] Undoubtedly it is this orientation that relates him to Jesus—although nothing is known of any previous connection—and enables him to undertake the bold act of claiming his corpse from the Roman procurator. Jesus' premature death astonishes Pilate and necessitates its confirmation by the centurion who was in charge of the execution, for crucified victims generally lingered on in living death for a longer time before they expired.

Because there is little time before commencement of the sabbath, Joseph is unable to prepare Jesus' corpse properly for burial. His naked body is simply wrapped in a linen sheet, a *sindōn*, which Joseph had purchased specifically for this purpose. Significantly, it is the same kind of cloth that the young disciple wore who attempted to be loyal to Jesus at Jesus' arrest in Gethsemane but who lost his nerve, slipped out of the sheet, and streaked into the night naked, when the soldiers apprehended him. It is this relationship between the linen cloth and the dead body of Jesus that furnishes the key to the interpretation of the brief episode of the fleeing youth of 14:51–52. Like him, Jesus was seized and, although he was sentenced and executed, like him, he will escape; but in the process he will leave behind his corpse. Shrouded in linen, he is buried in haste and without ceremony but in a rock-hewn tomb that was prepared and intended for someone of wealth, apparently, however, not for Joseph himself. The witnesses of this event and therefore also the guarantors of its truth are Mary Magdalene and Mary the mother of Joses, two of the three women named by the narrator who were present during the hours of crucifixion. The latter, of course, is the mother of Jesus, who once again is identified indirectly but with only one of the two sons named in 15:40. Both women "were observing where he has been put."

WITNESS TO THE RESURRECTION AND
FINAL INSTRUCTIONS
(16:1–8)

The Gospel's unusually brief but climactic Easter story begins with a seemingly redundant qualification of time that is typical of the narrator: "When the sabbath passed . . . very early in the morning on the

230. Why Joseph of Arimathea, a member of the upper class, should be a millenarian is indeterminable. One can only speculate about him being involved in some form of relative deprivation. See David F. Aberle, "A Note on Relative Deprivation Theory as Applied to Millenarian and Other Cult Movements," in *Millennial Dreams in Action*, ed. Sylvia L. Thrupp (New York: Schocken Books, 1970), 209–14.

first day of the week . . . as the sun was rising." The Easter event occurs on the **morning** after the sabbath, not in the evening after sundown, when, according to Jewish reckoning, the new day begins. That, of course, would imply the beginning of a new week, but nothing is left to assumption. Such a pronounced qualification of time appears to be theological rather than chronological—as are most of the other time references in the Gospel. The resurrection of Jesus is linked to the dawning of a new day and the beginning of a new week signifying the inauguration of a new age in human history. Three women make their way to Jesus' tomb, but they are not yet aware of the meaning of the time in which they are acting. They are not yet conscious of the epochal transition from one age to another that has taken place.

Mary Magdalene, Mary the mother of James—who is also the mother of Jesus but is now identified with the other of the two sons named earlier (15:40)—and Salome evidently intend to complete the burial of Jesus, which Joseph of Arimathea had initiated, by embalming his corpse with the aromatic salves they had purchased. Only after they are under way does the problem of opening the sepulcher by rolling away the stone occur to them. However, before any comment on the size of the stone is made, the addressees are told that the women "gaining sight . . . observe that the stone had been rolled up." Therefore the placement of the parenthetical remark, "for it was very great," after their surprise discovery, is disturbing; and it prompted later copyists of Mark's Gospel to improve on the narrator's art by relocating it at the end of 16:3. "And they were saying to each other, 'Who will roll the stone from the door of the tomb for us?' For it was very great."[231] Nevertheless, the text critical principle that the more difficult reading is preferable supports the location of the parenthetical remark at the end of v. 4. The women have suddenly become aware that they will be unable to gain access to Jesus' tomb. It is only when they look up, that is, when they gain sight, that they observe that the stone has been rolled away; and at that moment the narrator adds, almost as an afterthought, "for it was very great."

This compound verb of v. 4, *anablepein*, was used in 6:41; 7:34; 8:24; and 10:52. In its first two occurrences it clearly means "to look up," but in 8:24 and 10:52 its sense is more ambiguous and prepares

---

231. This is the reading of Codex D, the Koridethi, and a few other manuscripts.

the addressees of the Gospel for its final use in 16:4.[232] Blind Bartimaeus especially, who gained his sight immediately prior to Jesus' entry into Jerusalem and the beginning of his passion, looks up and thereby sees. He has empirical vision, but more important, he has gained the perception necessary for insightful seeing and understanding. As the Gospel reaches its climactic end, this same kind of seeing is indispensable for comprehending the resurrection. By looking up, the women gain sight that the stone which obstructed their view of Jesus' grave has been rolled away. Only in the context of this perceptive seeing does the size of the stone have any significance. For it intimates—and this is what the addressees realize—that the power that was operative in opening the tomb is to be identified with the power that overcame death for the corpse that had been placed inside it, and this can be perceived only by looking up and gaining sight, as the women did.

Although the corpse is gone, the tomb is not empty. As the women enter, they see "a youth *(neaniskos)* seated on the right hand wearing a white robe." This is the second episode in the Gospel involving a *neaniskos*.[233] At the beginning of the passion a stouthearted disciple, who had attempted to be loyal to Jesus at the moment of his arrest, slipped out of the linen sheet he was wearing and fled naked into the night. Now at the closure of the story, on Easter morning, a youth is encountered inside Jesus' vacated tomb "seated on the right hand wearing a white robe." Undoubtedly the two must be one and the same disciple. In his appearance he is no longer naked. The new garment he is wearing signifies glorification,[234] while the position of being "seated at the right hand" is reminiscent of the enthronement to "the right hand of Power" which Jesus claimed for himself as the New Human Being at his trial before the Sanhedrin (14:62). Once more the youth serves as a mirror reflecting the destiny of Jesus. Like him, Jesus has

232. Surprisingly it does not occur in the feeding of the four thousand, as it did in 6:41. Is the narrator shifting to another meaning in 8:24 in order to prepare for 10:52 and 16:4? Is this verb a "shifter" in Mark's Gospel? Shifters indicate the extent to which all meaning is context sensitive.

233. See Herman C. Waetjen, "The Ending of Mark and the Gospel's Shift in Eschatology," *ASTI* 4 (1965): 114–31.

234. Compare with the significance of the white robe in LXX Gen. 41:42 which symbolizes Joseph's glorification. Joseph's career, as recounted in Genesis 37 and 39—42, seems to be a paradigm of these two separate but related episodes of 14:51–52 and 16:5.

not only escaped the tenacious grasp of death by leaving behind his corpse; he has also been metamorphosed and reinstated in his enthronement to "the right hand of Power." Indeed, the white robe, which the young disciple is wearing, reflects the unveiling of Jesus' deification in the transfiguration during which "his clothes became very **white** such as a bleacher on earth is unable to make them so white."[235] Jesus' apotheosis, foreshadowed by his metamorphosis on a very high mountain, has been completed in his resurrection from the dead. Consequently, the declaration that he issued in 9:1, immediately prior to his transfiguration, has been fulfilled. **The rule of God has come in power.**[236] The eschatological reality which Jesus actualized by his deeds and words during his ministry has been reconstituted ontologically. Moreover, the New Humanity which he embodied is co-established with it and can never be eradicated, because it is co-enthroned with the Creator and therefore transcends all the forms and forces of death that struggle to prevail in human existence.

This youth, who mirrors the realities of Jesus' death and resurrection, represents the ideal disciple and may also convey to the addressees of the Gospel a glimpse of "the ideal reader," the image of the reader which the text wishes to actualize in order to have its full effect.[237] In his identity he continues the flesh-and-blood reality of the New Humanity, which Jesus embodied, by being co-enthroned with him "on the right hand of Power" and therefore also participating in

235. John Dominic Crossan ("Empty Tomb and Absent Lord," in *The Passion in Mark*, ed. Kelber, 148) notes the link between the transfiguration and the resurrection in the whiteness of the garment but draws no immediate conclusions. His essay contains some seminal insights, but they are not pursued in the light of Mark's story world. Crossan's stronger focus is on the historical development of the Easter tradition of 16:1–8.

236. In his essay "When Is the End Not the End? Literary Reflections on the Ending of Mark's Narrative," *Interpretation* 34 (1980): 157–59, 163–66, Petersen does not differentiate between the fulfilled eschatology of 9:1 inside Mark's story world and the yet-to-be-fulfilled eschatology of Mark 13 outside Mark's story world and therefore is unable to resolve the literary problem of Mark's ending satisfactorily.

237. The ideal reader may also be a mirror of the implied author who in Mark's Gospel may be identified with the narrator. As Wolfgang Iser says in *The Act of Reading: A Theory of Aesthetic Response* (Baltimore and London: Johns Hopkins University Press, 1980), 28–29, "An ideal reader would have to have an identical code to that of the author; authors, however, generally recodify prevailing codes in their texts, and so the ideal reader would also have to share the intentions underlying the process." Mark's ideal reader seems to have done so, but this does not appear to have made communication superfluous.

his transcendence.[238] Having died and been resurrected with Christ through the rite of baptism and therefore also having entered into a reordering of power, he has been called into being as God's son.[239] Consequently, Jesus' deification as the One New Human Being is simultaneously the deification of the many, this youth as well as all of his followers. As they, personified by the youth, continue Jesus' work of actualizing God's rule, they are undergoing the same metamorphosis that was disclosed in his transfiguration.

Perceiving all of this at a glance because they have looked up and therefore see, the women are stunned into speechlessness. They can only gape in awe at the mystery that is being revealed to them. "Don't be stunned!" the young disciple exclaims, and by bearing witness to the reality of Jesus' resurrection reinforces their understanding of what has happened: "You are seeking Jesus the Nazarene, the one crucified. He was raised! He is not here! See the place where they put him!" Since they have witnessed his death and burial, it is vital that they comprehend as fully as possible the reality of what they are experiencing in the tomb that was opened to them by divine power. The bondage of death has been ended!

At the same time, they are commissioned to serve as messengers to the disciples and Peter. The latter is specified by name not only because of the leading role he has played as the spokesperson of the disciples but probably especially because of the self-inflicted "death" he experienced by disassociating himself from Jesus through a threefold denial. Indeed, because he renounced Jesus at this point in the story world of the Gospel, he is no longer a disciple and must be referred to separately. The women, however, are not charged to proclaim the good news of Jesus' resurrection. Jesus himself had foretold it on five different occasions (8:31; 9:9, 31; 10:33–34; 14:28). Evidently that is not what they need to hear. Rather, they are to be reminded of the promise Jesus made shortly before his arrest: "After I'm raised I'll go before you into Galilee." Hearing the good news of the resurrection is not enough. They must experience the reality of the risen Jesus for themselves, and that will not happen in Jerusalem. There will be no post-Easter appearance in the canceled architectonic center of Judaism,

---

238. Crossan ("Empty Tomb and Absent Lord," 148) has also noted this implication.

239. Again, see Scroggs and Groff, "Baptism in Mark: Dying and Rising with Christ," 531–48.

because a new exodus has occurred. Jesus has exited from the tomb of death and departed from Jerusalem. God has vacated the temple. Now the divine presence will be experienced wherever the living temple of the New Humanity is encountered. Jesus, the resurrected pioneer of the New Humanity and the bearer of God's presence, is returning to Galilee, where he originally entered into his career of inaugurating God's rule. "There you will see him, even as he said to you," the youth promises.

On the one hand, Jesus, by his resurrection from the dead, has transcended mortal existence, and as the New Human Being he is co-enthroned with the Creator. For him, Dan. 7:13–14 has been fulfilled. The glory and sovereignty of God's rule belong to him. At the same time, however, he is also on his way to Galilee. For, on the other hand, he is only coming to enthronement. The second half of his confession before the Sanhedrin in 14:62 must also be actualized. For he will not be "seated on the right hand of Power" until his fellow human beings are co-enthroned with him. Therefore it is necessary for him, the One, to launch a second career in order to draw the many into an equal share of the glory and sovereignty of God's rule which he has received.[240]

For the narrative world of the Gospel According to Mark, Galilee is the appropriate region for Jesus to resume his activity of actualizing God's rule. It is there that he began his first career. But more significantly, it is the world of the rural countryside, inhabited by the peasantry which lives at the edge of subsistence and removed from the controlling center of the capital city and its wealthy and powerful upper class.[241] It was with the poor and dispossessed of Galilee that he

---

240. This also needs to be said against the prevailing view of the authors of *The Passion in Mark*, who have concluded that 14:28 and 16:7 look forward to the parousia. The dialectical eschatology of 14:62 and its continuation in 16:1–8 in both Jesus' co-enthronement with God and his return to Galilee to continue his mission is not considered. Generally their studies are dominated by the relation of the text to its historical world. Elizabeth S. Malbon's study, "Galilee and Jerusalem: History and Literature in Marcan Interpretation," *CBQ* 44 (1982): 242–55, more correctly insists on a literary critical approach that analyzes Mark's Gospel as a story world. She simply needs to press her studies further vis-à-vis the text of the Gospel as a literary unity and the production of meaning through interaction with the text.

241. The differences between the city and the rural countryside in antiquity are delineated by G. E. M de Ste. Croix in *The Class Struggle in the Ancient Greek World* (London: Gerald Duckworth & Co., 1981), 9–19. See also Lenski and Lenski, *Human Societies*, 189–98; and Stegemann, *The Gospel and the Poor*, 14–31.

had identified himself. It was among them that he had exorcised dehumanizing demons, returned ostracized lepers to society, enabled the blind to see, liberated women from the oppression of the pollution system, raised the dead, fed multitudes of hungry people, and re-established communication for the mute and the deaf. It was also from Galilee that he had entered the Decapolis and the boundaries of Tyre and Sidon to open God's rule to the gentiles. By resuming his work among the powerless and the exploited, the ostracized and the outsiders, he will continue to draw them into God's rule and its reordering of power and thereby enlarge the family of the New Humanity which he has constituted.

As the Gospel nears its closure, Jesus is also continuing to fulfill the role of the forerunner which he had expressly assumed in 10:32. By going before the disciples, he had constructed the way for them into Jerusalem and into a vicarious participation in his death—symbolized by the youth of 14:51–52. That, however, is where they have remained. What they lack is a vicarious participation in his re-creation or resurrection—symbolized by the youth of 16:5—but this cannot be realized in the necropolis of Jerusalem. To experience it they must participate in the exodus which Jesus has inaugurated. They must follow the forerunner once more, and he has left Jerusalem behind and is now constructing the way for them into resurrection from the dead. Like Jesus at the beginning of the Gospel, they will be re-created by the Spirit and called into being by the Heavenly Voice as God's beloved daughters and sons. At that moment the New Human Being, embodied by Jesus throughout the Gospel, will become a truly corporate reality, a community participating in the glory and sovereignty of God's rule. In collaboration with Jesus they can press on toward the universalization of God's rule and the co-enthronement of all humanity with the Creator.

The two introductory Old Testament quotations of the Gospel (1:2–3), which established the dialectical riddle of Jesus' identity and its correlated activity of actualizing God's rule, also govern the closure of the narrative. Initially John the Baptizer served as the messenger who shouted repentance and by baptism constructed the way that led to death and resurrection. Jesus entered upon the way and prepared for "the coming of the Lord" by submitting himself to the death experience of John's baptism. God came, as the Baptizer had promised, and Jesus was called into being as God's son and surrogate. Eventually, however, he also assumed the role as forerunner for his disciples and constructed the way for them into a vicarious participation in his death in Jerusalem. Now, as the Gospel reaches its end, Jesus the Christ, the glorified and enthroned Human Being, is still the forerunner constructing the way for his followers into the reality of their own resurrection and simultaneously with it their deification as God's sons and daughters. Whether they will follow him into Galilee remains ambiguous. In fact, it is the tantalizing question that the end of the narrative—which is really not the end![242]—leaves with the addressees.

For the women, after receiving the command to remind the disciples and Peter to follow Jesus into Galilee, flee from the tomb, overcome by "trembling and ecstasy." Emotionally they are overwhelmed with joy, but physically they are shaking at the enormity of what they have perceived inside the tomb. "And they said nothing to anyone, for they continued to be afraid." With these words the narrator ends the story. Since the last sentence contains two negatives—literally: "And to no one they said nothing"—and in Greek the second negative reinforces the first—the narrator's strategy must not be circumvented by postulating a lost ending. The efforts of ancient copyists of Mark's Gospel to create a more satisfactory conclusion for the story indicate how early in the transmission of the Gospel the unusual closure was no longer understood, a condition that has prevailed into this century. The women simply said nothing! A more stunning ending of the narrative could not have been fashioned.

The silence of the women is one of the great ironies of the Gospel. Throughout its narrative world, Jesus has demanded silence. Demons, which recognized him, were muzzled. A cleansed leper was intimidated to prevent him from publicizing his cure. The synagogue ruler and his wife were forbidden to make known the resurrection of their daughter. The deaf-mute was charged to remain mute. The blind person, who saw clearly after Jesus touched her or his eyes a second

242. Petersen ("When Is the End Not the End?" 151–66) recognizes that nothing is explicitly said about what will happen to the disciples, only that the consequences of the encounter will be disclosed. But what consequences? What will happen to the disciples? In the light of the reversal of 16:7 in 16:8, the closure is indeed stunning, but not as Petersen insists because the "second shoe is not dropped" and a prediction is not fulfilled.

time, was not permitted to return to Bethsaida. Peter and the disciples were censured not to speak about Jesus' messiahship to anyone. The transfiguration was not to be disclosed until after the resurrection. Now, however, at the culmination of the Gospel, when the revelation is finally complete, the command is issued: "Go and tell . . . ." Surprisingly and disconcertingly the narrative concludes, "And they said nothing to anyone, for they continued to be afraid."

"The Beginning of the Good News of Jesus Christ" ends in failure, the failure of the women to remind the disciples of Jesus' earlier promise to precede them into Galilee. Consequently the story tells only the beginning of the good news. But why should the women be afraid to communicate the message of the youth to the disciples and Peter? Actually, their continued fear has no object, or at least none is offered by the narrator. The Gospel simply ends with a two-word sentence: *ephobounto gar* ("for they continued to be afraid"). Nevertheless, it is out of this fear that they persist in silence. Why they fear or what they are afraid of remains a perplexing question. Apparently the narrator wants the addressees to puzzle it out, to deduce it from the story that has now been concluded. Reminding the disciples and Peter that Jesus is going before them into Galilee would probably lead to their participation in the exodus that he has inaugurated. As a result, *the story* of "The Beginning of the Good News of Jesus Christ" *would be continued*. But at what price? Would they really want to pay it? Are the women willing to pay it? The consequences of following Jesus into a reordering of power and collaborating with him in his second career to reconstitute reality are awesome. Do they really want to take up their cross and follow him? Can they survive, much less prevail, in a world in which the powers and the principalities, and the demons which they generate, appear to be predominant? Can they live holistically in a society of pyramidal structures which foster oppression, dispossession, alienation, and brokenness, while they themselves acknowledge no absolutes which define a priori the realities of good and evil, the sacred and the secular, the clean and the unclean? Can they live without the reference point of an architectonic center by casting their *axis mundi* into the sea and follow Jesus into a new wilderness journey in which they have to commit themselves to: All things are possible to those who believe? Can they really join Jesus in walking on the waters of chaos and exercise their sovereignty over the meaninglessness of human existence while they cooperate with him in creating a new world of justice, love, and peace? Perhaps even the women, who have been true and faithful disciples, prefer to retain their old world mentality and its necessity of an established and controlling center of reality, even if it means continued dehumanization by oppressive pollution systems. A fixed and immovable partition separating good and evil, the holy and the profane—even if they as women are its victims—guarantees at least a measure of life and security. The prospect of continuous ambiguity, insecurity, and anxiety that would arise from following Jesus to Galilee naturally engenders a paralyzing fear. In spite of the glory—and the ministry of Jesus reveals astonishing glimpses of it—silence is the safest response to the possibility of reinvolvement in a new exodus and its accompanying liberation.

Because the women remained silent, the disciples and Peter did not receive the message of the youth in the tomb reminding them that Jesus was going before them into Galilee and would meet them there. However, that does not necessarily imply that they remained in Jerusalem indefinitely and that therefore the prediction of 16:7 was never fulfilled.[243] They may have remembered the promise of 14:28—without the women's reminder—and followed him to Galilee, as they had accompanied him up to Jerusalem. What actually transpired is indeterminable. The ending is deliberately equivocal and confronts the addressees with the alternatives of continued silence and inactivity—all the while trembling in ecstasy at the awesome significance of Jesus' resurrection and his return to Galilee for a new career—and, on the other hand, following Jesus into Galilee and all that that signifies in the narrative world of the Gospel. Remaining in Jerusalem means con-

243. Contrary to Petersen ("When Is the End Not the End?" 154–58, 162–66), the narrator does not simply create an expectation in 16:7 and then cancel it in 16:8, nor does the closure of 16:8 tell the readers "to forget it." For the possibility continues to exist that the disciples themselves remembered 14:28. Consequently continuity can be imagined, but not as Petersen poses it. He is, however, correct in asserting that "the ultimate closure to Mark's story comes in the reader's imaginative positing of the meeting in Galilee." But what kind of meeting? The closure is not disclosed by the predictions of Mark 13 but by the significance of the new exodus, Jesus' resumption of his career, and the reader's existential decision whether to follow Jesus and collaborate with him in expanding God's rule. See also Petersen's essay " 'Point of View' in Mark's Narrative," *Semeia* 12 (1978): 110–13, where the same mistake of determining Mark's narrative world according to Mark 13 is made.

tinued death. No resurrection appearances will take place there. Jesus' sacrificial death may impart forgiveness of sins and even generate "the courage to be." But it is only participation in his exodus to Galilee and involvement with him in actualizing God's rule that will result in liberation and justice, love and peace. Which of these two alternatives the disciples chose remains unknown. Ultimately it is unimportant. The true closure of the story is determined by the addressees who, as has become evident, must generate a meaning that is not denoted by the signs that the narrator has employed.

If the women said nothing at all to anyone, how does the narrator happen to know the details of this culminating episode? The logical answer, of course, is that the youth in the tomb is to be identified as the narrator of the Gospel who simultaneously provides a glimpse of the implied author as well as the image of the reader which the implied author hopes for. He has inserted himself or she has inserted herself into the plot of the story at two points. The youth of 14:51–52 fulfills the strategy of the implied author by serving as the ideal disciple in mirroring the reality of dying with Christ in baptism and its witness to the judgment of the Day of the Lord, which Jesus inaugurated and suffered. The youth of 16:5–7 who is seated at the right hand and wearing a white robe testifies to Jesus' resurrection from the dead and proclaims the new exodus while reflecting both Jesus' destiny and his disciples' co-enthronement with him.

Consequently in the closure of the Gospel the narrator, who mirrors the image of the ideal disciple, is drawn into the dialectical reality of the coming of the New Humanity and its actualization of God's rule that was initiated by John the Baptizer and consummated by Jesus. Originally 1:4–11 disclosed the identity of the three parties delineated in the opening composite quotation of Mal. 3:1 and Exod. 23:20 in 1:2. God sends the messenger Elijah personified by the Baptizer before Jesus' face and he, John, constructs the way for Jesus into death and resurrection; and by entering upon it Jesus is called into being as God's offspring and surrogate. This set of identifications, however, must be revised at 10:32 when Jesus expressly assumes the role of forerunner. Accordingly, God sends the messenger Jesus—who also fulfills certain aspects of the Elijah typology—before the disciples and constructs the way for them by leading them into a participation in his own death and, potentially at least, his own resurrection.

Finally, at the end of the Gospel, the identification of the three parties of 1:2 must be revised once more. For in and through the extraordinary closure of the story, the narrator himself or herself, mirrored in his or her ideal discipleship by the youth, is drawn into the dialectical character of this opening quotation. Although seated on the right hand of Power and wearing a white robe, because he has followed Jesus the forerunner into death and resurrection, he too has assumed the role of forerunner: "Look, I God send my messenger," the narrator who is also the ideal disciple of the story world, and behind him or her the author, who, by creating this literary composition of the Gospel, has constructed the way for the lower-class addressees of the rural countryside of southern Syria.

Will they, the addressees—both hearers and readers—enter upon it? Will they follow Jesus into resurrection as well as death? Will they be called into being as God's beloved daughters and sons and bear the integrity and the responsibility of their new identity by continuing the actualization of God's rule? Finally, will they also, like John, Jesus, and the author of the Gospel, become pioneers and forerunners who will construct the way for others into the same reordering of power and co-enthronement with the Creator which they share with the First Final Human Being?

Biblical and Extrabiblical References